WHY NO REVIVAL!

Why No Revival!

What's Gone Wrong
How to Seize the Initiative

J.R. SOARS
with L.J. Lambert

OAKTREE PUBLISHING
Eastbourne

Published by Oaktree Publishing
P.O. Box 3019, Eastbourne, BN21 9DJ.
E-mail: <Oaktreeword@aol.com>

ISBN-13:   978 0 9553083 0 7
ISBN-10:   0 9553083 0 5

Book design and production for the publisher by
Bookprint Creative Services, <www.bookprint.co.uk>
Printed in Great Britain.

CONTENTS

FOREWORD

To contend for the faith by standing before the leaders of our nation is an important, apostolic part of our calling as disciples of Christ (Acts 9:15), yet the muzzled church is largely ill-equipped, unprepared and unaware of the depths to which it has allowed the powers of darkness to invade all realms of society in our nation; a nation uniquely used of God to carry the glory of His kingdom rule throughout the world.

This book presents a brief overview of our rich Christian heritage. It seeks to identify and to analyse ways by which we may, even at this late hour, recover our *God*-ordained role and prepare ourselves to contend for the faith in the midst of the rapidly rising tide of secular humanism. Thus, through obedience to God and His mercy, to cry out for another undeserved revival in our land.

In speaking with His disciples, Jesus said, 'You are the salt of the earth; but if the salt loses its flavour, how shall it be seasoned? It is then good for nothing but to be thrown out and trampled underfoot by men. You are the light of the world. A city that is set on a hill cannot be hidden . . . Let your light so shine before men, that they may see your good works and glorify your Father in heaven' (Mt 5:13–16). As the bride of Christ, the church has, urgently, to prepare herself for the coming of her Bridegroom (Rev 19:7), and in Part 2 the author focuses upon this preparation, before moving on to examples from the Gospels as to ways in which our Lord builds His 'house'.

We are only too well aware that our culture, increasingly dominated by postmodernist thinking, is inherently hostile to Christianity and does all it can to supplant, ridicule and illegitimise its basis of belief. As we reflect on many examples of the current climate within the nation, we find a marked similarity with the conditions that confronted Christ as He walked here on earth 2,000 years ago.

It is the author's belief that the church is able to respond, in spite of evidence to the contrary, to the high calling that it carries and that, as persecution increases, social cohesion crumbles and the economy is shaken, it will arise from its slumber and take the Great Commission as seriously as Jesus Christ clearly intended us to do in His final exhortation (Mt 28:19–20).

This book is presented as an aid for the equipping of the church, as a warning of the consequences should we continue to slumber and an encouragement to strive to contend for the faith at this crucial hour in history. We must not leave the task allotted to us for our children to accomplish because, as the Lord and His early disciples urged us to understand, 'Behold, I am coming quickly, and My reward is with Me, to give to every one according to his work' (Rev 22:12).

Michael Fenton-Jones FRICS
President ICCC
December 2004

'One of our greatest allies at present is the Church itself. Do not misunderstand me. I do not mean the church as we see her spread out throughout all time and space and rooted in eternity, terrible as an army with banners. That, I confess, is a spectacle which makes our boldest tempters uneasy.' (Screwtape in C. S. Lewis, *The Screwtape Letters*)

INTRODUCTION

Have you ever suffered the dreadful irony of carrying a life-or-death message so desperately needed, only to have it perceived by Bob your squash-playing partner as sounding like Homer Simpson's manic church neighbour? I have.

When I was a new Christian, I was immediately put to work 'witnessing' by playing my guitar sitting in a circle with my new friends in the local park; I experienced acute embarrassment and got nowhere. In fact, during the thirty years since then I have played guitars on many streets, handed out many leaflets and heard many doors, windows and hearts closing to my beloved Saviour. I have worn the religious coats of Pentecostal, house church, Restoration, National Revival and free evangelical movements while enduring this crying frustration of fruitlessness, the sum effect of my evangelism.

I feel as though I am in the Christian goldfish bowl mouthing, 'I'm in the bowl, but *you* are the prisoner,' or relating directly with Halle Berry's sane Gothika who is locked in an insane asylum by mad guards who mumble meaningless platitudes. Painful? Oh yes. For if, like me, you have lived the experience of God healing your spinal disease and saving you out of pain, desperation, bad circumstances and meaninglessness, yet do not have the power to reach out from the goldfish bowl to others, then you feel your failure most keenly.

The slide

For in this time, this thirty years of mine, what has happened to this nation? We have slid into a degree of lawlessness that makes one wonder if the nation is becoming ungovernable. For example:

- *Suffering children*: 100,000 children run away from home each year; 1.3 million children have addiction-problem parents; young offenders now constitute one third of all criminal convictions and more than half of them have absent fathers. Over 110,000 adults are convicted child sex offenders.
- *Despair*: 140,000 annual attempted suicides; 4,000 daily calls to ChildLine; 750,000 children have no paternal contact; UK teenage asthma rates are the highest in the world.
- *Crime*: Only 1 in 16 criminals and 1 in 50 child sex offenders face conviction; the 2.5 million offences recorded in 1980 rose five times to 12.3 million recorded in 2004; the prison population levels are at about 80,000 (an all-time high); gun crime doubled between 1997 and 2004 to 10,000 offences recorded in 2003–4; there are an estimated 4 million guns on the streets of Britain; crime costs the nation £60 billion annually.

- *Drugs*: HM Customs seizures rose from 30,690 in 1987 to 137,340 in 2002; in 2001 there were 930 drug gangs involved in the UK's £8.5 billion drugs trade; 60 per cent of mothers and 85 per cent of fathers who are drug-addicted no longer look after their children; in 2002 there were 5 million regular users of cannabis, 3.4 million of ecstasy and 2 million of cocaine.

After thirty years of this I began to cry to God, 'Where is Your revival in this nation of mine?' I believe I heard Him reply, 'Where is *My church* in this nation of Mine?' It was then I understood that it is the body of believers, the *ekklesia*, who are responsible for the state of the nation, rather than its rulers, pressure groups, press barons or industry generals, its natural resources or even its culture.

Ideas vs numbers

There is a contemporary church belief that if only the Lord 'would pour out His blessing' and save countless souls, then the nation would turn to God, and its institutions would begin to conform to a godly agenda. But the Scriptures and history suggest otherwise. When society's institutions are challenged by Christian ideas, and Christian light is seen in distinction to darkness in the public forum, then the people of the nation in the valley of decision can see clearly to make a choice between the two kingdoms of light and darkness.

To give an example, the extraordinary success of the Alpha course has seen more than a million participants pass through into church membership, but this has made no difference to the culture of the country. On the other hand, Brian Souter and Cardinal Winning worked together from a very small base to fight the promulgation of homosexuality in schools, and helped to overturn parliamentary votes in their favour *three times*! Were they from the same church group? No. Were they even from the same denomination? No. But were they from the same *ekklesia* (*ekklesia* = body of believers = church)? Yes, they were.

And thus I came to see that 'revival in a nation' depends upon revival in the whole national *ekklesia,* which in turn depends upon revival of individual believers, and this makes me responsible, and if you are a believer you are responsible too. I wept and cried to Him for His mercy upon our nation and the way forward for our people.

'Awake, you who sleep, arise from the dead, and Christ will give you light' (Eph 5:14)

I believe God has been trying to awaken His church in this nation to prayer and repentance for a very long time. He has permitted the increase of pressure from secular humanism and lately the Islamic movement until at last we are beginning to see prophets and movements raising the alarm of irreparable harm to our nation reminiscent of the Israelites reduced to making bricks for Pharaoh and further pressured by having to make them with no straw. (Prominent in this call to the church include those such as the Christian Institute, Dr Clifford Hill, the Lawyers' Christian Fellowship, the Barnabas Trust, Prophecy Today, David Pawson, the International Christian Chamber of Commerce (ICCC), the Evangelical Alliance, and the City Link Movement.)

The persecution of the Israelites continued until they started to cry to God, and now I believe it is our turn! Make no mistake, God is fully in charge and we have no option but to respond to His call if we are to fulfil our duty and our destiny to carry out those 'works which God prepared beforehand that we should walk in them' (Eph 2:10). The alternative fate hardly bears thinking about.

The future

But revival in the *ekklesia* is not an end in itself. It is the first step in the process of a much bigger task: that of *discipling* the nation according to the Lord's command (Mt 28:19). For, once the life of the church is revived, it is at a point in readiness and strength to obey the Master in discipling the nation by impacting the issues of the day, influencing the nation's course towards righteousness and bringing in all such as would be saved. This is true revival, for a discipled nation becomes a blessing to other nations as a light in the darkness to the glory of God.

Why no revival?

I have found the cause of 'Why no revival' to be twofold: first, the *ekklesia*'s immaturity in contending for the faith against the advance of the philosophies of secular humanism and its apprentice and current ally Islam in our nation. And, secondly, a damaging neglect of the roots of our faith from where we get our very identity and nourishment. In this book we will seek to address and redress these faults. We will then be able to see how the Lord Jesus Christ might begin to command His people with some hope of their obedience to bring a revival of life to His body, the *ekklesia*, the church, by the power of the Holy Spirit (*not* by the organisational skills of men).

We follow the Master as He trains His disciples, tracking their progress through the Gospel of Matthew. As you and/or your local group or church follow the Master you will be able to seek both individual and corporate tasks the Lord has for you in your locale and in the nation. As the national *ekklesia* matures in a diverse unity of the Spirit we will see the issue of righteousness become the biggest hot potato of national politics, and the *ekklesia* once again the source of righteous influence that our national government sorely needs.

Reviving and empowering the disciple

Since the eighties there have been a multitude of Christian discipling books, tapes and conferences showing us a better way to behave, and that is laudable. However, in order to command us in His Kingdom, Christ Jesus shows us in His own discipling process that this is just a beginning, for the real work of His cross is on the inside of a man, not the outside. This inner change is not a product of willpower and a willing mind, but the outworking of a powerfully changed inner life by the working of God Himself according to His promises (Eph 1:19; Phil 1:6).

In this book we follow the Master's training and empowerment of His disciples' inner life from His discourse in the Gospel of Matthew 5 to 7, examine this training in detail to enable us to understand how it works (or rather how He works in us), and explore the personal implications for us by applying it daily through the accompanying training session and tackling the very real issues in our lives. Jesus is seeking a behaviour change in us which comes not out of our willpower but out of an increased intimacy with Him and leads to a strong walk of faith upon which He may call.

Reviving the *ekklesia*, His church

We follow the record from Matthew 8 onwards as the Lord Jesus Christ then leads His disciples through a course of how groups of people behave and how to contend for the faith when confronted by them. He demonstrates, sometimes most dramatically, how to turn the tables on those who oppose Him, win the argument and win the hearts of the people watching.

As much as the individual has issues and problems to overcome, so the *ekklesia* has both local and national issues also, some of leadership and some of policy and tradition. In this context we examine one of the biggest obstacles to growth and national influence, that of the place of Israel in our affections. Rightly seen and understood our acknowledgement of our root links with Israel and the Hebraic covenants leads to blessing from God, spiritual warfare support and the feeding of the richness of our inheritance without which we will wither and die. Without jumping on any bandwagons we will examine in detail and as unambiguously as possible the conclusions and exhortations from Scripture, and the implications for our daily life.

Once the church understands its destiny and its members are seasoned and toughened faith-walkers it can set about the revival of the nation following the Holy Spirit in obedience and courage.

Reviving the nation

Jesus describes His *ekklesia* as a city set on a hill, as salt and light and as a lamp held high in a darkened room, and this involves contending for the light of the faith in the nation's dark marketplace of ideas. This book trains us in this 'ideas arena' to take up our place to contend for our faith in whatever sphere of influence God has set us. However, I believe He will not loose us on the national scene until we are ready; the risks are too great. For example, in the providence of God we are currently denied the national platform we need in order to address the nation. However, we will see also how church support for Israel will give us all the open platform we can handle in the national media so that we may also influence the nation in all the other areas of its need of discipling. But only in His timing and our readiness of motivation and competence.

Jesus, both Saviour and King

The Christian church is, and has been, competent over centuries in clearing up the social mess caused by a nation that flouts God's laws, creating the homeless and hungry, the drug and drink dependent and lonely, and others who are weak and helpless: this is our role in following the Saviour. But now it is time we also took up our role to begin to tackle the *causes* of this chaos. We look at examples not only from Scripture but from our own national story describing how Christian men and women boldly change the conduct of the nation bringing hope to the common folk and reining in the excesses of the rich and powerful. This is following Jesus the King and bringing in His Kingdom of righteousness, peace and joy (Rom 14:17) without reaching for the reins of power ourselves (Phil 2:5–7).

Ruling vs guidance

Because the Protestant church does not have ambitions to rule or influence the country for its own benefit, or on its own account, or to introduce a latter-day theocracy, it is and always has been in a unique position to counter the baleful influences of powerful interests such as political parties, lobby groups, the TV and news media, industry or commerce, and even foreign religions. The distinction between ruling and guidance is important because few who follow the precepts I am pointing out in this book will end up ruling anything! For in 'guidance' we are the prophets and priests (1 Pet 2:5–9) of the only true Ruler, the Lord Jesus Christ, to present national and personal choices before our nation. Providing choices is what we, the body of Christ, are all about; we will have lived in vain if we fail to fulfil this destiny.

Meanwhile, back at the nation . . .

At the same time as we reform and disciple ourselves, we can perceive that our nation is also in the flux of change as it articulates a cry which is gradually clarifying as a painful longing for a sense of identity, justice and truth, or, in a word, for *guidance*.

This rising cry in our nation comes from the roots and stumps of our 1,800 years of Christian inheritance; it is entirely natural then that in this extraordinary timing of God the body of Christ can step in to provide that guidance by contending for the faith and giving the people of our nation choices for life. In fact, it is the church's *duty* to provide this guidance.

The *Guardian* newspaper's leader column of 2 March 2002 concerning the choice of the next Archbishop of Canterbury articulated this national hunger as: 'This search for an authoritative voice – one that is spiritually profound, of deep conviction and intellectually coherent – ought to occupy the [Crown] Commissioners, not the elusive magic to reverse the emptying of pews ... The job of a Bishop – above all an Archbishop – is to inspire our spirit with a vision of truth and justice.'

Scripture and our nation's history show that guidance is the role of the Christian apostle and it is to the support of this prophetic ministry that we are all called, even if it might be unwelcome to those with power to lose, such as industrialists, media commentators, politicians and others who have a stake in the status quo.

The ball is in your court

This book is about preparing and training the prophetic church (Ezek 33:1–3) to provide choices for the people of our nation. It is not about a new marketing strategy to sell Christianity, or a new image makeover, but it is a rallying cry to those who are searching for the living Lion of Judah to reach and teach our nation once again (Mt 28:19).

Does that include you?

Note to readers

This book investigates trends within the nation and the Christian church. Not all Christians will agree with the views expressed within these pages, but I hope that the perspectives depicted are helpful in the call of the Master to Christian service.

I am against all forms of racial discrimination and incitement to hatred, and I have no intent to cause distress to, or to insult, any individual or group, but rather I am seeking to promote to the church a better understanding and awareness of the religious and cultural diversity within British society.

Part 1: Reviving the Disciple

When we consider what a challenge it is to prepare our-selves to participate in the discipling of our nation, we have to start thinking about how on earth we can get moving out of our own personal bunker and into contending for the faith.

In considering this I realised that Jesus had the same problem in motivating the multitudes that flooded towards Him (Mt 5:1–2). His solution to the problem was to propagate His teaching by multiplying its practitioners, so He sat down to teach His disciples to do the job on His behalf. We can do no better perhaps than to follow in the Master's foot-steps and follow His teaching programme of personal revival designed to get a disciple to that place where he can assume the role of Christ's ambassador.

Make no mistake about it, the Christian idea of salvation and righteousness is powerful and unstoppable once it is launched by a willing people in the timing of our God. The key is to be based in heaven but acting upon the earth: 'I have given them Your word; and the world has hated them because they are not of the world, just as I am not of the world. I do not pray that You should take them out of the world, but that You should keep them from the evil one . . . As You sent Me into the world, I also have sent them into the world' (Jn 17:14).

CHAPTER ONE

WE BUILD OUR HOUSE

The building scheme outline

The idea of 'building our house' is taken from Matthew 7:21–27, where Jesus exhorts His disciples to build a house of life in which they would be secure, and further explains that this is inextricably bound up with living under His authority, or 'entering the Kingdom of God'. The 'how to' is very simple in principle, i.e. 'he who hears these words of Mine and acts upon them', referring to the discourse with His disciples He had just finished in Matthew 5:3 to Matthew 7:27.

However, the process often goes against our instinct rather like that of a soldier in basic training when he obeys the voice of his commander rather than his immediate sense of self-preservation. As we shall see, training means overcoming the priorities of our flesh. Indeed, should our flesh not feel endorsed at a particular stage of training we have a very good indicator that we are finding out how to obey! It is also important to learn to discern the difference between overcoming in this way and sinning; if we are students under training we are not hypocrites if we cannot eliminate our old ways of living right away.

And so our intention is to look very closely at what the Master has instructed, and see how we might apply it to our own lives to build for ourselves what He calls 'a house built upon a rock'. If you choose to follow this course, I guarantee you will be changed for ever, and your life will be enriched immeasurably.

What is meant by the Kingdom of Jesus Christ?

Chapters 5–7 in Matthew hold a concise yet comprehensive course given by Christ Jesus on learning to build our house and live under His rule (in His Kingdom). For it is *His* Kingdom. Psalm 2 promises it, Acts 4:24–25 sees it and Jesus confirms it in Matthew 28:18 and again in Revelation 3:27.

There are several mentions of the Kingdom in Matthew 5–7:

- *'Blessed are the poor in spirit, for theirs is the kingdom of heaven' (5:3)*. The poor in spirit are those who have given their own priorities over to God so that His will is dominant in their lives.
- *'Your kingdom come. You will be done on earth as it is in heaven' (6:10)*. The Kingdom of God is wrapped up in the doing of His will.
- *'He who does the will of My Father . . . shall enter the kingdom of heaven' (7:21)*.

So entering the Kingdom, or rule, of God is about yielding our will to the Father and doing His, which is logical really. And the Kingdom itself might then be described as 'the operational will of Christ upon the earth'.

This will of His is the same as He now exercises in heaven; that is, total, full power, with nothing that could present anything resembling opposition against Him. I must confess that this came as a bolt of lightening out of the blue when I first saw it (I was studying that part of the Gospels when the disciples return after their first ministry journey crying that 'even the demons are subject to us in Your name. And He said to them, "I saw Satan fall like lightning from heaven"' (Lk 10:17). I realised that in this act of delegated authority the Kingdom had been established on the earth and the consequence was that in eternity Satan had lost his previous access to the Most High).

The moment we see that the rule or Kingdom of the Christ is a present-time reality and fact then our concept of Christianity takes on an entirely different perspective, especially as we consider the Great Commission: 'All authority has been given to Me in heaven and on earth. Go therefore and make disciples of all the nations . . . teaching them to observe all things that I have commanded you' (Mt 28:18–20).

Does one need a personal revelation from the Holy Spirit to grasp the magnitude of this? Yes, I believe so, and it might be opportune for any reader at this point who does not see the living reality of the Kingdom of the Christ to pause and ask for an entrance by grace into that understanding.

However, given that understanding, the next question we might ask is where we might go from here. How and where do we begin the pilgrim journey into the Kingdom?

Where to begin

If we start at where Jesus started with His own disciples we will see that the Lord had to introduce His own inti- mate disciples to the concept of an invisible Kingdom to which their hearts, like ours, are irresistibly drawn ('Lord, to whom shall we go?' (Jn 6:68)), and helpfully His course is laid out almost like a textbook in chapters 5–7 in the Gospel of Matthew. What was a systematic part of their training can also be good for us with the Holy Spirit as our guide. You might view these teachings as the keys to the Kingdom, that is, the keys to the rule of Christ Jesus in our lives.

This is the Christian's version of the humanist search for self-actualisation and identity; it can be seen that our search is into the eternal King who is the Rock that never changes rather than the humanist's hopeless search for meaning inside ourselves – selves which change like a weather vane with the emotions, and with the afflictions of the body and circumstances. And again, it is the difference between an Ordnance Survey map of unknown country ahead and a child's map of the sea; one is trustworthy and the other is a nonsense.

Jesus is seeking a behaviour shift in us springing from a life change where we can enjoy increased intimacy with Him and attune our lives to His ruling operation. It is not, generally speaking, about sin, righteousness and judgement. This is important to understand, for when we begin to strug- gle to enter His Kingdom, the Accuser will have a field day with us. That is his job, of course, to accuse, so we have to develop the skill in discerning what is of God and what is not.

What are the underlying stages of His training?

'In all that He began to do and teach . . .' In this phrase is the key to the method of the Master.

First (5:3–12, the Beatitudes), He describes the litmus tests that reveal the character traits that He would have us adopt. These character traits are the building blocks of our new house.

Second (5:11–7:20, the daily tests), He describes the daily instances of how we can practise developing these traits by presenting us with straight choices that we can take or reject. If we decide to take the testing choice then the Holy Spirit comes behind us to back it up with His control of our circumstances, our personal character failures and development of our relationship of trust and love together. This is the building process as God works in us (Eph 2:10).

Third (7:21–27, 'Therefore, whoever hears these sayings of Mine and does them . . . [is] founded on the rock'), He describes the goal, the house of our life that we are to build to shelter us and our purpose, for when the 'house' is operational, Jesus Christ is then able to launch us out of our personal struggles to contend for the faith in the world. This is the reason for building the house; that is, that we might find our purpose in His.

The problem of obedience

Of course the scripture quoted above of the house built upon a rock (from Matthew 7:21–27) is a definition of obedience, but as we unpack it in our experience, it develops from a straight 'knuckling under' into a pilgrim journey into life, wisdom and capability. Obedience is the key active ingredient on our part that links us to Christ; but fortunately that obedience comes from faith, which in turn comes as a gift from God Himself: 'the obedience that comes from faith' (Rom 1:5 NIV).

GIFT of FAITH → OBEDIENT ACT

So the problem of obedience (that we all have to face) becomes in fact an issue of faith; and all you need is faith the size of a mustard seed (Lk 17:5–6) in order to obey and enter the Kingdom of God. If we find we do not have enough faith to overcome the obstacles, temptations, errors, fleshly issues and so on, all we have to do is ask for it. The kingdom rule of Jesus Christ in our life really is an easy burden, even a pleasant one (Mt 11:29–30). It may appear difficult and onerous, but that may be deliberate to keep out the casual lookers and make way for the seekers and finders.

Faith and obedience are inextricably linked in Scripture. For example, the New Testament cites Abraham as being justified by faith (Jas 2:23) and the Old Testament cites his justification as by obedience (Gen 22:18). Another example is the encounter between Jesus and the centurion (Lk 7:8–9), where again the centurion talks about authority and obedience, but Jesus calls it 'faith'.

So it can be seen that obedience of this kind needs faith, and the good news is that this faith which is needed to obey is promised to us as a gift (Rom 1:5), coming in the forms of options that we can take and accompanied by the faith needed to take the right one. When the obedient act is complete, righteousness is imparted to us by the Lord.

GIFT of FAITH → OBEDIENT ACT → RIGHTEOUSNESS

This is not the *imputed* righteousness that He gives us in the act of believing Him for our forgiveness and redemption.

Instead it is an internal gift that begins to change our very nature in a lifelong process. Of course this is still a gift, as we cannot earn righteousness by any act of our own; it is all a gift through the sacrifice of Jesus and the mercy of God.

We may conclude then that the Kingdom of Jesus Christ is a tightly integrated process designed by God so that His Son the King can rule in the hearts of men and women who in turn might be salt and light influence in the earth. It is a noble and worthy challenge for all of us from the small to the great and to which we can all aspire.

So let us concern ourselves with the preparation of the house of our life to be strong enough to house the Master's purposes and to withstand all assaults. We start in Matthew 5 where the Master begins to outline the keys to His Kingdom.

The Seven Motives and Attitudes (Mt 5:3–10)

The celebrated passage of Matthew 5:3–10 (the Beatitudes) contains life-changing explosive. If we follow it through it will identify what we are, what we want and what we do; an exposure that can be quite painful at times but entirely worth it. It will change us for ever. We will begin to understand the process the Holy Spirit is employing as He takes us further into His training programme so that we can be willing and ambitious participants, rather than feeling like war victims. There is nothing worse than to appeal helplessly to the sky when circumstances have gone inexplicably pear-shaped. Far better to know what is going on and submit gracefully.

Motives and attitudes

The Holy Spirit will allow circumstances to develop which place us in a dilemma and reveal in us one of several motives and attitudes (M&As) that the Lord opens up in the Beatitudes as common to us all.

The choice of action will be quite clear: one to follow Him, or one to satisfy ourselves. This is not necessarily in a 'sin' area, but it is always in a growing area. By choosing to follow Him, we will be dealing with the M&A that Jesus has highlighted. We then audibly ask the Holy Spirit to take care of the consequences.

The power we need to choose is willpower, and indeed that is all willpower can do. It is like a small battery, it is not really up to controlling behaviour when further down the line of negative decision or opposed by great temptation. This requires something much stronger from God, and that is self-control, the ninth and last fruit of the Spirit (Gal 5:23), a much more potent source of power than mere willpower. It is important for us to recognise the difference so that we know when we are out of our depth and need help.

There is another most important principle to grasp before we go on that will help us handle what the Holy Spirit exposes in us. We must understand that we do not get condemned when we see who we really are but look ambitiously for our release in the area that has been highlighted. I remember when training in athletics how exhilarating it was to pass a difficult, painful new time target. This exposure process is similar, except that the experience is not transitory as in athletics but is an enduring 'high' as we enter into the Master's rule to develop faith rather than muscles.

When we get the hang of the Holy Spirit's *modus operandi* we get to respond quicker and better and build up a new, unexpected trust in the capacity of the Lord to look after us – perhaps another description of faith. And we are also learning to yield control. *These encounters are about developing a deep intimate relationship with our God that will produce the building bricks of our new house. They are emphatically NOT some esoteric exercise in breast-beating holiness by gigantic efforts of willpower. Do not allow the accuser to take advantage of you!*

The process is one of taking straightforward everyday decisions against our usual practice and trusting Jesus that we will be all right, like walking on thin ice. Have you ever dieted, fasted or exercised? Choosing to diet or fast goes right against the grain and it can be a painful process. Building our new house feels similar, as we don't have to like the process to love the results!

The routine goes something like this

First, we recognise in a particular set of circumstances that Jesus is doing something with us at a fundamental level. We ask the Holy Spirit what it is He is getting at in our motives or attitudes and we take the decision that yields control to Him and trust Him to get us out of trouble. Feels dangerous? You betcha! Although the everlasting arms are around us it still takes guts to choose for Jesus. But be encouraged. This is boot camp stuff, readying us, training us and strengthening us for the day when we will be doing this in contending for the faith!

Second, we must remember that it is an ongoing process, and one we have to experiment with, like walking on ice that we think will hold our weight, and which is, by the way, the operational act of growing our faith.

Third, it is almost certainly progressive, not instantaneous. We must learn to trust Him, and celebrate every little mark of improvement, such as when we don't lose our temper, seize control, lie to enhance ourselves in the eyes of others, or claim the revenge that is rightfully ours.

Fourth, we must be aware that we can become bogged down whenever we confuse the difference between fighting sin and the process of growing in maturity. It is the same as confusing a soldier with a drug addict where both are under training but one is training for greater responsibilities and the other merely to control anti-social behaviour.

The difference between fighting sin and growing in maturity

We are doomed to fall into deep discouragement and even apathy if we confuse our tendency to sin with the quite separate, challenging process of growing into Him in relationship and maturity, or what Paul calls putting off the old self and putting on the new self (Eph 4:22–24).

There is provision for our sin right from the beginning of our relationship with God, the Scripture making this quite clear in, for example Ephesians 1:7–8: 'In Him we have redemption through His blood, the forgiveness of sins, according to the riches of His grace which He made to abound toward us', and 1 John 2:12: 'I write to you, little children, because your sins are forgiven for His name's sake.'

The apostle John helps us here with his explanation of growth in his epistle by contrasting the little child in the faith with a father in the faith. He starts with the little child's 'forgiveness of sin' and concludes with the father 'who has known Him who was from the beginning', a reference to the Christ. To 'know' Christ in this way is to be able to obey Him, and to obey Him is to know Him as our Ruler, or King, by definition. This passage is therefore an indication that we grow from the basics of a relationship based upon one of pure baby-like forgiveness to one of increasing maturity as we become more practised in being able to obey and thus relate to Christ as King. We are familiar with this process in everyday life, for we clearly expect more responsible behaviour from a mature person than we do from a child. Paul echoes the process often, for example in the familiar passage in 1 Corinthians 13:11, 'When I was a child, I spoke as a child, I understood as a child, I thought as a child; but when I became a man, I put away childish things.'

This is clearly not an easy process and continues through our lifetime as we continually mature and grow closer to Christ. However, it is clear that the process can be taught and exampled as Paul makes clear in Ephesians 4:20 through to 6:18 and his remark to Timothy 2 Tim 2:2.

To obey or not to obey; that is the question

Ephesians 2:1–10 is a most revealing section of Scripture because in it Paul characterises the Christian as one who longs to obey because of the new birth, contrasted with the unbeliever who by nature longs to disobey. Wanting to obey is therefore a useful self-diagnosis tool, one for rejoicing and not for self-condemnation and sorrow, for if we find we long to obey then we know that the Father is at work in us. And when we see the contrast between our imperfection and His holiness, then that is again a cause for rejoicing and not sorrow, for we have been privileged to see where we are heading.

Of course the works of the flesh and sin are connected in the same way as your leg and your knee are connected, but although connected, they are quite different. One can grow into the other, as described in James 1:14–15 where the progression from flesh to sin and death is graphically described as first lust and enticement coming together to produce temptation, and when lust is conceived, it brings forth sin, which in turn brings death. These stages take a little time and it is within this time frame that we can begin to act, accessing the power of faith to obey which God offers us (Rom 1:5). It might take us a month or a year to make our first breakthrough, but it will be one we remember for a long time. And when we have done it once in a small way, we realise we can do it again, perhaps in a bigger way, and so our confidence grows in this God-managed experiential process, doing 'exceedingly abundantly above all that we ask or think, according to the power that works in us' (Eph 3:20).

Is a student a hypocrite?

This differentiation between God's provision of redemption from the effects of our sinning and our struggle to overcome the works of our flesh is thus most critical to discern and identify, because if we confuse the two then we can become mired in the distress of our immaturity and lose sight of the goal, which is the growth of obedience by the powerful working of the Father within us.

It can be seen immediately that such a confusion can be a rich source of accusation for our enemy the accuser, also for our flesh in depression, and of course also for the world, which is quick to criticise anyone who might seem to be trying to get a little above themselves. But we must not be deceived nor dissuaded, as this rite of passage is necessary in order to teach us about what is real and what is illusory. As we progress in maturity, we also become familiar with the scriptural promises that constantly reassure us that God is with us in the process of change and growth; for example: 'God is at work in you for His good will and pleasure', and, 'we are His workmanship', and 'the exceeding greatness of His power to us who believe'.

Progress in the overcoming of the flesh is by and large one of the greatest processes of growing in the faith that we will ever undertake: all other Christian achievements pale into insignificance. Jesus Himself gives it honour when He recognises how hard this move can be and He exhorts us to take up our cross daily and follow Him (Lk 9:23). But we must note two things: first, progress is often painfully slow while we take decisions to obey, and second, nothing comes in a rush, because like all natural growth, it is incremental.

Also, we have the privilege of working in an enterprise with the Father Himself in the singularly precious project of building our own house of faith founded upon the Rock Himself. And from this house, if we build well, His works will be able to spring into the full power and effectiveness of the gospel of the Kingdom of His dear Son. If the house is not built securely then we will not be able to withstand the demands that our calling will place upon it. Jesus Himself gives this quite stark warning in Matthew 7:27: '. . . a foolish man who built his house on the sand: and the rain descended, the floods came, and the winds blew and beat on that house; and it fell. And great was its fall.' *For we are concerned with a very real change of mind and perspective that goes deep to the roots of us, not mere surface behaviour, because the change has to be real in order to endure the high pressure that will be put upon it if ever we are to venture out of church ghettos and into the world to contend for the faith!*

Jesus is the model and the teacher for our ambition to follow Him and to be like Him in His remarkable and clear teaching in Matthew 5–7, so let us now look at His words in detail, starting where He starts when He describes 'poor in spirit' as the prerequisite for the Christian's progress.

'Blessed are the poor in spirit, for theirs is the kingdom of heaven' (Mt 5:3)

Jesus says that being 'poor in spirit' is the key to realising the aim of living in the Kingdom, which is the freedom to obey and to join with Him in His purposes.

I once had a great friend whom I thought of as rich in spirit. As I witnessed again to him one day, he said to me, 'What need do I have of a saviour? I have a lovely wife and family, a large house and a thriving business of my own. I am content. What am I to be saved from?' Although I answered creditably enough according to my church training, I was troubled by his position, because I did not understand the drives at work in him to make him rich in spirit. I later realised his satisfactions crowded out all thought of greater canvasses in his life, and that to a greater or lesser extent the crowding-out process affects all of us.

We might be tempted to say that we know the theory – that is, the greater the room in our spirit, the greater the potential for the presence of God there can be – but what we really need to know is the 'how' of making more room for Him.

The good news is that Jesus instructs His disciples how to crowd out competitive demands by becoming 'poor in spirit' through His training course, and guarantees that we shall enter His kingdom if we keep to what He says (Mt 7:21–25). We will be concentrating on this 'how' in the following pages.

So what exactly *is* 'poor in spirit'? The next few verses in Matthew explain (to be 'poor in spirit' we must mourn, be meek, hunger and thirst for righteousness and, be merciful, pure, a peacemaker and persecuted). As He takes us through the training, we should remember that each step of training will reach down into one or more of the deep motivations that would come against our desire to change and reveal our true selves as in a mirror. We can then begin the change under His tutelage and enabling power (see section on 'The Kingdom Dynamic'), His will and His legal covering by His blood covenant.

As we do, the changes become the new building blocks of our lives with which we begin to build the new house of our life; one which will be powerful enough to accommodate His presence as He directs our lives in His higher purposes (Eph 2:10).

I remember 'building a house' as a young lieutenant in the army, learning to manage a huge army mail room with some 120 staff. My captain told me he would show me how to control men, and then he walked over to a lance corporal and started to bawl the poor man out for no other reason than to instruct me. I learned the lesson and began to practise bawling men out in a superficial understanding of leadership. My mentor had taught me and that is how I built my army 'house', and to a certain extent it worked. But the fruit of it became damaging to me, my family and others, as I developed a constant boiling pot of anger. The day came when I had to dismantle that house and learn from the Holy Spirit, my new Captain, who, thank God, put His finger on this crippling spiritual disability.

So build carefully, or indeed the house will come tumbling down when unexpected stress is put upon it (Mt 7:27). -ask me how I know!

**'Blessed are those who mourn, for they shall be
comforted' (v. 4)**

During our lives we usually find some form of comfort to
depend upon in times of crisis or conflict, but this is often a
false comfort that in time grows to dominate us. I call it the
Lollipop Principle.

I could always rely upon anger and aggression to help me
out, and it was with great reluctance that I finally began to
relinquish this device as my comfort, as it was reliable, satisfying and it worked. For others it may be envy or jealousy,
drink, self-righteousness, self-pity and resentment, revenge
and of course all the usual bodily comforts. You will know
your 'lollipop' as soon as the Master puts His finger on it.

As the Scripture suggests in this passage, this voluntary loss
of comfort is accompanied by what might be called a mourning process, a yielding up, a sacrifice. I can vouch for the fact
that it can certainly be traumatic and painful.

But we are not alone; Jesus promises that by taking His yoke
upon ourselves, He will be with us in our struggle. This is a
dual process between Him and us by which two objectives are
achieved: first, the loss of illegal comfort and, secondly, a new
joining between our Lord and ourselves. This is a new intimacy
which develops into the source of the compensating comfort
He promises, and of course into a rich source of faith for us.

The opening gambit is a decision on our part, but the
empowerment comes only from God; the new position will
break down under pressure if we are not dependent upon the
Holy Spirit. I cannot emphasise enough that *willpower alone
is not sufficient*. This is not a course in life management, where
we learn to be independent and self-reliant, but rather it is a
course where we learn to be reliant upon the Holy Spirit and

enter into the way of the King and leave our own way far behind. 'I did it my way' is a song of failure in the Kingdom.

Why should we let these wretched tawdry 'lollipops' rule and ruin our life? I got into the ludicrous position of being angry about being trapped by anger! Christ points our comfort need out to us in His training to release us so that we become the true person He had in mind 'before the foundation of the world', not leaning upon false crutches for our ego. He promises here that we will receive a new kind of comfort in compensation; one that does not enslave us, which is freedom indeed.

There are other secrets hidden in this promise of blessings for those who mourn; for example, being given the gift of repentance for sin, particularly repetitive sin. I have majored on this promise of comfort, however, because of the hope that it gives us for the secret workings of our heart which we find very difficult to expose even to ourselves, and for which there is available a very real transformation of motives and attitudes.

'Blessed are the meek, for they shall inherit the earth' (v. 5)

Always the blank wall for the sceptic! But *Nelson's Bible Dictionary* defines meekness as 'Strength and courage under control, with kindness'. Does that sound like wimp city? I have found that meekness and gentleness are no handicap in the world of commercial sales. Some years ago I was being given the cold shoulder by a professional buyer in London and started to pray silently for a miracle. Suddenly the door opened and in walked the bluff, loud production director, who barked at me, 'What do you want?' Had I not been prepared for this intervention, the gentleness of my reply, with its humour and lightness of touch, would not have been mine. 'Give him an order!' he barked to the buyer and stormed out. Praise God!

You don't have to control in order to be in control and we all recognise the man who is in control and independent of our power. He doesn't need us and is good to be around, hence the order that was given to me.

Being meek and in control means that you do not need what the world has to tempt you with and it is well worth pursuing even for its own sake, as it is a sublime form of freedom. We will see in our training that Jesus will point out to us the times when we want to control the agenda, the people, the outcome, the rewards, for if we insist upon control, that rather leaves Him out of the equation, doesn't it? So we need to go back to square one if we are in controller mode and learn to let Him control the environment we are in, our advantages and rewards, and our need to show off.

'Blessed are those who hunger and thirst for righteousness' (v. 6)

This is a great idea for those on a desert island, but for those of us in the real world it can be an intimidating choice, as it may seem to threaten our security and well-being.

I remember being asked by a possible customer about my sales product at a time when I badly needed some business. In response I hedged a little and exaggerated its merits, and, well, got the order. After replacing the phone, there was a worm of discomfort wriggling in my insides which worsened throughout the afternoon, despite my silent self-justifications. I felt I could not retract my statements because I would look like a fool and completely untrustworthy, and yet I began to feel so bad that I did not want the wretched order. I was stuck fast by my own duplicity. I could go neither forward nor back!

In the end I seized the telephone, called the customer and apologised for misleading him. He took it all in his stride and from that moment we became his primary supplier, because of course he now knew he could trust me. Is that not a paradox? Honesty and integrity are difficult in business because we are in the devil's backyard and he is up to all sorts of tricks to trap us. But the Holy Spirit was there first and He knows a few tricks Himself, and the greatest of all is that He knows our frame, that we are but dust, and He is all-sufficient for our cowardliness, humiliation and neediness. We really can trust Him at the moment of feeling utterly alone or helpless, which is actually an opportunity to build into our relationship with Him, crowding out the devices of the world that are screaming in our flesh to be used.

'Blessed are the merciful, for they shall obtain mercy' (v. 7)

The oil of human relationships is mercy and kindness, and Jesus requires it of us. We can offer mercy every day in all our inter-personal transactions in our family, in our workplace and with the saints; for example, by relinquishing power over people that we maintain for our ego's sake. There is a perfect example of this principle in the film Schindler's List, when Schindler persuades the Nazi concentration camp comman-dant that it is more powerful to give mercy to the inmates than to take life. The revelation is profound both to the comman-dant and of course to us watching the process.

Mercy is a power far more heady to operate than transient revenge, or rights, or self-righteousness, and it is a builder of relationships and communities. Its fruit reproduces and the benefits abound to us, not only from others but from God. He loves the merciful, maybe because it delights Him to see one of His own growing His fruit.

Nelson Mandela has been merciful and forgiving to his erstwhile captors, and it has returned to him a thousand-fold. He is revered as a saint all over the African continent, and honours are heaped upon his head. I wonder if it would have been the same had he launched a pogrom against his enemies once he had gained his freedom.

'Blessed are the pure in heart, for they shall see God' (v. 8)

This is a very difficult one, at least for me as a sales and marketing man, for it is about the agenda in our heart when we are engaged with God and with our fellow man. Is it to take advantage for our own benefit? Normally we take a shopping list of what we want into most of our personal transactions, even if it is only to emerge from the meeting looking good and smelling of roses!

But if we are open about our objectives, completely open, then people can respond accordingly and deal with the issues rather than deal with us. This is subtle, but it bears the fruit of building trust, which I have found has enormous practical benefits even in the business world. It risks a dive into the deep but is exhilarating in the extreme. As always, the trust you put in the Lord as your Companion and Tutor is the essential component that complements your decision. His element is the dynamic which saves us in all circumstances.

I sympathise with you if God puts His hand on this one in your life, for getting rid of your secret shopping lists and yielding to God's shopping list can be the greatest (silent!) sacrifice. The biggest help for me was when I recognised that neither God nor others mind an openness of one's aims and objectives, for they can respond or defend their position accordingly. But what we all find most disquieting is when we discover hidden plans by which we can feel manipulated. I am reminded of the tax collector and the Pharisee, who had completely different attitudes to opening their hearts to God when worshipping in the Temple (Lk 18:14). Which did God receive? The one who was hiding nothing, who in fact sought Him in spirit and truth although apparently he had nothing to offer.

'Blessed are those who are persecuted for righteousness' sake' (v. 10)

Fear of persecution is our first defence against the pain of change to obey the Lord, and especially to keep His sayings. If we find ourselves being persecuted for righteousness' sake, we should take heart because this is the test of whether we have absorbed the sayings into our life at a deep enough level to enter His authority. Clearly this particular kind of pressure tells us how developed and ingrained are the new life principles in our soul, and how fully we have surrendered our old way of life.

It is hard that the experience of persecution as we begin to enter the rule of Christ is painful, but it is a mark, a signal that we are reaching for the truth. So we can be encouraged by the experience of persecution: it is like finding out if the boat floats!

I once had a very painful decision to make when my company directors instructed me to agree and enter into some very doubtful business dealings following a refusal by the bank to extend a credit trading facility. I knew I would be seriously compromised in my faith walk if I agreed, but the directors threatened me with the sack if I did not. What do you do under such circumstances? We all have responsibilities, and I was no exception with a family and a mortgage, and had no obvious career alternatives on the horizon.

In despair and no little fear, I appealed to the Lord to help me (the third option!). He pointed out to me what the directors were doing wrong that had got them into the mess we were, by now, all in. I persuaded them to return to the bank and the bank promptly agreed to extend the facility to enable us to trade our way out of the problem. Praise God!

Looking back I can see it was part of the proving process, designed by God to see if the boat floated, and one which in some other guise He would have repeated at a later date had I not chosen correctly. It also showed me that His reach, His 'operational will', extends deep into the affairs and institutions of men.

It is clear to me, remembering this occasion, that there is a big difference between making a choice and exercising willpower. Remember that willpower is like a small battery. Most of the time I just do not have enough courage or willpower to be holy. I find it far easier to simply make choices which He then backs up with His power and also takes care of the consequences.

Understanding His Ways

Our daily tests of choice that we start studying in the next section are designed by God so that we might get to know Him better, strengthen and grow our relationship with Him and trust in Him in adversity. Each test reaches deep into the motives and attitudes Jesus described in His mountain-top seminar with His disciples (Mt 5:3–11). The tests also have a hidden ingredient in that they are not internal wars of self-control but one of the kingdom power and influence of Christ Jesus the King as it pertains to us personally. These struggles with our tests become the building blocks of our personal house, the house of our calling. It is important to realise that we do not struggle alone, as there is the kingdom dynamic of Christ's rule and power at work in our individual life!

Before we begin to study the daily tests, however, there are three overarching principles that will help guide our reactions to studying how we move increasingly into the will of Christ. First, is how we react to injustice; second, is how we relinquish the desire for power in favour of influence; third, is how we learn to develop dependence upon the Holy Spirit as our sufficiency rather than upon our own resources.

Principle 1: Reaction to injustice, betrayal and rejection

Blessed are you when they revile and persecute you, and say all evil against you falsely for My sake. (Mt 5:11)

(*Check M&A ref: meekness.*) This is the first test of our independence from men and the power they have, and is a deep kindness from God. He does not want us to enter the practice of the kingdom rule openly in the world until we are really ready, for He truly cares for us.

If indeed we understand that each test of motives and attitudes actually reaches down into our very being where Jesus really wants to meet us as we make our choices, then we are ready to face the beginnings of contending for the faith. The experience of injustice is invariably one of the first tests that

Jesus arranges for us, as it very quickly reveals the secret attitudes of our heart.

Injustice and rejection are two of the most potent weapons the enemy of our souls has, and he uses them without mercy on us the moment we try to struggle out of our religious womb and into the bracing freshness of seeking the Kingdom of Christ.

What M&As are affected by our reaction to injustice?

(*Check out meekness.*) As we have seen from our definition of meekness from *Nelson's Bible Dictionary* (i.e. 'Strength and courage under control, with kindness'), as we reach into the provision of internal strength and resolution God has arranged for us (Eph 1:15–23) we begin to see the Kingdom of God work on our personal behalf and we move out of the 'battle against our soul' and into a divine peace, even though the attack upon us would normally drive us to drink.

Anger at injustice is a natural reaction, but if we bring to remembrance that all the issues involved can be transferred to the King's control by choice, then this makes us extremely powerful 'in the field'; it is as though our little world has just received reinforcements, say by acquiring a spiritual heavy artillery gun. It also hands the initiative to God, who can use it any way He thinks fit, from an impressive witness to achieving supernatural results for the Kingdom. There is ample evidence in the book of Acts of how clashes between the apostles and the institutions and individuals of the day produced powerful proclamations of the Kingdom, conversions and the growth of the church (a brief overview is included in Chapter 5). But these clashes did not take the initiative from God. On the contrary, the apostles' suffering meekness produced a harvest that endures to this day because they stepped away from the controls and let the Master take command.

Principle 2: Influence not power

> You are the salt of the earth . . . you are the light of the world . . . Let your light so shine before men, that they may . . . glorify your Father in heaven. (Mt 5:13–16)

(*M&A ref: meekness, poor in spirit, pure, comfort.*) Salt and light are the key principle of the living way; that is, we are to exercise influence not power! The way is prophetic not kingly; serving not ruling. We note that being a ruler is in fact the lesser role because any ruler in the world is bound up with 'many things' such as the compromises of power, the limitations of logistics, or satisfying the various competing blocs in his realm. This is a fact of life superbly described in Professor Michael O'Shea's management book *Influence*. The disciple of Jesus, on the other hand, can inspire upwards towards a better way and is not restricted by the requirements of people or groups. The contrast can be seen with the prophet Elijah and the king Ahab, for who had the real power to influence events?

And so it is with our role under God as we seek to influence rather than to rule. Already even in that concept you can see we are touching the motives and attitudes of our heart, say meekness, poor in spirit, even pure in heart!

What M&As are affected by seeking influence rather than power?

(*Meekness*): Do we have our ego under control? For example, do we desire to manipulate, dominate or control in confrontations for the sake of our ego? Are we really in charge of ourselves, bearing in mind that meekness is defined as 'strength and courage under control, with kindness' (Nelson), and also as 'teachable'?

(*Poor in spirit*): With our ambition and lust for recognition and the 'rewards' that power brings, can we make room for the will of Christ to operate in the events and meetings that we get involved in? Do we like to 'take the wheel' too much?

(*Pure in heart*): Are our motives really hidden under a secret agenda? What do we truly want? Maybe we need to lift our eyes to the bigger picture of the kingdom will of Jesus and look to take part with Him in His ambitions for the world.

(*Comfort*): Is the price too high to yield the prizes of men's admiration, of our competitive spirit, of status, of domination?

So which bells are ringing in our motives department when we know that we are in a kingdom issue involving the operational will of Jesus Christ and there is a choice between influencing and controlling? If we are clear, then we can proceed; if not, then we have to deal with the underlying problem before we can advance further in our journey. Notice that this exercise is not necessarily to do with sin and repentance, but decisions about how we choose to behave.

Principle 3: Dependency vs self-sufficiency

Do not think that I came to destroy the Law or the Prophets. I did not come to destroy but to fulfill. . . . Whoever therefore breaks one of the least of these commandments, and teaches men so, shall be called least in the kingdom of heaven; but whoever does and teaches them, he shall be called great in the kingdom of heaven. For I say to you, that unless your righteousness exceeds the righteousness of the scribes and Pharisees, you will by no means enter the kingdom of heaven. (Mt 5:17–20)

(*M&A ref: poor in spirit, comfort, gentle/meek*) The law is really Christ operating on the earth as He does in heaven. It is the written expression of His will, so we cannot ignore it; as He says, 'Not the smallest stroke shall pass away until all is accomplished.' But we tend not to like to obey and so the law finds us out quicker than anything and we discover in ourselves sin, self-will, selfishness, self-preservation and so on – in fact the whole gamut of motives and attitudes problems. The law finds us out for our sake. We now begin to know what we are truly like and realise our constant need of Jesus the Saviour to keep us clean; we are actually learning the first stage of dependency upon Christ Jesus. And this dependency keeps us safe because we know what we can do within our own sphere and we are learning what is His to do. Think of Gideon and the reduction of his forces from 30,000 to 300. That was dependency, and that is where we are going. Dependency means we are yoked with Him to work together.

What M&As are touched upon when we take up dependency?

(*Poor in spirit*): Do we want to be a master, or to serve *the* Master? Again, we need to seek the bigger picture; that is, the national, world picture, the long-term generational picture, the mystery of God's will which He purposed in Christ that 'He might gather together in one all things in Christ which are in heaven and which are on earth' (Eph 1:10). Our own ambitions are pitifully puny and, in the long run, stupid, because they lead nowhere that is ultimately secure and assured for us and our loved ones.

(*Comfort*): What humiliations will we experience as the result of letting go? Well, maybe quite hard ones. I was once offered a much-needed job if only I guaranteed never to mention the name Jesus Christ. What do we do in these circumstances? I was out of work and financially needy, but the thought of this prohibition was more than I could take and I refused the job. As though it were a test, God looked after us for clothing, food and our own roof, and I began to understand what dependency was. I must say I did not like the process at all – in fact it scared me – but now I see that it began to release me from my neediness of others' approval and the fear of the power others might have over my circumstances and I got to know my God a little better.

(*Meek*): In the instance of the job loss, I learned a little courage and control over myself, and I also learned the lot of many who were always in the place of helplessness, and my compassion and kindness increased from a very basic level.

The Daily Tests

Introduction

Now we understand something of the motivational drivers Jesus has identified that are common to man, and how God wishes to bring them under control in order to serve His kingdom rule, we can progress to the practical daily tests. Jesus trains His disciples to check out the motives and attitudes as daily personal tests come their way. Each one we face is designed to expose and identify the secret drives within us so that He can go to work with us to bring that area under His operational control. This is emphatically not a guilt trip or a breast-beating exercise, so if you find yourself going down that route, rebuke the accuser and he will flee from you. This is about kingdom rule by voluntarily submitting to the training regime required by this pilgrim journey (1 Tim 4:7). Just like an athlete (1 Cor 9:24–27) or a paratrooper (no scriptural reference!).

Matthew 5:21–24. Reconciliation with brothers. Check out M&A ref: meek, pure, mourn

> I tell you that anyone who is angry with his brother will be subject to judgement . . . Anyone who says 'You fool!' will be in danger of the fire of hell. Therefore if you are offering your gift before the altar and there remember that your brother has something against you, leave your gift there in front of the altar. First go and be reconciled with your brother; then come and offer your gift. (NIV)

This is a difficult lesson to learn, but I have found that our competent handling of personal conflict brings a significant building stone to the construction of our house of life. In the process, we may find that the separation from our brother touches deeply on the motives and attitudes; for example, pure in heart (our shopping list?), merciful (personal power), mourn (comfort), meek (we do not need the posture), righteous (are we?). When looked at in that clinical light rather than the emotions of the moment we can become like surgeons in control of events rather than at their mercy, and cut away the bonds of mistrust, anger, injustice and so on to reveal the real picture. How marvellous to be aware of the larger kingdom picture right now in the present rather than bitterly remembering and repenting years later!

Sometimes there may be an instance where separation is unavoidable because of persistent sin or wrong-headedness, but only accept this if you have passed the motives and attitudes with flying colours, have appealed repeatedly to your brother for reconciliation with clarity, and only then part in sorrow not in anger.

5:25–26. Cutting your losses. Check out M&A ref: comfort, meek, mercy, pure

Settle matters quickly with your adversary who is taking you to court. Do it while you are still with him on the way, or he may hand you over to the judge, and the judge may hand you over to the officer, and you may be thrown in prison. I tell you the truth, you will not get out until you have paid the last penny. (NIV)

If we cut our losses and get out of futile personal disputes as quickly as possible, we escape involvement in useless time-wasting, in distracting and exhausting efforts when all the time the treasure we really seek is safe in heaven! I recognise that sometimes it is not. For example, I know of a worldwide Christian business ministry which was being bullied by a secular organisation to give up its name. They stuck to their guns under considerable pressure and God delivered them. Nevertheless, it is possible to lose all our substance in lawsuits when in the end we would have been better advised to cut our losses early.

What M&A roots is Jesus getting at?

(*Comfort*): Are we clinging on to a so-called point of principle when in fact it is only our pride or our tradition that is at stake? What is the Holy Spirit saying to us about changing our old wineskin? If we should consider that our rights are being violated, perhaps we should ask what rights a servant has in the Kingdom.

(*Meek*): Are we being aggressive for fear of looking weak? Remember Jesus is training us not to react to the world, situations, conflicts or even attacks, but to react to Him, to depend upon Him – a mental and emotional capacity that takes great inner strength and maturity, and is something to be sought with all our strength.

(*Mercy*): Is there an opportunity to demonstrate the forgiveness of Christ by showing mercy when in fact you are in a powerful position to 'win'? Who knows, maybe the situation might develop into a powerful time of introduction to Jesus? We must learn to think of the bigger canvas!

(*Pure*): Although our outward position looks good and even innocent, how are we doing in the inner man? Before Christ, are we really as innocent as we claim? Perhaps we are not aware of how dominating or strong we appear to others, or perhaps we are not truly aware of how our social impact can cost others in anger and resentment.

After checking through the M&As, let go and settle for the best terms as long as there is not a big kingdom principle at stake in contending for the faith, such as there was for Paul in Philippi. When I was negotiating for a director's employment contract, there were several areas of dispute where we had reached an impasse. My wife advised me to cut my losses and let go the particular point of BUPA healthcare, which I did. The board were so glad for the concession that broke the impasse, they nodded through all the other points without a murmur.

5:27–32. Renounce sexual hunting. Check out M&A ref: meek, mourn

> You have heard it was said, 'Do not commit adultery.' But I tell you that anyone who looks at a woman lustfully has already committed adultery with her in his heart. (NIV)

The sexual predator is spotted a mile off by a member of the opposite sex. Sexual pursuit is a form of control and pride, and it takes a lot to beat it in oneself. There has to be a special yielding at root level, which can involve the giving up of some considerable comfort, otherwise it can make us a high risk if Christ uses us. If we burn with passion and are not married, then we ought to get married. If we are married then, as a major project in our life, we must go through the motives and attitudes to start a recovery job of our married sexual relationship. The task, which the motives and attitudes will identify, is to isolate the roots of this out-of-control passion. Once that is done, real repentance and healing can take place and the fruit of this particular plant will just drop off.

What M&A roots are being addressed here?

(*Meek*): The sexual relationship teaches us very quickly about how we are in the self-control and courage department. The meek person, under our definition above, will learn more about themselves and about their spouse than they can possibly glean from counselling or videos, and can also fast-track towards developing the Christ mindset that brings great satisfaction to the marriage relationship.

(*Mourning and comfort*): What compensation is this predatory lust giving us? Use that indicator to get to work on your marriage, or recognise that you need to get married in order to order this passion righteously. An honest look at the roots can mark a new chapter in the enjoyment of our marriage, and even talking about new possibilities with our spouse can be an adventure in itself. There is a lot of humour in married sex, a lot of warmth and mutual understanding, and we deprive ourselves of more than sexual climaxes if we neglect the closeness that married sex brings. This intimacy also brings a better understanding of who we really are in all our strengths and weaknesses, and offers an opportunity to support and love each other more in an encouraging and exhortive way.

If we conquer this one we are well on the way to building our house, for it can be a formidable obstacle to our progress.

5:33–37. Mean what you say. Check out M&A ref: pure, meek, mourn, persecution

> . . . Simply let your 'Yes' be 'Yes', and your 'No', 'No'; anything beyond this comes from the evil one. (NIV)

Since Jesus points out that there are few things in our power by which we can swear (that is, guarantee our word), it is enough if we let our own words speak for themselves. This is one of the hardest things to do, and yet it speaks volumes about us. We *are* our word, so if it is not good enough for ourselves, it will not be an awful lot better for our listeners. Just how deep does our word go? Once again the daily test of our motives and attitudes will help us to find the weak spots!

What M&A roots are being addressed here?

(*Meek*): Are our personal agenda items under control? Are we being cowardly? Are we reluctant to accept the consequences of our convictions? Is it in our power to extend kindness but we are considering withholding it?

(*Mourn*): What old comforts are beckoning? Is this a time to stand up and be counted? Will this be embarrassing?

(*Pure in heart*): Is our personal agenda being challenged, maybe by God? Is our comfort zone being invaded?

(*Persecution*): Does the boat float? Just how precious is our reputation to us? Can we stand against conventionally held wisdom? Is it time to bring into this environment a new idea of a bigger canvas – one that involves Christ?

In being tempted to act for our own advantage (meek), yielding to comfort (mourn), personal agenda (pure in heart) or even wanting to renege on our position because of persecution, the daily tests help us identify what would let us down when in real conflict. We need to sort it out in the shallows, for if the boat sinks in the shallows, then at least we don't drown!

5: 38–48. The battle is the Lord's. Check out M&A ref: meek, persecution, mercy

> I tell you, Do not resist an evil person. If someone strikes you on the right cheek, turn the other to him also . . . If someone forces you to go one mile, go with him two. . . . But I tell you, Love your enemies and pray for those who persecute you. (NIV)

Turning the other cheek is hard to believe as a strategy, and must only be attempted when you are on course pursuing the rule of God, never as a religious exercise, or to tempt God, or to identify with others like pacifists or peaceniks. But given those caveats, it really is a strategy for victory in all our life if we are on the Lord's business and we are letting the Lord retain control, because He will deliver us, sometimes miraculously.

What M&A roots are being addressed here?

(*Persecution*): The natural reaction is anger, violence, retaliation and so on, and to look for weaknesses and exploit them. Suppose we do not, through choice, but instead withhold our ability to strike? What then is the scenario? Check this out:

- We wrong-foot expectations.
- We pay a price for peace.
- We are unpredictable.
- We are out of the enemy's control.
- We are dependent upon the Kingdom acting on our behalf.

There is often a paradox acting on our behalf here; by giving up our advantage things will go our way. We can make friends or at least neutrals out of enemies. Remember Paul and Silas in the jail at Philippi, when God miraculously opened the prison doors? The jailer was so much at the mercy of events that he was about to kill himself, but instead Paul took spiritual authority, recognising God had given him a priceless opportunity to advance the Kingdom. The temporary advantage was rejected by Paul, for he was looking at a larger canvas, and we can have the same attitude when we look past temporary setbacks in order to be seen to react well.

God is not mocked, especially when it is His son or daughter who is involved and at risk, and He often makes 'all things work together for good to those who love God, to those who are called according to His purpose' (Rom 8:28). Jesus is eminently practical.

(*Meek*): The *Nelson's Bible Dictionary* definition, if you remember, involved being courageous and strong, under control, and persecution gives us an opportunity, a platform to speak and represent ourselves, because curiosity is inevitably aroused when people are confronted by unconventional reactions. The defence and persecution of Stephen, for example, burned into the conscience of the watching and abetting Saul, and stayed with him for the rest of his life as an example of Christian behaviour. Take this platform with a rapid prayer to God and seize the moment with grace, humour and a will to win yet another person to Christ. Again, expand the canvas of the moment to see what the angels might be looking at, such as the possible saving of an enemy of Christ.

(*Mercy*): In the intimacy of someone's confession of faith, remember the 'with kindness' of *Nelson's* definition of the word 'meek'. Your being merciful might quite possibly be a unique moment in someone's life and they may never encounter that integrity again.

6:1–4. Intimacy for others. Check out M&A ref: mourn, meek, hunger, mercy, pure in heart

> Be careful not to do your acts of mercy before men to be seen by them. If you do, you will have no reward from your Father in heaven . . . let your giving be in secret. Then your Father, who sees what is done in secret, will reward you. (NIV)

Charitable deeds are gifts of the Father to those in need, so if we get in His way, we may ruin an ongoing exchange between the recipient and the Father which the Father may have to begin all over again. We must be sure to check our motives and attitudes if we manage to scrape rewards out of charitable deeds; there may be a deep-seated need in us for recognition and reward which is dominating our life. We want to get to the stage where we are independent of the world's rewards and are totally usable and dependable to fulfil the destiny He has for us. Anyhow, the Father has promised to look after us later, off-stage. Take a strategic view of charity, let go of the comfort of recognition and be content with the privilege of seeing Him at work behind the scenes.

6:5–8. Intimacy for ourselves. Check out M&A ref: hunger, pure in heart

> And when you pray, do not be like the hypocrites, for they love to pray standing in the synagogues and on the street corners to be seen by men. I tell you the truth, they have received their reward in full. But when you pray, go into your room, close the door and pray to your Father who is unseen. Then your Father, who sees what is done in secret, will reward you. (NIV)

If we let our super prayer technique get in the way of intimacy with the Father, then we are idiots, but it is very easy to do! If our intimacy with Him increases, however, He will show us secrets and give us understanding of His ways or visions of His creation or insights into His thinking; he will give us greater union with our loved ones, a greater sense of security and of peace and satisfaction and the sheer joy of being alive.

Intimacy with the Father is worth pursuing for the rewards alone, but it has another purpose, which is that we might hear Him with greater accuracy and promptness so that our obedience has greater and greater relevance to our circumstances and the areas over which we might have influence.

The greater the intimacy grows, the greater our will to please Him, and as our trust grows, our capacity to withstand hardship and pain grows with it. All soldiers know the strange experience of initially loathing their drill sergeant, and then experiencing the strange reversal over a period of time as this changes into revering him as a father figure.

What M&A roots are being addressed here?

(*Hunger and thirst after righteousness*): We pray as a response to the Father, not as a demonstration of religion; this is a real relationship we are considering here, between two beings who truly love each other. And for our part, the Father holds the key to developing a greater understanding of His Kingdom and our part in it; we are also seeking to mature in obedience to Him and this certainly involves issues that we would not wish to be broadcast to all and sundry.

(*Pure in heart*): I suspect that if we are praying in order to impress men, this relationship with the Father is in a very early stage, or maybe we do not even believe it really exists!

So if we are playing to the gallery, the implication is that we are not very serious about prayer, we do not care about the wasted opportunity and even that we do not truly believe that the Father, our Father, is listening!

6:8–13. The Lord's Prayer. Check out M&A ref: poor, meek, hunger, merciful

In addition to the countless commentaries on this passage, I would add a few thoughts in the context of our study together.

Clearly the prayer is God-centred, not just upon His person but also upon His desire to rule the earth as He does in heaven.

And in praying this prayer, we follow His desire by applying ourselves to His tutorial which continues in this prayer:

- *Give us today our daily bread* – that is, give us what we need to survive.
- *Forgive us our trespasses* – that is, bring us over to Your side in support, not in opposition.
- *Lead us not into temptation* – that is, our character changes are quite enough to deal with and we do not want to be delivered like the man in 1 Corinthians 5:5 for the devil to attack.
- *But deliver us from evil* – that is, we are in the middle of change, desiring to keep to our journey into intimate service and fellowship; do not let the evil one get to us as much as he might try.

What M&A roots are being addressed here?

In the context of our study, what might be the roots that are being addressed here? Well, the prayer is such a wonderful and compact study in appeal, yearning and petition that the immediacy of expectation in the daily intervention of God in our personal human affairs might be missed.

In the sections extracted above, it is clear that the petitioner is keen that his pilgrim journey into intimacy with God the Father should not be interrupted, distracted or diverted, and that his main purpose should be encouraged and protected in its development. This prayer is the benchmark of the level of communication and intimacy into which Jesus is training us in order that our relationship with the Father should be incredibly close, forthright and practical.

6:14–15. Forgive. Check out M&A ref: poor, mourn, merciful, persecution

> For if you forgive men when they sin against you, your heavenly Father will also forgive you. But if you do not forgive men their sins, your Father will not forgive your sins. (NIV)

We cannot afford to keep long accounts in the Kingdom; there is too much else to do and achieve. So in forgiving sins against us personally, we release the other person from their obligation to us and we get on with life. If you cannot do this from choice, then run through the list of motives and attitudes found in an earlier section to check out what is driving your passion. Often it can be rejection and/or injustice; the motives and attitudes will lead us to peace in our soul by means of the decisions with which we are presented.

Of course forgiveness does not necessarily mean not confronting the offender with the truth. However, in so doing do remember you have to have integrity in truly representing your part without defence caveats. If they do not recognise their part in guilt at all, in fact see themselves as snowy white, forgive them anyway. You have done your part and your load is now lighter.

Sin that would tend to bring the body of Christ into disrepute is dealt with by Jesus later on (Mt 18:15–17).

What M&A roots are being addressed here?

(*Poor*): Harbouring resentment, bitterness and anger as a result of being attacked is an understandable but nevertheless dangerous practice. In my own experience, it was because of certain vulnerabilities in my life, and while I am sure that is not the universal cause of unforgiveness it is certainly a powerful one and a common one. We simply do not have room in our spirit to accommodate this self-indulgence and at the same time seek the kingdom rule of Christ in our lives. Something has to give and go. Unforgiveness is a life-dominating condition and can infect the lives of many around us as it descends into bitterness (Heb 12:15). We need to be alive to the dangers and brave for the remedy.

(*Mourn*): We must ask ourselves whether we are taking comfort in an inner sense of self-righteousness, superiority, imagined revenge or other imagined scenarios like being publicly vindicated to the discomfort of our tormentor. The mental gymnastics we get up to are a total waste of time and emotional energy; we should instead aim for a higher path, a bigger canvas. Let us therefore recognise the triviality of our mental scenarios, repent, ask the Holy Spirit to lead us into a proper perspective of the situation and remove our soul from the conflict it is now in (Ps 55:18).

(*Merciful*): Is this an opportunity to show the kind of mercy that has so often been shown to us? If we find ourselves at a moral advantage in confrontation, suppose we just give it away? Just let go of our advantage? Have we really lost so much? Do we not instead move into a different realm and share something in common with our Lord in exercising the nature of His mercy? Kindness is a real power in relationships and can often break through barriers that seem insurmountable. It builds (at a cost!) bridges of bonding that will stand the test of time and pressure where mere 'compatibility' fails at the first fence.

(*Persecution*): The first reaction to persecution is often a swift response in kind! Sometimes, however, that is not possible because of the relative power disparity. So how do we react then? Well, it depends on us, whether we wish to be the head or the tail; to be a victim or to be above the events that impact our lives. Alexander Solzhenitsyn was stripped (illegally) of his Russian Army colonelcy, decorations and privileges and thrown into a prison camp in the Gulag. Within a week, he testifies, he felt free, even though he was incarcerated in one of the most life-threatening gaols in the world. How was that possible? Well, he was subject to events, but he was his own man inside himself, a free man and in control of the one place that he could truly call his own; that is, his mind. If we can accept that victimhood is a state of mind not of circumstances, then we can be free even in the face of vicious persecution.

6:16–18. Fasting. Check out M&A ref: meek, hunger, mourn

> . . . when you fast put oil on your head and wash your face so that it will not be obvious to men that you are fasting, but only to your Father who is unseen; and your Father, who sees what is done in secret, will reward you openly (NIV).

The object of fasting is to increase intimacy with the Father privately by diligent seeking. It is not an ego exercise to promote our spirituality publicly. In fact Jesus exhorts us to go to great lengths to conceal the fact that we are fasting and keep it just between God and ourselves.

He will be found by us according to His promises, and according to this verse and others He will even reward us for looking for Him. We may have a situation in our life which we truly do not understand, and about which all our earthly reasoning fails. Our objective in fasting may be to obtain a new kind of comprehension, or a mindset change to increase our capacity to understand; the fasting discipline, combined with being quiet before God and learning to listen, is a very good way to give God access to us to do a necessary new work in our heart and mind.

In pursuing this course, we become quieter, more confident, more sure of ourselves, because Jesus Christ is helping us to build the house of our lives We enjoy life more, our sense of thanks to God increases and we become more aware of life itself, living every minute.

What M&A roots are being addressed here?

Our reactions to fasting may be explained by the motives or attitudes pointing out our need for recognition, competition, anger, fear, false comfort and so on which need dealing with.

(*Meek*): The repetitive nature of this exercise may begin to convince you that these inner struggles are common to all of us! What you are going through in your growth in intimacy and trust with the Lord Jesus you can be sure is shared by everyone who begins this journey. With this understanding, make room as soon as you can in your spirit so that the Holy Spirit is able to lead you into all truth without stumbling over anger and fears.

(*Hunger*): The marvellous thing about seeking God is that He wants to be found! If we wish to share His secrets, we shall become increasingly aware of our need to be clean before Him and we shall prepare ourselves automatically. Fasting will help us in this hunger to know about and to be transformed by righteousness; the developing sense of how perfect He is, and all His works, clearly goes on until we see Him face to face, but it is the most powerful incentive in the here and now to experience it and be profoundly impacted in all our senses. The paradox of this hungering and thirsting after righteousness is that it increases in intensity, and is never satisfied; it is the most profound sense of falling in love with our Creator, and becomes its own drive.

(*Mourn*): The desire for recognition is a potent drive and one which can seriously cloud our judgement because it is a need, and one moreover that we shall sometimes satisfy at the expense of our longer term objectives. But in seeking to satisfy this need in the wrong place, at the expense of our journey into Him, we can prolong that journey unnecessarily. So once we recognise and identify this need, we must repent of wrongly satisfying it and ask the Lord exactly where we can get it appropriately met. Ideally, of course, we may be able to hear the Lord say the precious words 'Well done, my child', and be content with that, but we are not always on this kind of direct line to Him. I had given up my ten-year part-time pastorate and was standing in St Mark's Church, Kennington, after one of their extraordinary services, and watching the bustle of a dozen ministries as they served the people. In contrast, I felt so lost and aimless after this surrender of my status, role, busy-ness and being needed, as though I was washed up on some spiritual shore or other. Suddenly the Lord whispered in my ear, 'Do you want to be honoured by God, or by man?' 'By You, Lord,' I whispered back. And so began my pilgrim journey with Him and I have not once looked back.

How We Build Our House

How you do something in the Kingdom is as important as *what* you do; not for the Christian the socialist excuse 'You can't make omelettes without breaking eggs'. We are always responsible – the Father accords us that dignity.

Mathew 6:19–23. Treasure and lamps

> Do not store up for yourselves treasures on earth, where moth and rust destroy, and where thieves break in and steal. But store up for yourselves treasures in heaven, where moth and rust do not destroy, and where thieves do not break in and steal. For where your treasure is, there will be your heart also. The eye is the lamp of the body. If your eyes are good, your whole body will be full of light. But if your eyes are bad, your whole body will be full of darkness. If then the light within you is darkness, how great is that darkness! (NIV)

We are always vulnerable if we have treasure on the earth. For example, we shall be reluctant to move, either geographically or doctrinally or circumstantially, if it means abandoning dearly held earthly treasure. Treasure may not be money or possessions; it might be a position, a role, a location, a club – in fact anything that claims a priority on our heart and prevents us from fulfilling our destiny in Christ. If the treasure is in heaven, however, we are free to follow the Master and not be hidebound by our need for possessions, tradition, habit, comfort or esteem. The kind of treasure we are referring to is, for example, the fruit of this pilgrim journey of ours into intimacy with the Father, and as this gradually displaces all other things it becomes all we desire because it brings with it the greatest satisfactions that a heart can embrace.

Interpreting events, opinions, decisions, actions and deeds, frameworks, objectives, motives and conditioning circumstances takes more than the mind of Solomon, so we can take the lead from Jesus, who always sought what His Father spoke and did first before He did likewise. So if this is our standard practice, we can trust the lens because it is clean. Otherwise we have to clean the lens with the motives and attitudes before we dare to proceed to make judgements.

It is really exciting to admit to the Lord that we are out of our depth and for Him to drop the wisdom needed for the moment into our mind the second before we speak. Or to have the guts not to speak if we have not heard from Him. I have found that I might only get a sentence from the Holy Spirit, but as I speak that sentence, the whole idea unfolds before me and I continue to explain (more accurately, report!) what I see just in front of me. The same principle applies in counselling, in sales and marketing, in strategising in business, or in trying to help in interpersonal situations. It can be quite unnerving, this walking in the light, but totally exhilarating.

What M&A roots are being addressed here?

(*Blessed are those who mourn*): Obviously by 'cleaning the lens' we might be giving up a psychological advantage over someone, and the loss of satisfaction of that may cause us mourning. Again, sometimes we may have to seriously consider a beloved pastime like, say, golf if it negatively impacts our marriage or the development of our children. As we run all our judgements through the prism of our frameworks of reference (see later chapters for full coverage of frameworks and metanarratives) it behoves us to ensure they accord as closely as possible with our scriptural norms. If they do not, the Holy Spirit may show us, for example, that we are prejudiced in some way or other, so that it is we ourselves who are in need of the correction, rather than the object of our examination!

The mourning over revelations of progress we need to make may be quite painful for a time, but the Holy Spirit will be our Comforter, especially over the extended period. The reward of dying to the flesh in these pleasurable areas will be repaid to us many times over as the recipients of our sacrificial love grow and develop. It is like seeing a garden grow, but with people rather than things.

(*Blessed are those who hunger and thirst after righteousness*): As we get the picture, our standing before the Lord becomes more and more precious to us because it gives us the pleasure of 'treasure that does not rust', and that internal satisfaction becomes like oxygen to us, necessary and exhilarating.

(*Blessed are the merciful*): When the situation of someone else's vulnerability is before us, we are in a position of power, and how we handle that power is a measure of our grasping of the M&As. If we lay that power aside, like Jesus did (Phil 2:7), and become like a servant to that person, we not only receive mercy from God, but in the future when the situation may be reversed we will also receive mercy from them.

6:24. God and Mammon

> No-one can serve two masters. Either he will hate the one and love the other, or he will be devoted to one and despise the other. You cannot serve both God and Mammon. (NIV)

'You cannot serve both God and Mammon.' In this materialistic age this should be burned across all Christian chests. We simply do not understand that there are only two real bosses out there and we engage in 'playing church' at our peril, for truly the enemy waits at the gate to devour us. I have found an extremely useful key when judging some new phenomenon is to look for the dollar sign, as it often points to hidden commercial motives. Christianity is the only interest group that defends the interests of other groups in the cause of righteousness; one time it is on the side of the government and then it is on the side of some other interest or group, such as children or unborn babies, in opposition to the government of the day. The body of Christ is apostolic to the nation and prophetic to the church; it is entirely unpredictable because it follows the Spirit (Jn 3:8), and is *always* in contradistinction to the interests of Mammon.

What M&As are being addressed here?

(*Poor in spirit*): Should God wish that we move to another department at work or stay where we are or accept promotion to another part of the world, then that would be to accomplish work for His Kingdom. The same motive can clearly be attributed to Mammon. So which do we follow? The ability to make this kind of choice makes us independent of this alternative kingdom and enables us to fulfil our true purpose in life and be truly satisfied. A shadow of this principle is already being seen in UK commerce, where executives are downsizing, downshifting or refusing promotions to avoid the outrageous demands now being made by the god of business, Mammon. How much more then should we of the Kingdom be able to act in this fashion?

(*Meek*): Can we control our reaction to threats, bribery, persuasion, appeals to our ego and lusts, intimidation and so on? If we can learn from Jesus, we can resist external pressures and truly become our 'own person' under His inspiration. This is true freedom and independence, but within the limits of His kingdom rule which provides for us the very deep-down challenges that we are seeking anyway. The ambiguity of the scripture 'He shall give you the desires of your heart' (Ps 37:4) becomes delightfully ours in both meanings. This is the way to go!

6:25–34. Be not anxious

> Who of you by worrying can add a single day to his life? . . . But
> seek first His kingdom and His righteousness, and all these things
> shall be given you as well. Therefore do not worry about tomor-
> row, for tomorrow will worry about itself. Each day has enough
> trouble of its own. (NIV)

You might say, 'It is all very well for you to preach this to us,
but we have to survive and care for our dependants.' But
as you may know by now the commercial and political
forces in the world are wilful and completely unreliable
when it comes to ensuring our security. It is becoming clear
that not even our pensions and mortgages are in safe hands
any more.

God is exhorting us in this passage not to be taken in by the
physical evidence of security in the world because it can be
wiped out in a second, but rather to take refuge and shelter in
His rule over our lives, abandoning ourselves to His care and
mercy. Mighty commercial companies like Enron, Parmalats,
LTCM or BCCI tumble overnight and the giants of last
month, like Vodaphone or BT, have trembled on the edge of
disaster with colossal losses.

At the end of the day there is not a lot of point in being
anxious for our life (vv. 25, 27–28, 30–31, 34UK (NIV)).
Instead Jesus offers the Father's alternative: 'Seek first His rule
and His righteousness and all these other things shall be
added.' In other words, throw your lot in with Him and He
will provide. It is surely a recipe for a more peaceful life, as we
only concern ourselves about today – in other words, the issues
right in front of us. We find ourselves in an age when anxiety
is almost fashionable, so to break out of what is almost a social

expectation takes an extraordinary leap of imagination on our part, as well as the empowerment of the Holy Spirit.

What M&A roots are being addressed here?

(*Poor in spirit*): This may seem unfair at first sight because of the struggle we have in survival. But not so, for if we develop our intimacy with the Father by following the sayings of Jesus and taking the decisions that invariably arise when we look at the M&As which drive our reactions to life's many challenges, that intimacy will help overcome the fear and intimidation we feel, and replace that fear with confidence. 'Perfect [or mature] love drives out all fear' (NIV), as the apostle John reminds us (1 Jn 4:18).

(*Meekness*): Remembering the definition of meekness by Nelson (above) of 'strength and courage under control, with kindness', the growth of strength and control can be seen to be very relevant in the present world, but of course it only comes through intimacy – that is, faith – in the Father and the Lord Jesus Christ. So the strength may be obtained from outside of ourselves, from the source of all strength Himself as we seek to obey Him by deciding to keep His sayings (Mt 7:24).

7:1–5. Judgement

Do not judge, or you too will be judged. For in the same way as you judge others, you will be judged, and with the measure you use, it will be measured to you. Why do you look at the speck of sawdust in your brother's eye, and pay no attention to the plank in your own eye? How can you say to your brother, 'Let me take the speck out of your eye,' when all the time there is a plank in your own eye? You hypocrite, first take the plank out of your own eye, and then you will see clearly to remove the speck from your brother's eye. (NIV)

There are several kinds of judgement here:

First, making judgements without hearing from God, where they are personal assessments and an ego exercise or worse, bigotry. It is a simple quid pro quo that if you deal out bigotry you get it back with interest, such as tribal bigotry of any kind where we can see daily on the news programmes that the response is equally or more violent. We have all got tribes in our nations these days, usually divided into indigenous and immigrant or into one philosophy or another, and the results of intolerance are frequently seen on the TV news.

Secondly, judging others in their capacity to evaluate the world. We cannot see their heart but only what they express, so a true evaluation of their competence to judge can only truly be made by God, and we are well advised not to interfere in the process.

If we are not hearing from God regarding others then we cannot see anything clearly, and the delicate operation of correcting them is completely beyond us. This is particularly important in any revival of the church, where God speaks differently to different people, and sets different agendas. So we must not criticise what may well be someone acting obediently on the Father's bidding. If God's agenda seems obscure to us then we must ask the Father and He may explain His business to us, and may even allow us to help if He thinks it appropriate. If in doubt, we should leave well alone. We must not take it upon ourselves to interfere with Him and His dealings with others, for that would be like saying that we are now His perfect handiwork, the finished apple of the Father's eye, and that is dangerous ground. None of us will ever have the full or final picture (1 Cor 13:9).

Thirdly, increased intimacy with the Father will almost certainly result in secrets vouchsafed to us that may not be safe or good to broadcast at that particular time, except to those the Father tells us to share with. If we share at the wrong time, we will almost certainly get hurt – anything from the mild 'I don't know where you're coming from' to the 'If you don't stop this nonsense you will get kicked out' variety. Our Father is very concerned that we learn to control our lust for recognition and approval (motives and attitudes again) to prevent the dogs turning on us.

Mark you, the process works in reverse: one day a prophet will share something completely outlandish with us and we will be tempted to assume the swine's behaviour and trample the treasure in the dust. No one is exempt from being like the elder brother in the parable (Lk 15:29), so it behoves us not to judge until we hear from God for sure!

What M&As are being addressed here?

(*Blessed are the Meek*): If we are able to exercise self-control in counselling or confrontational situations, we will find it the most useful of the characteristics of 'building the house', for we are then able to relax, listen to the leading of the Holy Spirit and proceed accordingly. This amounts to a strategy of cautious boldness. Not only are we privy to the extra information and timing of God; we are sure that we are acting in others' best interests.

(*Hungering after righteousness*): We may find ourselves in a position of ascendancy over someone, or in a morally superior position, in which case we must take extra care to avoid acting in our own self-interest. Examples of this might be by manipulating the circumstances for our own benefit, or by desiring to look good, to preach at our unfortunate victims, or to further our interests at their expense. Following the mindset we have been learning about, we can take action to cut at the root of self-interest.

Once when I was obliged to share a particularly difficult personal situation with a pastoral team, they moved out of their ascendancy by sharing a difficult marriage problem they had had to work at during their marriage. The interesting thing was that my reaction was to give them all the authority and prestige due to their role that they could possibly have asked for! They did not put on their pastoral surgical gloves to 'deal' with me, but rather joined me in my misfortune and supported me when I was so vulnerable. *That* is how to deal with the flesh that wants to pop up and dominate one's behaviour and attitudes!

(*Blessed are the merciful*): When given an insight into the life of another we can assume either the role of master, or that of servant. If we choose to take a deliberate decision to serve, we cut the ground from under the motives of our flesh.

(*Blessed are the pure in heart*): Taking our personal agenda out of the equation can equally safeguard us from falling into various temptations.

If we consciously work at these safeguards – that is, righteousness, mercy and purity – we may be able to help others, or, as Jesus puts it, be able to see clearly to take the speck out of our brother's eye. If we cannot, we know that the Holy Spirit has highlighted that we would be playacting if we tried to do so.

7:7–12. Snakes and fish

> Ask and it will be given you; seek and you will find; knock and the
> door will be opened to you . . . Which of you, if his son asks for
> bread, will give him a stone? Or if he asks for a fish will give him
> a snake? If you then though you are evil know how to give good
> gifts to your children, how much more shall your Father in heaven
> give to those who ask Him? So in everything, do to others what
> you would have them do to you, for this sums up the Law and the
> Prophets. (NIV)

Why the three-fold exhortation 'ask, seek, knock'? I believe it
is because it is like the Sussex local who, when asked how the
traveller could ride to Dublin, replied, 'You can't ride there
from here.' The subtext is that the traveller has first to find a
suitable port, take the sea journey, say to Larne or Waterford,
and then ride to Dublin.

Likewise when you ask God a question, He cannot always
answer it from where we are presently located. We may have
to move to an accessible port!

It works rather like this: first you ask the question and it is
registered in heaven. A life roadmap is prepared so that the
object of the desire can be reached from somewhere more
accessible. Provided we keep on asking, the Holy Spirit leads
us by the route map until we are at last in a position to knock
on the door, the other side of which is the answer to our original question. When we knock it is opened and we then have
a choice, to enter or to turn back, for we may not like what is
on the other side! The persistent rich young man was faced
with this kind of choice when Jesus challenged him to sell all
he had and give to the poor (Mt 19:22); at this time in his life
he was unable to take the plunge.

Entering after knocking usually involves a change of life-style, which is probably why the episode has been prompted in our mind by the Holy Spirit in the first place. We find that the whole process has been tailormade to lead us into new truth, new circumstances or new behaviour. If we find ourselves engaged on this kind of (bumpy!) process, we may assure ourselves that we are unbelievably privileged. The process can seem unpleasant, but that is only to dissuade the accidental poker, the casual looker or the drifter from picking it up free of charge. We are urged to grasp the scorpion, eat the stone, embrace the snake and it will turn before our eyes into bread and fish and eggs, real food for the hungry of spirit, and a lifter of the head and motivator of the heart.

As a guiding principle, we develop belief that the Father truly knows what is best for the new person, our new self, because as we change and grow, the old desires pass away to be replaced by a longing for the new, *His* new, which only He can satisfy.

What M&As are being addressed here?

(*Poor in spirit*): Can we make room for God in the conduct of our life? For should we choose to do so, we will be learning new ways to solve problems, disputes and failures. We may have to wait for answers from God, or for situations to resolve, or for pieces of heavenly jigsaw to make their appearance. A good principle to adopt is 'We know nothing as we ought', as this makes room for the wisdom that comes from above.

7:12. What do we want from others?

> So in everything, do to others what you would have them do to you, for this sums up the Law and the Prophets. (NIV)

In the context of this study, we desire others to exercise the checks and balances and the generosity of the Beatitudes towards us, especially mercy and kindness. So, as we exercise what we have shorthanded as the motives and attitudes, we find that the response tends to be along the same lines, with goodness begetting goodness. I suppose that is why growth in the Holy Spirit is called 'fruit', as it reproduces as well as feeds.

What M&As are being addressed here?

Jesus calls this a summing up of the Law and the Prophets, so it is clear that all seven M&As are being touched upon. To be able to stand outside the circumstances and assess all positions, including our own, against the standards set by Christ requires a good working knowledge of how to make the building blocks of our house. We are now moving towards being able to 'roof over' our house; that is, it is getting near to being fully workable in the Kingdom as we become more able to respond to the requirements of the King, having established ourselves in the faith; in a word, we are moving towards being useful.

Perhaps we could take a little time to think about the seven M&As (below) and fill in for ourselves an explanation and personal illustration of how they are touched upon by doing to others as we would have them do to us.

1. Poor in spirit
2. Mourning
3. Meek
4. Righteousness
5. Merciful
6. Pure in heart
7. Persecuted

7:13-20. Knowing which path to take

> Enter through the narrow gate. For wide is the gate and broad is
> the road that leads to destruction, and many enter through it. But
> small is the gate and narrow is the road that leads to life, and only
> a few find it. Watch out for false prophets. They come to you in
> sheep's clothing, but inwardly they are ferocious wolves. By their
> fruit you will recognise them. (NIV)

This is not an easy path for us to take because it makes
demands upon us that we are not culturally used to meeting,
and requires decisions we are just not used to taking and risks
we have not been conditioned to face.

Our response really depends upon the depth of our desire
to follow the lion into the bush, trusting that it really is
the Lion of Judah! The rich young man who confronted
Jesus about personal prices 'went away sorrowful' (Mt
19:22) because he could not make the jump; at least not at
that time.

I have reiterated again and again the need to hear God for
ourselves so that we can avoid being deceived, distracted or
led astray by our own lusts or those of others. The daily, real-
life exercises that the Holy Spirit takes us through in the
Master's textbook course of spiritual development prepares
us for the sometimes unpleasant task of discerning what is
the narrow and what is the broad way. This may, as I have
heard for some thirty years, be an allusion to the unsaved and
the saved; that is, we enter the narrow gate once upon
our initial conversion, and the rest of mankind careers down-
hill to destruction. But if this were really the case then
God would not have found it necessary to institute the
role of prophet in the Church (e.g. Eph 4:12), whose tasks

include to exhort, edify, comfort and correct our corporate path if we are falling short of our proper role. So my conclusion is that the message of the 'broad way' is a message to the church rather than to the world. There is plenty of evidence of the church falling apart in destruction, and plenty of evidence of the contrary when the church struggles through the narrow gate and the narrow way to find new life.

It is new life that I desire for the body of Christ – life that turns the world upside down, life that disciples a nation. It is in the nature of things that this is therefore a prophetic message, and this very scripture exhorts you to judge its fruits; that is, is it the false message of a ravening wolf (v. 15) or is it good fruit from God (vv. 16–19)?

What M&As are being addressed here?

(*Meek*): Is the trouble you are experiencing in following the path of building your house worth it? Do you discern good fruit coming from the path you are taking? Are you more in control of your reactions to provocation or lust or persecution? In other words, are you more in control and does Christ have more access to your obedience?

(*Righteousness*): When you encounter the various ups and downs of life, do you seek the righteous road rather than the immediately advantageous road? Do you find yourself increasingly at peace with God? In the times of total inadequacy are you more confident that the Holy Spirit will support you and supply your lack?

(*Pure*): When the potential of the Kingdom begins to dawn upon us we can realise we could make a career here! Our motives of self-advancement, of status, of ambition can wipe away our original intent to promote Christ and Him only. We really do have to destroy this kind of personal ambition, not because it is particularly sinful, but because if we are caught in the wrong place at the wrong time we will get hurt and damaged because our calling was for some other purpose, which of course is now suffering and neglected.

7:21–23. Race according to the rules

> Not everyone who says to Me, 'Lord, Lord' will enter the Kingdom of heaven, but only he who does the will of My Father who is in heaven. Many will say to me on that day, 'Lord, Lord, did we not prophesy in your name, and in your name drive out demons and perform many miracles?' Then I will tell them plainly, 'I never knew you. Away from Me, you evildoers!' (NIV)

We used to live near the Brands Hatch racing track, and my son trained as a safety marshal there. The cars and motorbikes would roar around the track on the specified race days, and of course someone would end up winning the prize. But if someone stole onto the track without the proper accreditation and roared round a few times illegally, would they win anything? Of course not, because they had to perform according to the rules of the track, and the president of the track would have nothing to do with an illegal entrant.

Similarly, the Lord will disqualify anyone who meddles in kingdom business without His express command, even if they might know some of the ropes. Pretending submission by mouthing 'Lord, Lord' or by getting involved in contending for the faith when He has not commissioned us to is just asking for His displeasure. Obedience is the key to being trusted, along with pure motives.

What M&As are being addressed here?

(*Pure in heart*): Our motives will be surely tested when the Lord starts the miracles of the Kingdom around us. Let us get our agenda on the surface with Him and confess that we rather like it when the miracles start, when we know more than others, or when we can perceive the true state of things. When the Lord started me on this road He quite clearly said to me, 'Respond to invitation.' So I hid my insights away. I did not let them be known and I must say, I hated the experience. I was like a kid who wanted to tell all his friends about his new bike! In due time I was sought out to speak at various gatherings, but the self-control needed to keep my mouth shut nearly bust the buttons on my jacket.

7:24–27. And finally, the house of my life

> Therefore everyone who hears these words of mine and puts them into practice is like a wise man who built his house upon the rock. The rain came down, the streams rose, and the winds blew and beat against that house; yet it did not fall, because it had its foundation upon a rock. (NIV)

Nowhere is quite so isolated as the place that is cut off by a weather or other natural disaster. We have seen some awful tragedies over the last few years with the floods in India, the West Indies and Bangladesh, the fires in California and Indonesia, the earthquakes in Japan, Turkey and China, and most recently places cut off as far apart as the victims of the great Asian Tsunami and of Hurricane Katrina in New Orleans.

In this story Jesus asks us to imagine a flood rising around the house, high hurricane-like winds 'beating against that house', and torrential rain. This is bad weather! So will the house stand? Well, is it built according to the Architect's instructions? If so, you have His promise that it will. Each part has been bench-tested to a high tolerance by exposure to motives and attitudes. We are safe if we have taken this path to knowing Him and His ways.

What M&As are being addressed here?

(*Persecuted*): If you can withstand in your mind and obedience the assaults that would bully you into abandoning your obedience to Jesus, or to distract you into another way, then your house is withstanding the storms that Jesus describes. Not only is Jesus able to visit and eat with you (Rev 3:20), but others will as well because you and your life have become a shelter and resting place for the needy. These, by the way, may be like-minded warriors in the contending for the faith who just need the encouragement to keep up the fight. Similarly, you too will rest briefly on their shoulder when tired, lonely or dispirited; you have entered a brotherhood of pilgrims, of seekers and of servants of Christ whose history can be traced back to the very fathers of our faith.

Conclusion

Yes, it is finally taking shape. The results of my struggles with the motives and attitudes shown up by my daily struggles to obey the Master are finally giving me a blueprint for life. I can live in this structure; it will protect me, keep me and serve as my base in my work for the Father. It is strong enough to invite the Father to stay and to begin to count upon it for His plans in the area of influence to which He has brought me.

Not that the struggles cease after some kind of mountain-top or plateau experience. No, they go on and we are watched closely by friends and foes alike to see how we react to the pressures of this world. But now we know the score. We know what is going on, and the sense of the strategic struggle strengthens us in the battles to maintain our behaviour shift.

Because of this we begin to withstand pressures we never thought possible (neither did those watching!), and this walking with God in intimacy and awareness makes us true ambassadors for Christ.

CHAPTER TWO

THE WEAPONS OF OUR WARFARE[1]

Introduction

In this chapter we examine how minds may be influenced by skilful manipulation, and how, by making ourselves aware of the pitfalls, we can avoid being tied up in ineffectual knots. We then go on to see how both the private and public agendas are controlled and how we may combat them.

In understanding these devices, especially by examining biblical precedents, we make ourselves aware of the battlefield of the mind. Our task is to master these devices so that we, like Jesus Christ *the* Master, like Paul, like Wilberforce, may once again regain the high ground of national influence that our opponents held for the best part of the last century.

---

1. 'For though we walk in the flesh, we do not war according to the flesh. For the weapons of our warfare are not carnal but mighty in God for pulling down strongholds, casting down arguments and every high thing that exalts itself against the knowledge of God, bringing every thought into captivity to the obedience of Christ' (2 Cor 10:3–5).

The practice of recognising and engaging in the battle of ideas is both an invigorating and a maturing process, forcing us back to the Scriptures, to prayer, to intercession, to humility and, best of all, to a new intimacy with our Father and our King and God, Jesus Christ.

This is meaty stuff. Enjoy!

Michael's People

We are now in a new era, that of the joining of two interests that actively oppose the people of God: Islam and liberalism. Islam's present-day inspiration comes from Iran (Persia of old), and the secular postmodern world of liberalism is the successor of the Greek democratic ideal. It can be seen increasingly clearly that Christianity is the only religion which may be freely mocked by both these philosophical entities in our nation. This suits an Islam which has England firmly in its sights as a proselytising target and also a secular liberalism which aims to destroy the Christian idea of Jesus Christ as the absolute God whose word is law and whose truth is absolute.

This linkage of Persia and Greece is foreseen in the warning to Daniel by the Glorious Man: 'And now I must return to fight with the prince of Persia; and when I have gone forth, indeed the prince of Greece will come. But I will tell you what is noted in the Scripture of Truth. No one upholds me against these, except Michael your prince' (Dan 10:20–21). The Prince of Persia (now represented by Iran) and the Prince of Greece are described here as combined in their activities against the Glorious Man, who is described again in the New Testament and named as 'the Son of Man' (Rev 1:13); that is,

Jesus. And no one helps Him except: guess who? Michael the Prince of Israel ('Your prince' He says to Daniel).

So if we want to get help in our contention for the faith against the princes of Greece (secular humanism) and of Iran/Persia (Islam), the seat of modern Islamism, do you think it would be a good idea if we took the heavy hint passed to us through Daniel and were helped by Michael, the Prince of Israel? Well, perhaps a 'good idea' is not sufficient, so we should ask whether there is a New Testament reference to the connection and mutual support between Christians and Jews. There is, and it is found in the three chapters of Romans 9–11, where Paul discusses the predicament of his brethren the Jews, and the attitude which we the church should adopt towards them.

In these famous chapters, Paul refers to both the *nation* of Israel as a collective and the *persons* of his generation (his 'brothers') as individuals. If we bear this distinction in mind we can fathom quite easily the references he makes to both groups of people. Thus when he says, 'My countrymen according to the flesh . . . to whom pertain [present tense!] the adoption, the glory, the covenants, the giving of the law, the service of God, and the promises . . .' (Rom 9:3) he is thinking of men and women he knows by name, as well as the others of his generation. He is grieving and sorrowing for actual persons (Rom 9:2). And when he says, '*But to Israel He says* . . .' (Rom 10:21) he is referring to the nation as a collective, as an historical entity.

The Scripture in these three chapters warns us to honour the 'lump', the commonwealth of Israel, because we Gentile Christians are connected to the root through Israel the collective, the historical entity. The use of the term 'lump' here refers to the lump of dough made from the holy first-fruit offering of the harvest given to God through the priest (Lev 23:10). Thus if the 'first-fruit is holy, the lump is also holy' (Rom 11:16). The parallel here is made to the root also making the branches holy, both Jew and Gentile, and the root of the nation of Israel's relationship with God are the covenants He made with the Jewish patriarchs and prophets, particularly Abraham, Isaac and Jacob. So clearly we have access to the rich grace of those covenants through the last covenant promised through Jeremiah to 'the house of Israel and . . . the house of Judah' (Jer 31:31), which we celebrate as 'the New Covenant' (Heb 9:15), whereby Jesus 'is the Mediator of the new covenant, by means of death' (Heb 9:15) and is the one we ourselves depend upon to be saved. So we are inextricably linked with the Jews, the lump, the natural olive tree, as we partake of the richness of their root, their covenant with God, our New Covenant. The Greek used here (Rom 11:17) is *sunkoinonos*, which is to do with companionship and joint partaking together.

Thus if we are able to embrace both Israels – that is, the historical entity with whom Jesus has made His covenant and Paul's countrymen of today – then indirectly we will be attracting the support of the Prince of Israel against the princes of Islam and liberalism and will draw deeply from the richness of the root and lump (Rom 11:17). The heavy hint to Daniel expressly says that there is no one else to help. Furthermore, we will not risk the dreadful fate of falling foul of the 'severity of God' and being 'cut off' (Rom 11:22) or being overwhelmed by the manifestation of these two princes in our day. Do you think there are sections of the Christian church that are 'cut off' in our nation, where their members are going to heaven, but they are irrelevant regarding the contention of the faith in our generation? Should we not all have a part to play in establishing the Kingdom of God in our nation (as it is in heaven) once again?

The alternative to helping the Israel of God is neatly and frighteningly summed up in the famous banner God set over His people: 'I will bless those who bless you, and I will curse him who curses you' (Gen 12:3).

We are engaged in a struggle to the cultural death in our nation. The ISIC Report *Islam in Britain* (Isaac Publishing, 2005) lists the frightening Islamisation of our nation in British media, local and national government, education, law, immigration, national politics and foreign policy, language and dress as the nation begins to submit to Islamic influence.

Likewise, Maranatha's paper 'Evidence, State of our Nation Today' charts the frightful, agonising statistics of 100 years of secular social philosophy spelled out in terms of social disintegration, crime, debt, disease, drugs and so on.

We need help and we need to put our house in order. Let us obey God's word to us, turn from our neglect, or worse, of the Jews, repent and seek God's forgiveness and help in this our time of great need. If we help them, God will help us in our spiritual warfare; this is above all in the Christian church's own interest for self-preservation, as well as to help us in our calling to evangelise our nation, to teach our people once again to honour the Lord in our day.

If we have this mind, maybe we will also see the day when the Jews '. . . will look on Me whom they pierced. Yes, they will mourn for Him as one mourns for his only son, and grieve for Him as one grieves for a firstborn . . . In that day a fountain shall be opened for the house of David and for the inhabitants of Jerusalem, for sin and for uncleanness' (Zech 12:10; 13:1); and also the New Testament promise, 'And so all Israel will be saved, as it is written "The Deliverer will come

out of Zion, and He will turn away ungodliness from Jacob" '
(Rom 11:26).

In the light of this latter scripture, which is the conclusion
of the exposition on the olive tree, we may reasonably ask ourselves whether the process of both engrafted and natural
branches taking their proper place in the olive tree might have
a part to play in this end-time scenario of 'the Deliverer will
come out of Zion, and He will turn away ungodliness from
Jacob'. If so, we should not risk getting in the Lord's way in
His end-time purposes and it behoves the church in our
nation, both corporate and individual, to repent of its neglect
of the Jews, to turn and befriend them. In the context of the
princes of Greece and Iran/Persia, this in turn will be a most
potent spiritual weapon in our armoury, 'mighty in God for
pulling down strongholds, casting down arguments and every
high thing that exalts itself against the knowledge of God' (2
Cor 10:4), which describes exactly the help we need.

The issue of the Jews, Michael's people, is one of the major
stumbling blocks for the church and one we must grapple
with if we are not to be rewarded with irrelevance and
all our efforts to spread the gospel ending in frustration
and fruitlessness. We have addressed this issue in more detail in
Chapter 4, for we must put our house in order before God does.

Metanarratives

Catching the wise

I once watched Luis Palau confound everyone on the panel of
a religious TV programme chaired by a master of the debating forum, a Lord and senior broadcasting grandee. Palau's

stance was so simple, so reasonable, while all around him were gnashing their debating teeth, getting themselves tied up in knots! He just moved the debate to a stance of his choosing, led, I have absolutely no doubt, by the Holy Spirit. Until, that is, the presenter managed to corner him in an historical dilemma from which it was clear he thought Palau could not extricate himself. He had not counted on the backslidden history professor suddenly switching sides and robustly defending Palau, demolishing the attack with ease. Palau just sat back and smiled. I had just watched a classic battle of wits in which the Lord had trapped the presenter in a framework of his own making or, as Paul notes in 1 Corinthians 3:19: 'He catches the wise in their own craftiness.' It was an education to watch the Master at work.

The importance of engaging is that the struggle is watched by the multitudes in the valley of decision. And the conduct of the struggle gives them a chance to make their decisions about who they are going to serve for eternity as they stand in the valley. It is therefore our duty to engage – in righteousness – in order to discharge our duty to the gospel.

The book of Acts is full of the struggle for the minds of men. Think of Paul and Silas in Philippi – ostensibly losing the battle in public by being committed to jail, only to win the jailer and his family to Christ, then secure a public apology, then their release and then the establishment of the first church in the city!

And like Paul in Philippi, it is such a powerful struggle that we do not even have to win the primary contest in order for the righteousness to be seen and to win hearts and minds, and achieve all the objectives of the Kingdom for Jesus.

The issue is, do we engage or not?

Metanarratives

With a selected number of tried and tested meaningful truths we can construct a *framework of reference* or in philosophy-speak a metanarrative. We then use this framework, and others we develop (see the following section), to peer through in order to judge information that comes our way to see if it fits the frame. If it doesn't, we have the tendency to reject it, explain it away, avoid it or fight it. The framework enables us to skip the lengthy process of evaluation each time we are called upon to make a judgement. There are, however, several features of frameworks that we should be aware of so that we can use their strengths but be unhindered by their weaknesses.

Frameworks/metanarratives are exchangeable

What we might consider to be self-evident truth today may in fact only be the habit of measurement we are currently using. We only have to regard the fashions in thinking in areas such as politics, clothing, psychiatry, architecture, even education, cooking, art and literature. True, there are classics among the above list, but it is apparent that we make contemporary constructs so that we may conveniently order our thinking and therefore our actions without a major crisis several times a day.

How many times have we said, 'If I knew then what I know now, I would be in a different situation today'? Or sometimes the review is only rueful: 'How could I have said or done such thing? I don't believe I could be so stupid.'

But of course we were probably not so stupid. We took a decision that we may have taken many times before but perhaps didn't realise one or more framework factors had changed, rendering the result inappropriate.

Frameworks are part of verbal warfare

Establishing frameworks wins arguments. A good TV interviewer will try to get a politician off the safe territory of agreed policy PR and onto *his* ground. It is sometimes interesting to see the same interviewer put one politician on the spot and then immediately put the opposing politician on the spot using the opposite arguments! The skilled interviewer has been trained to become a master of the use of frameworks.

How is it done?

The mastery of framework-setting is the first skill in destroying the wisdom of the wise from within. Examine how Jesus used a change of ground in all His exchanges with those who challenged Him. He did this in His dealings with the scribes, the lawyers, the Pharisees and the Sadducees. He dragged His opponents onto the ground of *His* choosing. He never danced to their tune, He always set the agenda.

For example, Matthew describes how the Pharisees challenged Jesus about breaking the fourth Commandment by working on the Sabbath when He healed the sick man (Mt 12:11–13). Jesus first referred them to the Sabbath working of the priests making sacrifices (Num 28:9–12), then to the higher law of mercy over sacrifice (Hos 6:6); that is, He made the case for works of mercy on the Sabbath. The Pharisees were speechless.

He is the Master, the Teacher, the example of how to enter this marketplace of ideas and win in the beauty of righteousness. His debating stance in overcoming the wise of His day should be required study for all Christians.

One Christian biologist, a research scientist, when examining a morally repugnant Parliamentary Reply on genetics, thought the position was lost before her contention had even begun. The Holy Spirit told her to look again. Under His direction she was shown the threadbare science of the reply and how to respond. He even led her to the latest scientific papers to back up her position. She found that if Jesus Christ the King is the truth (Jn 14:6, 17) then anything that opposes Him is by definition not true and will contain internal contradictions that will destroy it in the hands of a trained servant. She was subsequently called upon to prepare a paper for the EU Commission who were investigating the issue.

The steps

First, ask the Holy Spirit to show you the frameworks being used.

Second, ask how you can avoid the traps contained therein.

Third, ask how you might follow the way, the truth and the life to reframe the discussion and drag it onto your ground.

Fourth, realise that His ways are not our ways. 'For the weapons or our warfare are not carnal but mighty in God for pulling down strongholds, casting down arguments and every high thing that exalts itself against the knowledge of God, bringing every thought into captivity to the obedience of Christ' (2 Cor 10:4–5). Some of the more unusual weapons are:

- We have access to the truth.
- It is the Father's good pleasure to join in alongside us.

- We are not wedded to a closed philosophy which inhibits our contention.
- The opposition are always at risk of turning upon each other.
- We have the Holy Spirit, the greatest power and the largest databank in the universe.
- Despite our feelings, we look intimidating.

Fifth, seek to destroy the opposing argument by way of its internal contradictions. This can come in a flash of a second or in a reasoned debating paper, and it is called 'destroying the wisdom of the wise from within'.

Even philosophers have moments of enlightenment! Spinoza wrote: 'Truth, as light manifests itself and darkness, thus truth is the standard of itself and error' (*Ethics*, Part II).

This is one of the main themes in the first four chapters of 1 Corinthians and needs to be studied at length with enlightenment from the Holy Spirit in order to master this debating tool. However, we have included a few help notes as an *aide memoire* in the following.

Destroying 'the wisdom of the wise'

First of all we have to come to the state of mind where we depend upon God totally and understand that His ways are not our ways (2 Cor 2:5–12), as David found in his remarkable restraint in asking God for instructions the second time the Philistines attacked. God gave him the famous 'Mulberry Tree' tactics and David once again triumphed (2 Sam 5:17–25). David could have been forgiven for going straight ahead and repeating the tactics he had used a short time before which had brought him victory, but in this 'Mulberry Tree' experience he had learned the fundamental lesson of this walk: 'His ways are not our ways.'

We must ask for instructions and in that way we can emulate the man of the Spirit Jesus describes in John 3:8; that is, we become completely unpredictable.

And these instructions will include where to attack, when, with what weapons and which allies . . . witness Brian Souter and Cardinal Winning in their joint campaign to fight the promotion of homosexuality in our primary and secondary schools. What an unlikely combination, and what power is available – the John 3:8 principle in action!

And God often uses the arguments of the enemy against them, so that He causes them to fall into the pit that they themselves have dug (Ps 57:6; 37:15). In other words, He destroys the wisdom of the wise *from within*! (See Paul's use of the principle in Acts 23:6–8 when he sets the Pharisees against the Sadducees by means of their own arguments.)

Destroying the wisdom of the wise from the inside is also a function of the thinking adult to teach us to develop judgement for ourselves, a necessary faculty of churchmen who are engaging in contending for the faith.

Where do we start?

1. Read how Jesus Christ handled the way of truth in Matthew 7–14 and the apologetics of Paul in Acts 17:16–34 and Acts 23:6–9. There is really no better tutor than the Scripture when we are enlightened by the Holy Spirit.

2. Start testing every received opinion you encounter against Scripture and the voice of the Holy Spirit, acknowledging God in all your ways. You might then start in private to

test newspaper articles, TV documentaries and discussion programmes. Do not necessarily express your thoughts publicly at this stage. Ask the Holy Spirit to explain the mysteries of the Kingdom when they just do not make sense (1 Cor 2:12) as there is usually a reason, and we develop a more wonderful intimacy with Him as He tutors us.

3. Develop gentleness and compassion for those around you. The Holy Spirit will not want to harm them by your careless use of the insight He gives you.

4. If you choose to reply to the media, avoid at all costs the tag '. . . as a Christian', or using Scripture references. Remember the aim is to destroy man's wisdom by its own internal contradictions; for example, the use of 'rights' is often the recourse of a weak argument.

5. Keep a diary. I was interested to note that David seemed to be a diarist, even in his banishments (see the header notes of Psalms 51, 52, 54, 56, 57 and others). In doing so, passing revelations are trapped and stored for future use, and not lost.

6. Be aware that the spiritual weapons made available to us really are quite dangerous, and if we engage, we will attract flak. Make sure you only engage in battles that the Holy Spirit releases you to with Him, and do *not* turn back like Ephraim in the day of battle (Ps 78:9; Lk 9:62).

This is 'contending for the faith' and really is what we are born for. It is exciting, stretching, breathtaking and deeply satisfying, developing a new intimacy with the Master and a new understanding of His heart's concerns.

Identifying Metanarratives/Frameworks

Forming the mind

Paul, in his letter to the Philippians, described the reason for his incarceration in Rome as the 'defence and proclamation of the gospel'. He likewise exhorted his readers: 'You stand fast in one spirit, with one mind striving together for the faith of the gospel, and not in any way terrified by your adversaries' and: 'And do not be conformed to this world, but be transformed by the renewing of your mind' (Rom 12:2). The disciple of Christ is truly free because he is free in his mind! Solzhenitsyn, one week into his imprisonment after illegally losing his colonelcy in the Russian Army, threw up his arms and cried, 'I'm free!'

We have studied and attended classes describing the fundamentals of our faith so that we understand the necessity for the vicarious suffering of Christ on the cross, His glorious victory and the eventual culmination as He sat down with the Father on His throne. We have looked very hard at ourselves to root out personal sins, and we have evangelised to the best of our ability. So far, so good. But the second part – that is, 'with one mind striving together' and 'renew your mind' – is neglected in our generation. We have lost the capacity to use our minds in the defence of the gospel because we do not know the issues our minds should address. We cannot prepare or equip our minds for contention in the world, and we are easily routed in the field of ideas by an (inferior) opposition.

One of the reasons for this is that we just do not have a convincing worldview of our own, a 'one mind', and at best we seem to try to accommodate, to tolerate, to be inclusive and 'loving', but we have no backbone of our own, no story to tell.

We will be looking at philosophical opposition later, but it is useful to consider some of the 'devices' of enemy philosophies right now and also consider what our own frameworks might be.

Oppositional metanarratives/frameworks

I would commend books by authors such as Paul Copan, Marcus Honeysett, Alistair McGrath and Ravi Zacharias for more exhaustive treatment of how to resist doctrines which oppose the gospel. However, a brief overview will serve to bring our attention to the underlying secular religious themes which have discipled our nation today.

1. 'I want to be free to do whatever I like' (or variations on the same theme)

Although this has been the cry of rebellious and irresponsible men down the ages, it finds succinct expression in Rousseau's 'All men are born free, but are everywhere in chains'. Rousseau's own behaviour was irresponsible, leaving several women to cope with his babies so that he might be 'free' to roam Europe and inflame others with his call. If you are on a desert island and solely reliant upon your own resources it might be possible to be free in this sense, but it is quite simply not possible in the interdependent world of the West. By the way, men are not born free but as dependent babies in the trust of those who have given up a measure of freedom to care for them!

2. 'There are no such things as absolute laws'

Variations on this theme are very common, and those espousing it are usually completely unaware of the contradiction in the statement. All laws require a basis in the absolute, or they are not laws.

3. 'There is no such thing as right and wrong, only injustice and oppression'

Again, the speaker is usually unaware of his contradiction in his recourse to a legal framework which presupposes a law of right and wrong (however eccentric). In which case it is right to question the basis for his law; for example, what right had he to frame it?

4. 'There is no such thing as truth'

This is a variation on objection 2 above, and contains the same kind of inner contradiction. This is clearly hypocrisy since no philosopher would accept subjective treatment of his salary or bank balance; he would soon be putting absolute arguments if his monthly pay packet or his bank balance were 50 per cent short!

5. 'Communication of original intent is impossible without the presence of the author'

A clear impossibility with most texts, which supposedly allows the reader to make of any text anything he likes, as he is the only authority present. However, if this were true, the individual would raise no objection if his hi-fi instruction book referred to another model, or if road signs pointed the wrong way.

6. 'Heterosexuality is oppressive'

Unless the speaker is advocating complete abstinence, then he is promoting variations on homosexuality as a logical alternative, which is as oppressive as his original accusation. The logical outcome of this position is a loss of identity, as definitions of gender, morality and behaviour are obscured, and a breakdown of social discipline that prevents sexual abuse such as paedophilia.

Supportive framework/metanarratives

So, in order to establish ourselves in the faith and know the issues the Lord Jesus Christ has decided for our generation and deal with them vigorously, we have to be masters of our minds and of the ideas that are the tools of our trade. We have seen briefly above how our spiritual opposition's stall has been set out (and there is a lot more and a lot more complicated in addition!). Now we must set ourselves the lifetime task of learning how to think and how to hear with which Holy Spirit intellectual treasures, both old and new, to fill our renewed mind.

The first thing to understand is that ideas come in parcels, neatly packaged as frameworks. The new term is of course 'metanarrative', but I prefer to call them frameworks because I tend to be a visual person, so I see ideas frameworks as concentric circles, each larger one giving the context for the one it encompasses, rather than the more common description of seeing them as 'over-arching' metanarratives. This is because 'over-arching' lends a kind of superiority to the larger concept which does not necessarily apply, as the significance or power of a concept should be clearly defined by its nature and content rather than its title.

Warning! Frameworks are exchangeable

Paul warns us in 1 Corinthians 13 that 'we see in a mirror, dimly', and Jesus warns His disciples, 'I still have many things to say to you, but you cannot bear them now' (John 16:12). He called Simon and Cleopas 'slow of heart', and they themselves described their experience with Him on the Emmaus road as, 'Did not our hearts burn within us?' Hearing revelatory truth involves the heart and attitudes of a man, and sometimes we are just not up to it, maybe because of entrenched attitudes (such as the apostle Peter on Simon's roof in Joppa – 'Not so, Lord!', Acts 10:14), fear of man, fear of novelty, or sheer lack of elasticity of mind. Our understandings are constantly enlarged, modified, grown and rejected as the Holy Spirit leads us further into greater truth. Like the pearl swapper in the Lord's parable, we are always ready to sacrifice what we have for what the Lord may give us next. Aren't we fortunate to be on such a journey!

But when our heart calls 'halt!' on us, we stop growing. There is no need to; we can continue to a ripe old age as the apostle John did, being able to receive greater and greater insights into eternal truth as we do.

And so it is with these 'concentric circles' I am describing now. They are without doubt dim and vague approximations of the truth, the real, but they will serve until you or I can replace them with something more accurate. Hold them lightly, let them help you contend for the faith and serve the Lord Jesus during your times of opportunity, but remember that these ideas, and others like them, are not eternal Scripture and will pass their time of use.

How it works

Each concentric circle of ideas interacts with those either side and also, to some extent, with all the others. So it is rather a slippery exercise to get into. But once we have established the concentric frameworks, we are then able to place statements, philosophies, procedures, arguments, logical analyses, criticism and, most important of all, contention for the faith into a context and understanding so that the most effective defence of our living faith may be undertaken. The Holy Spirit is able to shortcut laborious trails of revelation and lead us directly to the kingdom perspective so that we are acquitted good workmen, able to handle the dynamic of His intervention competently.

The first, inner circle: The church of Christ Jesus

So I see a succession of circles starting with the church of Christ Jesus as the inner core, as the yeast, as it were, which leavens the whole lump of the world of men and women in their context of space, time and events. I believe the use by Jesus of the idea of 'leaven' is potent. He uses this idea quite freely; that is, of a foreign entity introduced into a functioning body and converting its nature; He uses it when describing His Kingdom permeating every part of a life, as well as the seducing spirit of Pharisaicism. In itself, it is a neutral idea, describing the way ideas permeate and spread through a person or a group or a community. It is in fact a principle of seeds in His creation, so let me make it clear that I use the idea of leaven in the context of 'The kingdom of heaven is like leaven, which a woman took and hid in three measures of meal until it was all leavened' (Mt 13:3).

The second concentric circle: Contention for the faith

The church of believers contends for the faith, not God, as Paul encourages us (2 Tim 4:2–7); we cannot leave it to Him as though we are safe in some kind of religious ghetto cut off from attacks from the outside world. If this is not clear to us from Scriptures, it should be clear from the daily evidence of the newspapers and TV news that show the tip of the iceberg of persecution of Christians worldwide in the honourable tradition of brave martyrs throughout history from the book of Acts onwards. It is also made clear by the definition of the call of God upon Paul's life – the call of an apostle of the faith – in Acts 9:15, when Paul was told through Ananias, '. . . he is a chosen vessel of Mine to bear My name before Gentiles, kings, and the children of Israel. For I will show him how many things he must suffer for My name's sake.'

But the method of contention is critically important. First, Christians sacrifice and intercede for others, not to promote their own personal interests, epitomised by our Lord on the cross and His extraordinary 'Forgive them, Father, for they know not what they do'. That is why we have a Christian martyr tradition whereby its sacrifices for the proclamation of the Kingdom of Christ are, in the end analysis, for the sake of those who oppose the faith, not to advance the powerbase of its own cause.

Secondly, the engagement of the church universal in contending for the faith begins with the destruction of the philosophical frameworks that govern the thinking of a society, because all contention begins in the mind. Without significant advances in this area, there can be no convincing defence of the gospel when faced with ruthless and fierce opposition. The gospel of the rulership of the Lord Jesus Christ has all the intellectual material it needs to destroy the philosophies of this world, past, present and future, as promised in the Scriptures (see 1 Cor 1:19–20; 3:18–20). Fortunately, God has prepared specialists in this field, such as The Zacharias Trust and others, who can train our minds and provide us with all we need to overcome the Goliaths the intellectual world can produce. And it is this field which we must first master before we can even hope to contend in the open field of Mammon and the power structures of this world, even at the personal one-to-one and local level.

Thirdly, when we are fully equipped, the Holy Spirit may release us to move out into the fields of operation the Lord has decided for us, whether they are local, national or international, somewhere 'on the outer wall' of the church. That means we move into the arts, media, literature, poetry and other story-telling media and thus to the governing bodies to influence national culture and thus the policies that guide the nation in its behaviour in the world. *It does not mean, however, that we seek a theocracy in our land, but rather we operate the considerable power of influence.* It can be seen immediately that influence as a modus operandi fulfils the condition of 'salt and light' that Christ laid down, and that it is the apostolic role of the church.

Fourthly, personal preparation is of the utmost critical importance. It is no use presenting a message if we ourselves are somewhat divorced from its implications. We have to be trained in secret by the Holy Spirit in how to conduct ourselves, how we might be overcome unawares, how to sustain suffering, insults and/or forms of abuse that would seek to deflect, overcome, obscure or discredit our claims. For after all there is no better way to attack than to attack the messenger! The Lord Christ led the way in His discourse on the Mount as He taught His disciples and then demonstrated the lessons that would see the disciples fill Jerusalem with their doctrine (Acts 5:28).

The third concentric circle: The church is in a contemporary time–event context

Although the church, in effect, never dies, and even joins with Christ in heaven, its actions are always expressed in time and space, against a backdrop of events in the world. There are always events which challenge the church so that 'the hand of each generation is trained for war'. So, although we have an honourable history and examples of those who are fathers in the faith, each of us, to a greater or lesser extent, can become like them in the time–space–event context in which we find ourselves.

So, how do we go about finding the current challenges specific to this time–space–event context? I would suggest we start by asking ourselves the following:

1. What is the world time setting that we find ourselves in, and how do we define it?
2. What are the particular challenges of this age?
3. What are the *unresolved* but still significant challenges of previous ages?
4. What are God's strategies (King David's Balsam tree response, 2 Sam 5:22–25)?
5. Where are the stategists and how do we recognise them?
6. What are the challenges that these people face?
7. How are they to be reached, and what is the language that has to be employed to communicate with them?
8. What are the religious deceptions and oppositions to be aware of?
9. What are the worldly deceptions and oppositions to be aware of?
10. What are our strengths?

11. What are the opportunities?
12. What events are significant in opening up expectations and minds to the possibilities of new metanarratives, and how might these be taken advantage of?

Bear in mind that each of us should be involved in an expression of these issues, whether in a small group, or locally or nationally. The whole, building up into the body of Christ, presents His gospel in a comprehensive way from the least to the greatest across our nation, reaching into every home, institution and community of whatever background.

The fourth concentric circle: Church is priestly-prophetic not kingly

There is only one King, and that is Christ Jesus, the Son of God. The church, at any level, must not step into His role except as He directs, and then only with trembling. The greatest power we should aspire to is *influence*, for with influence, as Professor Michael O'Shea points out in his book *Influence*, there are fewer restrictions, fewer paradigms, fewer deals, fewer prices to pay than a ruler has to deal with. In the US the Moral Majority Christian lobby group found this to be horribly true when it became embroiled in national politics after aligning itself with the White House party of the day and found itself trying to defend unholy government policies.

With influence, we are free to present our agenda without compromise or concession and with the maximum persuasion possible and the utmost integrity! It is putting Christ's injunction of being 'salt and light' into practice. Where we see the church placing itself in the ruling position we see problems, as Oliver Cromwell found out when honest dissent became a conflict of loyalties. His and his sympathisers' positions became untenable when the king refused to hear and act upon matters which were commonsense and necessary for the nation. Cromwell found himself leading a revolt which led to the execution of King Charles and the institution of a theocratic commonwealth in place of the kingdom of England. Peter himself was also forced into this position and was obliged to answer, 'We ought to obey God rather than men' (Acts 5:29).

The fifth concentric circle: The world in a sandwich

Over the world of men and women, time and the natural universe, all things in heaven and earth there sits the Ruler, Christ Jesus the King. It is His operational will which is the nature of the Kingdom of God. So the world of men and women is in something of a sandwich: internally it has the church always with it, like leaven, and externally there is the Kingdom of Christ Jesus, to whom, one day, 'every knee shall bow and every tongue confess that He is Lord'. Vine describes the world as 'men and women organising themselves in alienation from and opposition to God'. Thus it can be seen that they really are in a fix, regardless of the extent of their desire to escape into rebellion. The presence of God is always with them, particularly when they persecute the church.

The sixth concentric circle: The Kingdom of God

The apostle Paul tries to describe the current, future and eternal operational will of Christ in time and eternity in the first few chapters of Ephesians, Colossians and Philippians. It is an epic of love, beauty and power unsurpassed in literature or human experience. In fact, possibly because of its sheer scale, we tend to glide over the texts. But pause a moment and read slowly, tasting each word, and see the passion with which the Father and His Son love us, sacrifice for us and prepare for us, not only now but eternally, those delights that meet every ache and aspiring desire of our souls. In fact so transcendent is the experience that He Himself, 'for the joy that was set before Him, endured the cross' (Heb 12:2). I am not trying to lessen His obedience to His Father, of course. I am just pointing out that there is up ahead of us exceeding joys at His right hand.

But here and now, God has prepared good works for us 'that we should walk in them' (Eph 2:10), and in order to do so, He has made us His workmanship, created in Christ Jesus for that purpose. It is this worldview, that of the sandwich, that inspires us to see our present time in the context of the rolling nature of the Kingdom in time, taking our place in the expression of His will in our particular time.

The seventh concentric circle: The Father

Behind the Scriptures describing the honour bestowed on Christ Jesus we mentioned earlier in the epistles of Ephesians, Colossians and Philippians there is the last and first and eternal figure of the Father of our Lord Jesus Christ. I really have nothing further to say on the subject – just that He is the limit of everything, summed up for me in His description of Himself, 'I AM THAT I AM', and echoed by Christ Himself: 'I AM' (Jn 8:58).

How to use the supportive frameworks

It can be immediately seen that if we are trying to deal with an issue by using the wrong framework, then it is doomed to be limited or even to fail. So for example, if we do not recognise the issues in our time–event context, but try to deal with them using our church's traditional methods, or address issues which properly belong to a previous age, then we will not achieve maximum effectiveness. If we seek to achieve in the church what God has given to the Kingdom, then the same applies. If we seek to dominate or rule as a church authority (like Cromwell), we have not understood the fourth circle. If we do not understand the 'sandwich' principle, then the world will always be confusing and unassailable to us. And so on.

Although you may have seen this simple mental help immediately, you will appreciate its potency as you apply it in daily life as you observe what is going on around you in both the world and the church. As the Holy Spirit leads you into all truth you will find that this worldview will help you take shorter time to understand newer mysteries (to you) of the Kingdom, or help you over painful readjustments.

The Kingdom Dynamic of the Interventionist God

From religion to relationship

We have been so used to going it alone in the Lord's business that we can easily lose the memory of Him waging the battles in our stead. But we are emphatically not alone, and should we find ourselves out where we should not be, then we are well advised to look for our King's banner and rally to Him quickly.

We must not pay lip service to an interventionist God because this, in the long run, only serves to sentence us to a prison of self-deception. The way we avoid this is to move from religion to relationship with Him, and this book is written specifically to help us develop in this respect. Are we accustomed to His presence in worship, or in prayer, or in signs and wonders in church services? If so we are fortunate to have some experience of the divine in, as it were, 'walking in the garden with Him'. But that experience is not meant to be confined to goose-bump time on Sundays or special occasions. It is far more vital as a dynamic when confronting everyday challenges.

So we must learn to transport this awareness into everyday life, and understand the correct contexts for looking to this awareness for wisdom, guidance, competence, power or deliverance.

For example, my son telephoned me recently and told me of the unpleasant experience of his Directors refusing to honour a 20 per cent part of his (successful) business tender to do with a certain profession. Ian had worked hard and skilfully on the preparation of his successful bid, and so his frustration was profound. At that moment his mobile telephone cut out and I took advantage of the break to quickly ask the Lord for guidance, although I know next to nothing about Ian's business. The word came to me: 'We are not lawyers.'

Ian reconnected a moment later and I told him what the Lord had said (i.e. that his company were not lawyers but contractors) and as I spoke, the prophetic word expanded to explain that his client really needed a specialist company with a legal department already set up to take that 20 per cent of the contract because liability for malpractice was on the increase.

Ian gave the word to the client, suited to his audience, and we were all astounded the following day by a national press conference given by the Hertfordshire police announcing that they had just broken an international internet paedophile ring centred on the very profession the word from God had spoken about! Ian had avoided a huge potential liability which his company would have been unable to handle.

Ciphers or friends?

What is there to learn from this? We are not ciphers in some cosmic game, but we are friends of the Most High, voluntarily locked into Him by the slavery of increasing love. By applying to the Holy Spirit for kingly wisdom as part of our ordinary daily life we develop from religion to relationship with God, an essential connection if we are to follow Him in the pursuit of His kingly objectives. It also means of course that we can begin to operate outside of our normal parameters of competence as we have increasing access to the one who knows the end from the beginning of all things.

'Dynamic' means lively, energetic, forceful, active, immediate, practical. This must match our expectation of the Kingdom of Christ Jesus.

The nature of His power, both personal and public

The active presence of God is a required accompaniment whether we are waging 'war in our members' or contending for the faith in our community. The Lord's Kingdom is a dynamic, it is power, it has plan, it has purpose. It is all to do with Him and His rule. The Lord's Prayer defines His rule: 'Thy kingdom come, *thy will be done on earth as it is in heaven*'. There, in a nutshell, is what it is all about, and how many times have we prayed that definition without examining the words? So what does it mean? Try this: 'The Kingdom of God is the will of Christ for your generation.' That, of course, immediately begs a number of questions which will keep us all occupied until the day we die. However, in order to begin somewhere, let us understand that there is a dynamic at the very heart of His rule to achieve what it has been sent forth to achieve (Is 55:11). We make a mistake if we think we are alone and must rely upon our competence to achieve kingdom purposes. This is not a religious position, a nod in the direction of piety. On the contrary, it is a given; that is, 'No kingdom power, no Kingdom'.

In following through the building of our personal house (see Chapter 1 of this book), we will become aware of His generosity and power on a small scale. Indeed, as we stumble about in half-belief that this is a sensible procedure at all, it is often difficult to look for the divine intervention that the building needs. But as we accustom ourselves to leaning on a person we cannot see and relying upon a power we cannot control or direct, we accustom ourselves to another way of walking through life with all its challenges, joy and pain. As we gradually shake ourselves loose of relying upon what we can see, touch, feel and control, we enter a newness of life which must be experienced to be believed. Without losing sight of that we must try to exercise the awareness of His power operating on the large scale at work, in our community and in our nation.

Although Pitt the Younger was an extraordinarily successful prime minister, he was something of a recluse, a very private man with few friends, except that is for Lord Wilberforce, whom he trusted above all others. How is it that Wilberforce was this central to the halls of power in a time of war when many priorities pushed out desirable social priorities? Because, of course, God had placed him and his small band of Christian lobbyists there so that in due time the call He had placed upon his heart would come to pass; that is, the momentous freeing of slaves. The change would not have been possible without the dynamic intervention of God and His chosen servant (Acts 9:15).

There is, then, as part of the discipling of the nation, the dynamic of the interventionist God. This must be remembered at all times, no matter how successful the walk, no matter how we may be lionised, no matter how lofty our status, or how humble our station and calling, or how obscure.

A very obscure man, Ananias, knew God intimately. So much so that he held daily conversations with Him! He pops up once in the Bible (Acts 9:10) to launch the great apostle Paul into his ministry and then he disappears, but he was essential to God's plans for the spreading of this marvellous gospel to us, the Gentiles. So thank you, Ananias!

In summary . . .

I see three main components that must be in place to bring about national revival through personal revival and church revival:

1. The dynamic of the kingdom rule of Christ Jesus, both personally and corporately.
2. The training and calling of the apostles.
3. The cry of His people, the church.

All three are from God, are energised by Him and return to Him.

Arché, Friend or Enemy?

Understanding of the concept

Arché, translated 'principality' in the New Testament and pronounced 'arkay', is a ruling entity that springs from the creation of an institution or 'corpus' by a person or group of people. A typical everyday example is the formation of a business that gets bigger than its creators, who end up serving it rather than the other way around. The process is that first it is formed by an act of a person's will in giving it life, then it begins to abrogate authority and power to itself that does not belong to it, then it begins to rule its creators. (In British law, a limited company is actually called a corpus, and has similar legal rights to an individual citizen!) Finally it can become, although not necessarily, demonised and controlled by spiritual beings. One might see Disney's cartoon story of the *Sorcerer's Apprentice* as a representation of this process, for example. If you are in business at any level you can see it every day and observe numerous examples.

Origin and purpose of arché

I believe God has allowed this method of the ruling of persons to exist in order to have a continuance of earthly governance without chaos at the end of any particular period. When the ruling *arché* is destroyed, however, chaos can often be seen to reign, as the ex-colonial history in Africa can show or, to a more limited extent, in Eastern Europe after the fall of the Wall, or the aftermath of Tito's death in Yugoslavia.

I think the origin of *arché* governance can be found in the Garden of Eden. Man reached for the fruit of the tree of the knowledge of good and evil (Gen 2:6); that is, he moved to appropriate law-making powers to himself. However, he really is not up to that act of creation, and he finds that his laws deteriorate over a period of time, necessitating finer and finer points of law to be made to cover unforeseen exceptions to the rule. The system eventually becomes top heavy and his

arché finally grinds to a halt in a welter of detail and recrimin-
ation and injustice.

Marx echoes this in his circular dialectic, whereby the
downtrodden ruled peasantry rebel to become the rulers, and
then in time, the new underclass revolts to become the new
rulers in turn. The Cultural Revolution in Red China was a
vain attempt to purge the ruling system or *arché* of the new
revolutionaries settling in to make governance their own.
Marlon Brando starred in a memorable film of South America
portraying the same process in a South American republic,
with the revolutionary hero-president recognising in his
middle age the new young bull of a revolutionary destined to
push him out of the presidency.

The significance of hearing in the Kingdom of God

The perfect form of earthly government found in the Garden,
that of man ruling by hearing directly the living word of God
(Gen 1:28–30; 2:16; 3:9), was eventually replaced in the
Israelite nation by a framework of law administered by local
authority, with exceptions to the rule and national emergen-
cies being dealt with by judges. This developed tragically into
the usual earthly government of a monarchical civil authority
as the Israelites rejected the intimacy they had with the living
God (1 Sam 8:7).

The operation of the Kingdom of God by hearing His word
of direction is the way God created governance to operate in
the Garden, and how He attempted to lead the children of
Israel by means of judges rather than kings.

With judges as the means of governance, the glory of governance is hidden in the heavenlies (Heb 8:5), but with kings,
the glory of governance can be seen on the earth, even if it is

but a pale shadow. The Israelites wanted their governing glory to be seen in competition with and set against their neighbours (1 Sam 8:11–20), a tragic ego-exercise. Hence they rejected direct governance by God (1 Sam 10:19) for governance by man.

How can the *arché* of human governance be controlled?

Perfect governance is by hearing and obeying the word of God, as instituted in the Garden. As kings cannot seem to combine governance with hearing, God has instituted prophets to shout at kings to change the course of their ways; that is, God guides the *arché* of human governance indirectly by the crude method of prophetic utterance (2 Sam 12:7), as in the prophet Nathan with King David. There is, therefore, influence upon the *arché* rather than control. Unfortunately, when there is little or no prophetic voice of righteousness, the ruling of peoples eventually goes haywire, as various ex-Communist states might now testify, and as the hardness of the Pharisees and the Sadducees in Jesus' day would be an example.

And today . . .?

If, then, this is an accurate description of *arché* in human affairs, we must now seek to understand from God the practical everyday way He would have us exert influence on the controlling *archés* of our day.

One answer seems to be in the prophetic voice guiding the transient, popular fashions of the day's thought with creative ideas and originality from a repository of wisdom, together with strategically placed men and women within the system who are trained and brave enough within their sphere to represent the voice of God.

For example, in the nineteenth century of British history, such men would be Wilberforce, Shaftesbury, Cadbury, Arch and Temple. The church (Anglican, Non-Conformist and Catholic) swung popular opinion behind these lone voices by prayer and their ceaseless representation of Christian-Judeo thought and example. There was no imposition of the Christian agenda upon the nation; the nation itself moved towards it to embrace it. The *arché* of British governance, the course of the nation, had been changed, however imperfectly, to follow in the footsteps of the Lord, fulfilling the duty of the church in the Great Commission in Matthew 28:19.

However, if this is not in place, the *archés* of this world are a fearsome and cruel force against which there is little protection. The only way I know to combat an *arché* is:

First, to behave in accordance with the M&As and the understanding that Jesus has already overcome the world systems (Jn 16:35) (that is, all *archés*) and this is a kingdom issue, not a church, intercession or spiritual warfare issue. In other words, realise that this is one of those occasions when the battle is the Lord's, not ours, and there is precious little we can do to influence the outcome, except get out of the way and let Jesus rule.

Secondly, we have to understand that only an *arché* can combat an *arché*, even in the world, so as Christ controls all *archés*, He can set one against another. Usually these are money-based, but there can be other power bases such as ethnicity/religion/family/prestige and so on. A good contemporary example is the way the paying customers revolted against the sale of GM foods in the EU, despite the most powerful high-level lobbying by multinationals such as Monsanto and Novartis. The press took up the theme of 'devil food' and the supermarkets followed their marketing nose and banned them. This was one *arché* against another or, in biblical terms, the Lord setting ambushes against each other. When the Kansas Christians lobbied for the reintroduction of creationism teaching in schools, they managed to set off the determinists (Darwinists) against the free-willers. But only the Lord can set the ambushes, because this kind of conflict is kingdom against kingdom, and the Lord fights these battles, not us. Our job is to stand in the evil day, be righteous, understand prophetically what is happening, and take advantage of the opportunities the Lord opens for us.

Developing Wisdom

Wisdom: the secret of power

While examining the frameworks and *archés* of our everyday world and taking part in proposing God's alternatives, we also need to keep in mind our own worldview, our own frameworks. There are three main fundamentals.

First, the rule that Christ exerts (His Kingdom, by definition) does not belong to us, so we cannot manipulate it, control it or own it in any sense whatsoever. In a phrase, the church of Christ is subject to the rule of Christ, His Kingdom, not the other way round, and we together with all things are or will be subject to Him. The church of Christ is His body (Col 1:24) and as such we must do what the Head expects us to do.

Secondly, we need to see our nation in an organic, developing, historical setting, vulnerable to change over the centuries, including the one we are in right now!

Thirdly, we need to perceive the lessons of the Garden of Eden experience as possessing the seeds of our present and our future.

Bearing this in mind, let us explore how we may seek the wisdom of Christ so that we may be entrusted with our part in bringing revival to the nation.

The nature of originality

The strategy of our enemy has been to conceal and confuse who we all are in relation to a just God. And, by and large, one might think he may have done a good job. In parallel to the proclamation of the good news of the Kingdom of Christ preached over two millennia, the enemy has sought to persuade us that we cannot really know anything outside of ourselves. There are two main philosophical methods: one the empirical (I will not believe unless I can see it, touch it and repeat the experience at will) and the other the rationalist (I cannot believe anything I cannot prove from inside my mind). These two principles, although dressed up in the modern uniform of liberal scepticism, date back to at least Aristotle and Plato respectively.

However, God already prepared the ground for these assaults in the Scriptures when He said His name was 'I AM' (Ex 3:14; Jn 8:58), for that statement is already outside of laboratory experiment and philosophical possibilities. His other claim, to be 'the Creator', also shoots holes in the fabric of scepticism as He announces He is the original Cause of all things (Jn 1:1–3), which include events, people and the material world.

The nature of derived identity

'I am' is the ultimate subject and 'you are' is the ultimate object. We are, then, the 'you are' of God. We are derivative. He is the original, the only 'I am', the authentic subject. Thus if we are the products of His will, we are the objects of His mercy, His wrath, His purposes, His relationship.

So, calling ourselves the subject or the originator is meaningless if we are obliged to refer to something outside of ourselves to give any measurement of meaning. Philosophers have great fun with students with this principle. As we are not original we cannot have originality within us, therefore the search for meaning within ourselves will be fruitless and despairing, a nonsense, a self-contradiction. Francis Schaeffer explores these issues at great depth in his masterful books *Escape from Reason* and *The God Who is There*.

So when a deconstructionist of the postmodern school asks the killer question 'Can you prove God exists?', the technical answer is 'Can you prove He doesn't?' This is not a cop-out because the postmodernist must then define his starting point, which is in fact that there is no God. But that is a preconception that has no proof in and of itself, and if held as a valid position from which to start, then the Christian position that 'there is a God' must be equally valid.

Further, by asserting a preconception that there is no God, the postmodern position is trying to introduce an outside influence to validate its starting point, but there cannot be an outside influence by which to measure value if the self is the measure of all things. Its values must of necessity have no value, therefore, as they cannot be measured by an agreed external-to-self standard. The best the postmodernist can say is, 'If there is a God, then I have no access to Him, therefore to me He doesn't exist.' But that statement is a cop-out, because that does not mean He does not exist and, further, as there is access to God through Christ Jesus, then it would be more accurate to say that he refuses to seek access to Him through the way that has been prepared for such as him. His position is therefore more like hypocrisy than scepticism.

The Christian, on the other hand, starts from the position that there is a God who can be known, and that He is the great 'I AM'; that is, the original from which all things are measured. Thus the Christian is by definition an object, not a subject, and can only be a subject by entering into the life of Christ, known technically in the Christian worldview as 'being born from above'. Because the Christian as an object can enter a subjective experience and has access to external standards to measure his existence and the world around him, he is in the unique position of knowing who he is, where he has come from and where he is going. It is unique because that existence is unknown outside of the union with Christ (Rom 6:5; Col 2:12, etc.). Thus when the Scripture calls those who do not know Him 'lost', it does not exaggerate.

Does all this seem somewhat esoteric, a little unnecessary perhaps, an exaggeration, a sideissue to the real business of getting on with evangelism? Unfortunately, to properly understand the road, you must read the map because the enemies of the gospel have moved too far and have taken too much ground for us to be able to 'wing it' any more. Thus if you are unaware of the philosophy that now pervades our educational system, geography, arts and the media, English, history, or the health industry, then you will simply be inadequate to follow the Holy Spirit into the areas that the enemy has made his own. The recent generations that have been going through our educational system have been fed postmodern philosophy as though it were mother's milk; that is, absolute truth. They have no means by which to know what has been done to their minds because we in the church have not troubled to enlighten them, and have thought it was enough to 'witness' in the high street with a guitar. Through ignorance perhaps we have not realised that our nation's future rulers, opinion formers and educators are being educated that self is the highest god and there is no other, and Christianity is an enslaving philosophical relic of the ignorant past that needs to be smothered and ridiculed.

We, in our generation, must find the means to arm ourselves in order to destroy 'the wisdom of the wise' from within their own house of cards.

The search for meaning

To look outside of themselves to establish a reference point in order to give meaning to their perceptions, people may define themselves by taking a mechanistic, deterministic view, such as, 'We are part of the cosmos, a random collection of molecules', or they may prefer the mystical by making a jump to Gaia, astrology, the elements, or gods that describe their circumstances, such as the god of fire, war, love, death or famine.

Christians, however, are on a different track in their search for meaning as they know where they have come from (born from incorruptible seed), they know where they are going (to be with Him) and they know who they are (sons of the living God). And yet even Christians, in attempting to deepen their perception of this great and precious salvation, can miss the mark of authenticity.

For example, we can attempt to find meaning in *circumstances*, which, while these are admittedly external, is doomed to failure, as there is no consistent way to react to them. We can also try to fill the void of lack of meaning by *activity* (particularly self-sacrificial activity), or by the *pursuit of goals*, or by *inventing an inclusive system* of explanations.

Christians are not exempt from these four blind alleys, all of which lead to despair and emptiness in the end. In fact, as Christians we can have a greater sorrow because we know the Scriptures promise complete meaning and more, '*I have come to give you life and that more abundantly*', and our reading of the great saints backs up this promise.

But if He is to give us this 'great and exceeding promise', it cannot by definition belong to the four deceptions above. For example, it is impossible for any of us to enclose God's purposes in Christ within a *system* of prophecy, of end times, of church structure or of any other man-made construct. This is obvious really, but would cost most of us a lot if we acknowledged the fullness of its truth.

The difference between meaning and data

There is a very precious experience in Christianity called 'revelation'. Revelation is when a biblical truth ceases to be words on a page (data), and becomes meaningful to us, an engrafted part of our lives. Establishing meaning in our lives is an essential process designed to help us make sense of our surroundings.

I remember a Mr Wrigden, a school history teacher, who could make history sit up and beg, even in our very tough class, and there would never be so much as a snigger when he took the lesson. He made the history of dates and kings live so well that we were there in our mind's-eye.

We have all had experiences like this, happily perhaps in church as well. I once took detailed notes of Pastor Hector

Gimenez's sermons at a summer camp. He started with a ten-minute strict biblical exposition, then he told stories of his experiences illustrating the main theme for about forty minutes and finally he summarised his experiences in the light of the scriptures first expounded. It was a master at work, transporting us from the draughty tent to his huge campaigns in South America, his 250,000-strong church and his experiences with national leaders both great and small. And the teachings live in the memory because we were alongside him in his adventures as we joined in his narrative to picture and take part in the scenes he drew with his word-pictures.

The use of narrative, then, is a way of conveying meaning. *Revelation is the inner process by which meaning is given to data that comes to life,* for we have identified with it by a vicarious experience. A story that illustrates the truth therefore has me myself as one of the characters, which thus enlists my endorsement of the truth it carries as I accept and participate in the circumstances of the story.

A perfect example is Jesus and His parables, when He would ask His listeners to imagine a lost sheep or a woman searching for her jewellery or a farmer sowing seed. Or the guy selling all he had in order to buy the field with treasure in it – imagine his wife's reaction! In Paul's apologetics, or Peter's or Stephen's, there is the use of narrative of the history of Israel to capture their audience.

How many books and audio tapes are languishing on our shelves, the contents forgotten and ignored because they only contain data – dead information – and have never caught us up to participate in lively truth? Therefore, in trying to convey something that does not belong in the hearer's currently accepted framework, we have to overcome the difficult problem of converting data (dead information) into meaning, whether we are the messenger or the receiver.

We must be aware, therefore, when Jesus describes the process in terms of new wine and old wineskins, or a new patch on to old cloth, He is explaining to us that newness of truth is an understood problem of progressing in the Christian faith. New truth often comes to us in the appearance of stones or scorpions or other nasties rather than in the nice, acceptable and familiar appearance of bread, fish or eggs.

We then have two alternatives: either examine the new truth to see how we might destroy its threat to our comfort zone, or embrace it and see if it accords with revealed Scripture. Or as teachers, preachers or apologists do our utmost to invite participation in the story of our truth. This is not as straightforward as it seems. I well remember the horrified reaction of certain evangelical Baptists in my village trying to come to terms with the baptism in the Holy Spirit – forgetting the equal horror their fathers in the faith had caused by their insistence on scriptural water baptism, and the terrible persecution *they* endured for this truth to survive!

How then can we be sure that God is calling us to move on, to change our perspective, our accepted measure of things? Well, the Scripture exhorts us to test the spirits to see if they are from God (1 Jn 4:1), to exercise our senses to discern good and evil (Heb 5:14), to be enabled with a Gift from the Holy Spirit (1 Cor 12:10), to discern good and evil, and to look for good fruit (Mt 7:20) and a pure fountain (Jas 3:11). And if the revelation is from God it will inevitably bring with it the peaceable fruit of righteousness (Jas 3:18), it will be easily entreated (Jas 3:17) – not defensive or aggressive – and it will have as its objective the building up of the believer and the church (Eph 4:12–13). New truths from Scripture will not require twisting and squeezing to fit and will not lead to the believer's destruction (2 Pet 3:16). True revelation then has to run through a testing hoop that will destroy the counterfeit and set the truth at liberty to change us more and more into His likeness.

We must likewise be aware of this holy process as we prepare our apologetic material for the new listener. We must also be aware that this is what our enemy is up to all the time in order to disciple this nation. We not only contend for the faith, we contend for the opportunity to expose truth and lies to the watching people, to allow them the chance to make informed decisions for life. The fields this shall embrace will include economics, genetics, history, community structure and education, and it will give a national voice to those helpless who do not have one.

The road to wisdom

There is a progression and development from receiving data from the Holy Spirit to when it becomes wisdom to us, as Jesus promises: 'He will guide you into all truth' (Jn 16:13). The steps have five elements:

Data

Data is the elemental material of communication, the first sight of raw information.

Knowledge

Knowledge is the capacity to archive data coherently. We may be able to see it, describe it and remember it, but that is about all at this stage ('. . . but you cannot bear [it] now', Jn 16:12).

Understanding

Understanding is the ability to handle, use and set knowledge in perspective. This is where we are 'getting a handle' on some truth by relating it to something in which we are already able to move. For example, once we are able to speak in tongues, it is a revelatory progression to receive ~~words of prophecy~~ but it is not outside of our comprehension because we can already move in a similar spiritual environment.

Meaning

Meaning is the skill to move safely and knowingly into the data and act in it as a principal in the story that the data represents. However, although we are able to use the data, we have now to learn when and in what manner.

Wisdom

Wisdom is the development of the ability to make judgements concerning the data that satisfies the righteousness of the cause being served. The highest form of wisdom is demonstrated by Jesus as He was able to gather all His actions and speech within the parameters of what He saw His Father doing (Jn 5:19). The data is now in safe hands.

Implementation of wisdom

So in understanding how truth is perceived we move to a wisdom whereby we may be able to do something about it. First, we understand that without the Holy Spirit's intervention even our own side will not understand what Kingdom of Christ is doing. And secondly if we understand how the enemy has worked his devices then we can plan our response accordingly. Our object is to disciple the nation in accordance with our Master's commission, but in order to obey Him, we must first understand the nature of the battle ('know our enemy's devices') and train our minds for war if we may by any means win souls for Christ, keep our nation in the bounds of Christ's Kingdom and not permit our rulers to 'cast off the fetters of the Lord and His Anointed' (Ps 2:2–3).

Fortunately, we are not sent on alone by our Christ. He is with us in several specific ways in order to facilitate our contention for the faith.

The two aspects of the kingdom rule dynamic

First, the outworking of God's will upon the earth is a dynamic, not a dead letter which can be examined, taken apart, defined, organised and controlled. Secondly, the dynamic can only be truly perceived in the generation of His visitation – it is present, organic and alive.

It may be possible to understand a little of yesterday's visitation, or (like C.S. Lewis and Francis Schaeffer) a little of tomorrow's. But the main thrust of the kingdom rule of Christ Jesus is today's moving dynamic of God's purposes. It cannot be defined as the culmination of past events (meditate upon Matthew 21:43–45), or even the precursor of future events (because there are always the missing jigsaw pieces of events that the Father keeps to Himself). It can only be defined as today's.

This is most marked at the national/global level and least at the personal level. It is like a small child on a long train: his own carriage is the limit of his comprehension; anything beyond is speculation.

This brings an immediacy to everything, both in my personal development and in my sphere of influence. It also makes our relationship with God personal, raw and hot.

The role of the prophetic

The attitude of the prophetic in all its definitions is to examine in Holy Spirit light the signs of the present times (Mt 16:3; Ezek 13:5), *not* to second-guess the future. In analysing the Holy Spirit revelation, it should always be acknowledged that we see through a glass darkly, that what we see is only the seeds of the future and that a large part of that future God has abrogated to Himself in mystery. Our task is to prepare our minds and thus our lives for whatever He chooses to bring about, nationally and personally, and be content to allow Him the freedom of action, mystery and unpredictable surprise that is rightfully His. We call this the Event Syndrome.

The event syndrome

The kingdom rule dynamic, being in the present, contains within itself novelties of its own that cannot be predicted. For example, it was foretold in Scripture that the Messiah would be born in Bethlehem, and also that He would 'come out of Egypt'. No old sage could in his wildest moments have foreseen the whim of the Roman emperor Caesar Augustus to hold a census which would require all Israel's people to return to their tribal home town, or that a jealous tetrach would start a murderous campaign to kill newborn children, obliging the Lord's parents to flee from Bethlehem to Egypt from which they later emerged. *The unknown future 'event' cannot be predicted and remains*

God's prerogative alone and renders nearly all foretelling mere speculation. (There, however are examples in Scripture of remarkably detailed foretelling, such as the prediction about Cyrus and the warning of famine in Acts 11:28, but on the whole there are usually large pieces of the jigsaw missing. God really is in charge.)

The personal dynamic

Thankfully, God does not restrict the action to a few Elijahs, but has prepared a personal aspect to the kingdom rule dynamic for each of us (Heb 8:11). Ephesians 2:10 tells us that we are His workmanship, created in Christ Jesus for good works, 'which God prepared beforehand that we should walk in them', and Philippians 3:14 exhorts us to press towards the goal of the upward call of God in Christ. It is essential that we understand it is our purpose in life to discover and develop our calling under God together with all the saints, because our objective in discipling the nation is to reach our nation from the least to the greatest, with no one left out.

Intimacy

Intimacy with the Father through worship

'Why worship?' has been an abiding battleground for both apologists of the Christian faith and its opponents. Typically a critic may argue (not ask!) that if God is so big and self-sufficient, why would He need to be worshipped? The subtext is that should the claim to holiness prove to be hollow by God exhibiting vain human characteristics of pride or bullying, then God is not holy and must therefore be an imaginary human construct which it would be illogical to worship. So the criticism is not really about God's characteristic of holiness at all; it is about His existence, and the response must answer at both levels.

But the questioner has in fact hoisted himself on his own petard, that of the holiness of God, when he asks, 'Why does God need to be worshipped?' because it allows us in reply to cover far more ground than otherwise.

God doesn't *need* us to worship Him in any sense whatsoever, for He is completely self-sufficient in Himself, and contains all that He requires within the loving relationship of the Trinity. On the contrary, it is we who have the need because our particular problem comes with how we can possibly communicate with that Being who is totally and completely the essence of all existence and from which anything that does exist, has existed or will exist is derived.

All Christians know, of course, that there is a new and living way – that of the cross of Jesus the Christ, the only begotten of the Father – by which the repentant Christian has had offered to him a possible approach to this Source of all life and existence. But even so the chasm is so wide and deep – if the real Person has in fact been perceived – that there is only one possible attitude for the applicant to have and that is of total and complete awe and overwhelming gratitude. And thus we have arrived at both a sound definition of worship and all that is required in response to the question 'Why does God need to be worshipped?'

(The background to this position of the vicarious work of the cross of Christ is not the subject of this book. However, it is hoped that this all-too-brief a touching on the cross has served its purpose as background to understanding worship as one of the most powerful weapons a Christian has in his contention for the faith.)

There are three main components of worship that underpin our stance before the world at this start of the new century. First, worship offers us the possibility to exercise and mature a living relationship with God's Son Jesus Christ in whose Kingdom we now reside. Secondly, it gives us a superior worldview. Thirdly, it gives us motivational pleasure.

Growing the relationship

This has the effect, first of all, of allowing me to know who I am in this age of deceiving and beguiling philosophies, because I know who He is and that I am derivative of Him by being born from above from His 'incorruptible seed'. This knowledge of identity is related to and dependent upon Christ as the Rock, the eternal Son of the Father of all creation, the God Jehovah, and it grows stronger as the relationship with Him grows through the intimacy of worship. The second effect is that as we begin to know ourselves through the illumination of the Holy Spirit and in the light of Scripture, we may then move towards fulfilling the potential God has placed within all of us. As we no longer feel like a square peg in a round hole, the intimacy of worship allows God to unfold the purposes we are being called upon to perform. And thirdly the sense of belonging gives us real security; that which is not dependent upon salary, status, position, education, power, inheritance, race or colour but upon being chosen by the Father and having His personal blessings and privileges showered upon us.

And although most of the above is to illustrate what God has provided for us through the maturing of our relationship with

Him, it is all directed towards the growth of His Kingdom, that area of His rule that He exercises through His saints on the earth. The Kingdom is about the Father's will and the Son's obedience and our part in it, not purely about what we can get out of it. As President J.F. Kennedy might have said, 'Ask what you can do for the Kingdom, not what the Kingdom can do for you.'

A superior worldview

We belong to a vision that the Father has had from the beginning, which St Paul takes a considerable time to outline, and for which the Son endured the shame of the cross for the joy of it. It stretches beyond our own time upon the earth, it is high and worthy and it encompasses all that is good and right within all that has been created. The vision is of the rule of Christ Jesus, which will be sublime in its beauty and wisdom and which knows no limits to our exploration. Compare this to a determinist who thinks his flesh is all there is to reality and reality ceases the moment that flesh loses its life. No wonder his temptation is to 'eat, drink and be merry, for tomorrow we die, and to hell with the consequences'. Which is of course exactly where his attitude will lead him.

This Darwinian, determinist view of human behaviour has come in for some severe criticism from some unexpected quarters because of its complete antipathy towards the weak and helpless. For example, not only is fascism derivative of survival of the fittest or most able to adapt and repudiated in most political arenas, but feminism has awoken to the licence determinism would give male behaviour in, for example, its attitude that rape is 'natural to men'. This posits that rape is programmed into the human male and that he is not therefore really personally responsible for any such sexual crime he might commit. Rightly, feminists are outraged by this entirely logical development to determinist thinking.

But intimate association with our God through worship motivates us to keep His most holy laws; that is, our very desires mature to accord with His, to protect the weak, the inarticulate and the disadvantaged because it is right to do so, even though there is nothing directly in it for the Christian protagonist himself.

Jesus confides to His disciples shortly before His last journey to Jerusalem that He had 'many things to tell them but they couldn't bear them now'. This was not about the things He would suffer or indeed the things that they might suffer. A very short while later, however, on the road to Emmaus, He began to share with two disciples the things He couldn't do so before. Those things were truths about Himself and His Kingdom that are unpalatable the first time of hearing. They disturb our sense of boundaries, our proprieties and our sense of what is a right worldview. The same goes for us as we too explore and learn more about Him and His Kingdom. What we learn can often seem like a stone or a scorpion, but if we persist and stick with Him, it turns into the very bread and fish we have been seeking for so long.

With our eyes opened in worship, we see His love and mercy poured out on all flesh and we cannot help but respond likewise. This is the superior perspective that worship gives in our worldview.

Additionally, worship helps to reinforce the purpose that God has given us in our calling, and develops the humility that allows us to evaluate our progress. It is a common experience for those who actively pursue the Kingdom of God in their lives that their perceptions and perspectives actively grow over relatively short periods of time. Lord Wilberforce started to pursue in 1798 the cause which would end up freeing slaves in all the Christian world. Along the way, however, he and his group also expanded to pursue better factory conditions for women and children, universal education, abolition of press gangs, freeing of 'chimney boys' and wider voting rights. The purpose just grows larger.

And in worship, communication develops both ways; we can express ourselves to God concerning all the issues of life which affect us and our effectiveness in His Kingdom, and we can begin to learn how to hear Him as well. Worship enhances all our meditation and listening faculties until it becomes natural to hear quite particular things from God. The key to worship is the attitude we described at first; that is, keeping before us the majesty of who He is and who we are and exactly how we are approaching Him at all; an attitude of awe and thanksgiving. This is another way of expressing humility. There is a danger of familiarity breeding contempt, which while we would be loathe to admit it, can in fact infect us in subtle ways so that we can become the arrogant guardians of personal revelation or 'leadings'. However, bearing this in mind and being careful about our attitudes, our growing relationship and communication with the Father and the Son can give us remarkable certainty in life, and cause us to develop a more relaxed demeanour when dealing with issues or with people, and an ability to enjoy life whatever the circumstances. And this leads on to the third area that worship gives us; that of pleasure.

The pleasure of worship

Does not the Scripture say that 'at His side there shall be pleasures for evermore' (Ps 16:11)? Worship certainly brings us to His side in this life He has given us and prepared for us. And we need the pleasure that worship gives us for very real reasons. There are times in life when things become fallow, unexciting, gritty and we have to draw upon our reservoirs of faith to maintain the vision given to us. The pleasure of worship helps incentivise us to continue our path and not give up, to heed the Lord's words and to be persistent. When there is a change required in our lives, maybe in our attitudes or maybe in sacrificing a loved post or hobby or political position or the thousand other things we become attached to, the pain of change can be ameliorated by the pleasure and consolation of worship. When we are lonely, maybe abandoned or sold short by others, worship reorientates us and comforts us in the only true centre in our lives – that of the love of the Saviour for us by name.

And by invoking God's eternal purposes as expressed in the Scriptures, by seeing Him as totally in charge of all things in time and eternity, we receive power and energy when we are down and out for the count. He is the source of all power and by plugging into that in worship, we can restart our efforts with renewed vigour and creativity.

Conclusions

Worship offers us three main benefits in our contention for the faith we hold:

1. We exercise a living relationship with our God:
   - fulfilling our purpose in Christ;
   - giving us identity;
   - causing us to belong.
2. We develop a superior worldview:
   - perspective, contrasted with Darwinism/determinism;
   - purpose reinforcement and evaluation of progress;

- communication, especially insight and expression;
- certainty.
3. It gives us pleasure:
  - incentivising us to continue, to change, to sacrifice;
  - energising us.

Eating Flesh, Drinking Blood

This title is a reference to the Gospel of John chapter 6 where Jesus scandalises His listeners by exhorting them to eat His flesh and drink His blood (Jn 6:53). When the multitude is reduced to His central core of followers, He explains that He was talking about His words and His Holy Spirit.

This section is devoted to the idea that in order to follow Him, we must eat His words and drink His Holy Spirit.

Eating the word

The maxim 'You are what you eat' may be a useful slimming slogan, but it is even more appropriate to growing in the knowledge and intimacy of the Lord. Reading the Scriptures is tantamount to quieting ourselves and listening to Him talk with us privately. I still remember the thrill of meeting a world famous preacher over breakfast when my wife and I had him all to ourselves! We asked the questions we really wanted to ask, and got answers which were the least expected but so very fresh. How much more will the Son of God thrill us if we learn to hear Him speaking!

When reading the Scriptures, ask the Holy Spirit to lead you into His truth, and when you run up against something you don't understand, ask Him to explain it to you, like the Lord did for His disciples when they asked Him (Lk 8:9). For example, I read a troubling newspaper column where an (ordained) writer had pointed out differences in the scriptural accounts of the birth of Jesus, in particular did the holy family return to Nazareth or Jerusalem after the birth in Bethlehem? I was led to open a Bible map which showed Bethlehem directly south of Jerusalem and Nazareth directly north, so they would have been obliged to pass through or by Jerusalem on their journey home. In other words, there was no discrepancy between the versions! There were other apparent discrepancies which the Holy Spirit explained through the Scripture so clearly I wondered how I could ever have missed them in the first place. There is a tremendous thrill when an opaque scripture is explained to you by the Holy Spirit – a thrill which becomes an expectation each time you read the Bible. And that expectation of course becomes a great motivator.

Bible reading also equips us with solid frameworks, philosophical answers and insights into stratagems that are used by the enemies of the gospel to come against the knowledge of God. The weapons of the Kingdom are truly mighty to bring them down, to destroy the wisdom of the wise from within, but we must understand our faith and have a solid grounding in the Scriptures from which the Holy Spirit may draw in this 'contending'. Very often, we may be able to draw people into a Bible scenario by means of Bible stories and the very real and human situations people found themselves in. In explaining the resolution of the story, we can perhaps draw our hearers into the biblical perspective of our interventionist and loving God, maybe paralleling the listener's situation. This is a very compelling way to get the Bible into a hearer's mind and heart.

We are also washed and refreshed by Bible reading and this is clearly detected by our listeners. It is as if they realise that they have been with Jesus (Acts 4:13). The Bible keeps us humble if we are approaching it with a disciple's mindset, and this attitude of servant–messenger rather than master–teacher is immediately perceptible.

Drinking His presence into ourselves

Prayer is a practical framework by which we can exercise ourselves and get used to the presence of our God so that we begin to become aware of Him all through the day. The section that follows is a short overview of a nine-part series called 'Prayer School' produced for businessmen. The living material comes from Scripture, so although we are concentrating on the act of prayer, do continue to bear in mind that we also need daily scriptural food and lively hearing! The Scripture gives us substance about which we can talk to God, and it highlights the true perspective to have when doing so.

How to start

Let's start by setting the Lord before us (Ps 16:8–9), because when He is at our right hand, we shall not be moved. Our spirit, soul and body also come into the sort of peace they were designed to exist in (1 Thess 5:23). Let's invoke this law as though it were like the immutable law of gravity.

Why are we praying?

So that we may establish our mindset before Christ afresh daily and be effective in withstanding both the blandishments and the accusations of our enemy.

When should we pray?

I would suggest that you start even before you open your eyes upon awakening! Continue in the bathroom, so that you are emphasising these truths to yourself as you see yourself in the bathroom mirror, as you shower and so on; pray even before the cup of tea, before the newspaper, before family business. You will banish shadows of worry, guilt, fear and so on even before you finish praying, without even addressing the problems of the day! Problems are then brought down to their proper size, ready to be addressed aggressively.

For whom are we praying?

I would suggest you make mention of yourself, your spouse, your immediate family, your closest friends and your ministers. Just name them at this stage, nothing more.

How do we pray?

We must pray aloud like the Hebrews did, and we can move about, maybe walking up and down the room, emphasising with our bodily movements the points we are making. I suggest you try the following for a month, every morning without fail (Is 50:4–5), and you will see the difference, especially if you keep a notebook handy to record your progress. In any case, record what the Holy Spirit says to you.

Start like this:

Father, I pray right now for You to establish in my thinking (Rom 12:2), and in the thinking of those I have named before You today, the covenant blood of Jesus Christ (Heb 12:24) in our conscious thinking and in our experience today.

First, I pray for justification (Rom 5:9); that is, through the blood of Jesus, we are acquitted, not guilty, reckoned righteous just as though we had never sinned, and that all the ordinances written against me and us today are wiped clean from the record against us.

Second, that we are sanctified (Heb 10:10), made holy, set apart for Your use today by the blood of the Lamb.

Third, that we are cleansed (1 Jn 1:7) from all sin by the blood of the Lamb as long as we walk in the light, and we are redeemed from the consequences of our sin (Eph 1:7).

Fourth, we are saved (Eph 2:1–13) from all the power of the enemy by the blood of Jesus.

Fifth, that we can draw life from the blood of Jesus, more abundant life (Jn 6:54).

Sixth, that we can overcome the accusations of the evil one by the blood of the Lamb (Rev 12:11).

Seventh, that we have passage into the holy of holy places (Heb 10:9) by the blood of the Lamb, no longer strangers and aliens from the covenants of promise (Eph 2.13), but now brought near to Your presence.

Don't forget, this is a prayer practice to make the covenant provisions won by the Lord Jesus on the cross for us actually real in our experience and daily life. So use the provisions when you need to. For example, should unworthiness because of your personal history assault you, you might draw on the prayer for justification like this:

Father, I thank You I am justified by the blood of the Lamb (Rom 5:9). The list of accusations against me is obliterated (Col 2:13–14). I stand before You just as though I had never sinned. I do not accept what these accusations are telling

me. Instead I decide to accept Your word. And as for the
accusations of the devil, I overcome them right now by the
blood of the Lamb (Rev 12:11).

Or if you should feel inadequate, pray something like this:

Father, You have set me apart for Your use (2 Tim 2:21), I
am Your servant, Your chosen one (Eph 1:4), I stand justi-
fied by Your choice. No other judgement is therefore valid,
including my own (Rom 8:30–31).

Should we feel 'out of it', then we must remind ourselves that
we are no longer strangers and aliens from the covenants of
promise, but we are now drawn nigh by the blood of Jesus
(Eph 2:13). And so on. There is total provision through the
sacrifice of Jesus for us to triumph over our feelings, or the
devil's accusations, or comparison with the world's behaviour
(1 Pet 2:9–20a).

But we must practise walking in this freedom as the tests
come: try it, the release is astonishing! And of course, as we
begin to set the mental framework that accords with the mind
of Christ (Rom 12:2), our thought life, attitudes, speech and
actions begin to follow suit. The Holy Spirit is teaching us to
go to war by the spirit in our mind; we will overcome internally whatever the evidence might seem to be in the external
circumstances. Then, with some mental victories behind us,
we are ready to move into new territory.

Holy Spirit diversions

Note that we can sometimes move through our prayer time
quite quickly with virtually no impromptu meditation or

diversions by the Holy Spirit for 'special cases' (the timings shown below add up to about seventeen minutes, including a time for meditation). Later in the day, however, He may prompt us into another prayer now that we are attuned to Him.

You may feel this is rather mechanical. All I can say is that the Holy Spirit manages to bless most good things and, happily, disciplined prayer is one of them. Try it and see!

To begin (about five minutes)

First, set the Lord before you so that you will not be moved during today (Ps 16).

Second, make mention of yourself, your spouse, your close family, your friends, your minister and others that the Lord has placed upon your heart. Keep the list as short as possible.

Third, pray for all those you have named, that the blessings of the covenant of the blood of Jesus will apply today in their conscious experience and personal acknowledgement.

Fourth, pray for justification, sanctification, cleansing and redemption.

Fifth, pray for life from the blood, for the power to overcome the accuser, for passage into the holy of holies to be consciously in the presence of the Father.

Prayer for equipping (about one minute)

Sixth, pray for greater revelation of the cross of Jesus Christ, more power in the Holy Spirit, more authority in the name of Jesus, more faith in the word of God and more understanding of the Kingdom of God.

Prayer for the armour (about one minute)

Seventh, pray that all the persons you have named are made aware that they must put on the full armour of God today;

that is, the helmet of hope of salvation, the breastplate of righteousness, the girdle of truth, feet shod with the gospel of peace, the shield of faith and the sword of the Spirit. And that we must become aware of the schemes of the devil and take the appropriate stand against them, resisting until victory.

Prayer for primary ground (about one minute)

Eighth, submitting to the Father, pray that all spiritual forces ranged against those you have named will retreat and flee immediately, especially those attacking areas of calling, marriage, relationships, healings and health, emotions, mindsets and attitudes.

Prayer for spiritual provision (about one minute)

Ninth, pray to be filled with the peace of God, joy and love.

Prayer for projects (about three minutes)

Tenth, pray directly against the mountains in your life to demolish them and provide testimony of the Kingdom of Jesus.

Eleventh, pray for local projects such as the spread of the gospel, greater prosperity in the area, schools, local council schemes and so on. Pray for the peace of Jerusalem and the blessings God promises for those who bless Israel (Gen 12:3).

Meditation (about five minutes)

Twelfth, open yourself to Jesus, expecting your attitudes to be challenged and future action to be outlined. Set yourself to obey.

Thirteenth, obey the King, over-ruling your will, stubbornness, pride and attitudes. Look to allow the Holy Spirit to show His fruit through you. Prepare for miracles, deliverances, new ministry areas, revelation.

You can expect to hear from the Holy Spirit all the way through your prayer time, and by making a record of these impressions, you will not clutter up your short-term memory and will be able to dwell upon them at your leisure and review them later. It is also interesting to track your path with Him over a period of, say, one month, to see the way He has brought you.

In ordering this practice in your life, you will dispel many problems and personal attacks of the enemy, and in conjunction with your Bible reading, it will give the Holy Spirit substantial material to work with. It will be harder for circumstances to rock you emotionally and mentally, and His peace and joy will be communicated to others. The Holy Spirit will be able to lead you into more challenging environments than you thought you could ever face, and you will have the material and the capacity to deal with them effectively.

Apologetics

Apologetics is the discipline of being ready to give an answer for the hope that lies within us (1 Pet 3:15). But . . . answers to what questions? Each age is probably different, but our task is to answer the questions of worldview and assumptions of belief, and by so doing challenge the alternative worldviews that have influenced our communities and the nation at large.

The Christian, with his roots in the patriarchal covenants of Israel, makes certain presuppositions in his worldview; for example, he believes that through His Son the Christ Jesus, God Jehovah of Israel, made the physical world and all that lies within it, and then delegated power over it to man. It follows that man, as the one delegated to, must abide by the rules laid down by his creator and owner (Gen 9:1–17).

Introducing the prince of Greece: Secular humanism

Although there are many fronts on which to confront the enemies of Christ, there is one single overarching enemy that manipulates them all and that is secular humanism. This spiritual force, to which I have referred in the section on Michael's People, is the prince of Greece in his latest form. And as we have already seen, he struggles against the church of Christ suborning an ally in the prince of Persia, the force behind the Chaldeans and Persians of old, and Islam of the present, as Islam's crescent symbol gives testimony.

Secular humanism has been described by at least ten manifestos and declarations, but all own a root in the saying 'Man is the measure of all things' (Protagoras, 485–421 BC), Greek rationalism, eighteenth-century rationalism and nineteenth-century freethought movements. In general these definitions would posit that there is no acceptance of anything that cannot be proved by experiment or logic, and is determinist by nature, supporting the theory of Darwinian evolution by species jump (even though this cannot be proved). Needless to say there is no acceptance of God, His creation, salvation, eternal life or authority. The earliest expression of this reach for autonomy is Adam's fall (Gen 3:5) and was the purpose behind the three temptations of Jesus (Mt 4:1–11); that is, to set up an alternative kingdom to God.

If we do not understand or accept this overarching reality then we are doomed to be a reactive force to manipulations, struggling often feebly on our opponents' ground on their terms and ignoring the major weapons the Lord has given us to defend ourselves and to advance the cause of the Kingdom on the earth in our time.

Foremost in this armoury is the issue of Israel in the thinking and behaviour of the Gentile church, for Michael, 'the great prince who stands watch over the sons of your people [. . . Israel] (Dan 12:1)' is 'the only one who upholds Me [Jesus] against these' (Dan 10:21). If we consider we need that support and God's covenantal blessing (Gen 12:3) then it is time for a rethink on our relationship with Israel and the Jews.

Coming a strong second is the struggle to create frameworks in our nation's thinking which govern behaviour and the spread of the gospel. Secular humanism has had its own way for decades. Now it is time to question its dominance and remove its influence. This section shows us how.

We must address both these issues (our view of Israel and how to frame our responses), ignoring the siren calls of secular humanism, which demands that its priorities are paramount, and we must seek God with all the single-mindedness at our command. For it is He who is our Commander and it is to Him we will give answer; it would be good if we learned as soon as possible what He is demanding of us and how His priorities are to be met.

Secular humanism's worldviews

Determinism

A Darwinian might posit that all physical matter has come together and organised itself by means of accident and natural selection. This accidental joining of forces, which would tend to favour the strongest or most adaptable at the expense of the weakest, leads logically in turn to a determinism that absolves people from responsibility towards others in the name of freedom, and is by definition intolerant of dissent.

The Christian with respect to law posits freedom within form, while the determinist posits anarchic freedom alone. From these basics flow many of the issues where Christians are challenged to give an answer for their hope.

The areas of challenge and the Christian response might be summarised as follows, but a more exhaustive treatment may be sought from authors such as Marcus Honeysett, Alistair McGrath, Ravi Zacharias, Norman Geisler, Jimmy Long and Paul Copan.

Area 1: All text is available for individual interpretation This is an attempt to eradicate authority in communication by downgrading a message to the level of its means of communication. By that I mean that the theory behind this asserts that as the reader cannot know the author or his intentions accurately, then the text has no interpreter and may now be used in any way the reader thinks fit. Hence the appropriation of certain classic texts such as Oedipus by the homosexual lobby and the dismissal of classic political history as propaganda.

The Christian response has rich potential to dispute this. For example, it is clear that the philosopher has confused the medium with the message, like discounting a telephone for the message that it has transmitted. As long as the message obeys the three simple rules of evaluation – it must be internally consistent, it must correspond with reality and it must work practically – then it stands on its own feet logically. It is not necessary to have the author personally explain his work, otherwise we would be stuck at traffic junctions all day trying to contact the road sign designer to see if he really meant us to give way at the junction, or whether it was an arbitrary suggestion for Thursdays only.

Moreover, it is interesting that the Scripture seems to anticipate this situation, as it calls Christ Jesus the 'Word made flesh'. He was, in other words, both the medium (the telephone) and the message (the meaning)! The philosopher is trying to establish interpretation as the new truth, regardless of what the original text intended as its meaning. But this means of course that the interpretation itself has no meaning as it may be subject to a similar exercise of interpretation. The philosopher assumes that the interpreter is the last stop of the conveying of meaning, but he may well not be, thus it would be impossible to express meaning to third parties under this regime. And so all learning, all training stops because it becomes impossible to reproduce original thought.

But this is demonstrably untrue as the proposition fails on at least two of the rules: it is not internally consistent (the teaching itself may be examined as the philosopher himself expressed it), and also it does not work practically as this philosopher clearly wishes to persuade his audience of a fixed point of view regarding interpretation!

Area 2: Absolutes The second area of contention is that of the dismantling of the idea of absolutes, because by so doing God, the establisher of absolutes, may be dismissed also. Unfortunately for the philosopher, however, he has to use absolutes in order to establish his parallel universe of relativities – thus statements such as 'There is no God', 'There is no such thing as revealed truth', 'There is no possibility of certainty in life', 'There are no intrinsic rights and wrongs in life' and the giveaway 'To think in rights or wrongs or absolutes is immoral and oppressive'.

Not only is the philosopher using absolutes in all his statements, he has no basis guaranteed to deliver on his pronouncements and must appeal to a moral law to justify them. Now apart from law being an absolute concept, a given law must have an author external to the fact, and so he is drawn inextricably to a lawgiver external to his universe who can guarantee his parallelism, but there is only one such, and that is God. Now God the guarantor can hardly deny His own existence, so the internal contradiction of the philosopher's argument is total and collapses his position.

His second charge that absolutes are oppressive in the form of the exercise of power is incorrect. If anything, in this kind of context 'absolutes' would be an expression of authority rather than power. Power is only expressed as a form of censure when the authority is abrogated, so the complaint is really about the censure that underpins authority.

But let us look at this closer. The philosopher says it is oppressive, unjust, that his behaviour might be restrained by censure that underpins authority. But the charge of injustice refers to a legal framework of some kind that supports in turn some kind of expression of authority. But if he eliminates any kind of authority, he eliminates at a stroke any justice upon which he might rely for support.

He is of course really talking about the *right* to be lawless, but this right necessarily depends upon an enabling authority, which in turn must have the power of censure over that which would prevent the lawlessness that he longs for becoming the new law. Far from revealing contradictions in the system of absolutes which require legal frameworks and empowered authority, he reinforces its inevitability and the implication that it is a necessary precondition for human interaction. In other words, it is built in, and if it is built in, it must have a builder, so he reinforces the reality of the Creator God and his argument collapses again.

This is not a theological oddity, for the philosophy already pervades our laws. For example, the 'offence laws' depend upon whether or not someone 'feels' offended, not whether something is true; in fact a misdemeanour has not been committed unless a so-called 'victim' says that it is true (for him!). This is developing to the stage where the police are arresting or cautioning people who might have offended a theoretical person!

Deconstruction

This is the distortion and magnification of a legitimate exercise to examine texts for accuracy to the point where any minor discrepancy discovered or any possible alternative meaning discerned immediately invalidates the clear meaning of the *complete* text under review.

This philosophy is another dispute against authority, in this case the authority of language as a defining medium for expression. By seeking to invalidate language the philosopher aims to invalidate any expression of authority, meaning, identity, definition and even personhood, and also to render communication impossible. It is an expression of total lawlessness.

Apart from its inhuman and destructive impact, the philosophy falls down upon the logic of its own position; that is, it can be deconstructed! For example, it relies upon structured linguistic logic to try to disprove structured linguistic logic, and if the philosophy itself may be defined and debated, then communication must be possible after all.

By now you can see that these philosophers have taken seriously the Psalm 2 scripture: 'Let us break Their bonds in pieces and cast away Their cords from us' (v.3). Nothing, absolutely nothing, is sacred, nothing is fixed and everything that is dependable, clean and right is up for grabs to be destroyed and mocked. If you care to follow the Holy Spirit into these areas, be prepared for a real battle of minds, hearts and harsh words, and remember that as you contend, the people in our nation, great and small, watch closely, keep score and make decisions.

Let me say that the above is just scratching the surface. I recently heard Dr Elaine Storkey interpret an episode of *The Simpsons* in the light of the postmodern philosophy it contained so that we could see the subtle persuasion it used through its humour. The Christian audience was really shocked.

I cannot emphasise enough your need to become familiar with the philosophical devices I have outlined above that set out to destroy the gospel of Christ Jesus. If you are able to, please get hold of books by the authors I have recommended above; they will open your eyes to what is going on around you, enrich your passage through this life and help arm you to fight the good fight.

Part 2: Church Revival

The outward dynamic

Whereas personal revival might be viewed as the inner dynamic of the Kingdom whereby we build *our* house, there comes a time of release when the Lord works with us as He builds *His* house; that is, the outward dynamic of His Kingdom.

He does the building of His house, of course (Mt 16:18), but we are commissioned with various tasks on His behalf. We must not appoint ourselves.

To introduce us to this idea, Jesus begins a stream of practical demonstrations of His kingdom power to the disciples to show that He is involved, He knows what He is doing and He has the power to achieve what He wants to. This is the visible sign of kingdom power promised in the Lord's Prayer (Mt 6:9–10).

CHAPTER THREE

CHRIST BUILDS HIS HOUSE

Running with the ball

As we know, church attendance has fallen off dramatically in this land of Wesley, Whitefield and Wigglesworth, despite our best efforts to stem the loss. *Operation World* reports that the UK's Christian affiliates reduced from about 85 per cent to 67 per cent of the population between 1980 and 2000, with total church membership down to about 4,630,000. In asking ourselves why this should be, perhaps we should ask ourselves if *we* have set an agenda which was the prerogative of God to set. In a phrase, have we been running with the ball?

What ball? What would most of us say is the number one priority of the church? Maybe we would say it is to evangelise and get as many new members as possible (what we might call strenuous evangelism); or to exhort the troops to greater holiness because the great outpouring will begin when we are holy enough (effortless evangelism); or to teach more about holiness, evangelism and leadership; or to plant churches, to seek out successful representatives from 'outpourings' elsewhere; or to develop the 'care' ministries to an even greater effectiveness than they currently employ . . .

Do we not often seem like the proverbial gerbil running ever faster on its wheel? 'It works in Indonesia, Columbia, Korea, Argentina, Eastern Europe; why doesn't it work here?' I have seen an incredibly gifted evangelist and teacher work the 'outpouring' oracle in Lithuania, Eastern Europe, following fifty years of Communist oppression only to confess publicly that he cannot get the same results here in the UK.

This is what I mean by 'running with the ball'. Perhaps we are simply not accepting anything outside the framework of reference that does not conform to our priorities of evangelism, personal holiness and the 'care ministries'. Of course these three are vital to any work of the Lord, but can they loom so large that they obliterate any other message the Lord may be trying to give us? We need to learn to repeat the mantra 'We know nothing as we ought, Lord. Please instruct us afresh in the way' until it becomes an organisational given.

We also need to orient ourselves as the disciples were obliged to and learn that the Kingdom of Christ comes not only in words but in power.

This is kingdom power

'Jesus put out his hand and touched him . . . Immediately his leprosy was cleansed.' 'And his servant was healed that same hour.' 'He touched her hand, and the fever left her.' 'Then He arose and rebuked the winds and the sea, and there was a great calm.' 'And He said to them, "Go." And when [the demons] had come out, they went into the herd of swine.' 'Then He said to the paralytic, "Arise, take up your bed, and go to your house." And he arose and departed to his house.' 'And the woman was made well from that hour.' 'He said to them, "Make room, for the girl is not dead, but sleeping" . . . and took her by the hand, and the girl arose.' 'And their eyes were opened.' 'And when the demon was cast out, the mute spoke.' (Mt 8:1–9:35)

The disciples' introduction to the stream of power from Christ's throne is a series of remarkable miracles that transcends their (and our) understanding of the natural world, which Jesus clearly demonstrates is under His authority.

While He is doing this, however, He is also commentating on what is happening; for example, when the centurion makes his statement of his understanding of authority (Mt 8:9), Jesus remarks upon his unusual understanding of faith: 'I have not found such great faith, not even in Israel,' and goes on to warn that faith is the doorway to the Kingdom, and those who think they know better but ignore this prerequisite will be 'cast out into outer darkness'.

He healed Peter's mother so that she was well enough to wait upon them, and then all those who came to Him (Mt 8:15), whether demon-possessed or sick. It had been a long time since God had appeared in such a tangible way in Israel, and the hunger was palpable. The people swarmed as they do today when God turns up.

Jesus was demonstrating He ruled over all things, even sickness and demon possession, because that is the nature of ruling: either He had this total authority or He did not. He was opening their expectation, their understanding of the total rule of God and His desire to intervene in human affairs. He was also building up to the time when He would be able to delegate to His disciples.

He began to demonstrate the essentials of operating under the rule of God; that is, first you are totally at His disposal and can call no place your place of rest until He gives it (Mt 8:20). Secondly, He emphasises that the essential social obligations come second place to His priorities (Mt 8:22). And thirdly, He demonstrates that if you are on business for Him then all things really will work together for good (Mt 8:24; Rom 8:28). In this latter demonstration, the waves were actually breaking over the boat and they (with expert fishermen among them) were convinced of their imminent demise (Mt 8:25). No, it would not happen while they were on kingdom business. Mind you, there is not necessarily protection if we are *not* on His business and decide to test Him out as an interesting egotistical exercise (Acts 19:16).

Kingdom authority

Jesus then leads the disciples into an ambush of ideas to introduce them to the concept that if you are on His business, then His authority overcomes all tradition and common practice.

First, He clashes with the scribes on the issue of the forgiveness of sins (Mt 9:2–5). They are talking about holiness and the law and He demonstrates that He *is* the law by asking whether it is 'easier' to forgive or to heal. Both are impossible of course and beyond us unless we have the power and authority from God to do so. 'But that you may know that the Son of Man has authority on earth to forgive sins . . .' (NIV) whereupon He healed the paralysed man. The people recognised that 'God . . . had given such authority to men'. (NIV)

Holiness can be used by priests as a control mechanism over their flock, whereas God seems much more interested in a faith relationship with Him. Clearly He can deal with the unholy, in ways ranging from the impartation of His righteousness to straightforward correction and punishment. After all, it is for His satisfaction that we work, not anyone else's (Rom 14:4). But unbelief, on the other hand, is in our province, under our control, and He has to wait upon our own decision to trust, adhere to, cleave to, believe, and as we do we grow in understanding of Him and His ways (Mt 8:26).

He then clashed with the Pharisees, who accused Him of associating with sinners, implying that He sullied His holiness by doing so, whereas they relied upon the holiness provided by ritual sacrifices and abstaining from such associations (Mt 9:11).

His reply is interesting. He reminds them of their first duty, which is to administer God's compassion rather than judge one's fellow man, and then goes on to outline His calling, which was to call sinners to repentance. In other words, He was carrying out the duty they had miserably neglected, and it was they not He who were lax. He turned the accusation on its head. The disciples were watching and learning, *as should we be*. This is how to deal with criticism from the 'holier than thou' brigade.

Dealing with criticism from your own side, such as the enquiries by John's disciples (Mt 11:2–6), however, is treated rather differently. It is done with compassion for any mis-understanding and with a full explanation: '. . . the days will come when the bridegroom will be taken away from them, and then they will fast' (Mt 9:15). He then continued upon a concentrated course of demonstration of kingly authority whereby nothing seemed too difficult (Mt 9:35). He raised the dead, gave sight to the blind, healed every kind of sickness and disease and taught the good news of the Kingdom, i.e. of His authority. It was a consummate display, designed to build up faith in His disciples, readying them for the great day of their first practice. He had taught them in word and deed about the ultimate authority He was operating under and demonstrated healings of every kind and also the suspension of natural laws if that was what was required to fulfil a kingly commission.

Delegated power (Mt 9:36–11:30)

The demonstration of Christ's authority had been essential because now it was time for the 'inner twelve' disciples to go out by themselves on Jesus' behalf. They had to believe that they were on a delegated mission and not relying upon their own gifts. Jesus told them in no uncertain terms that if they should fail to convince others in their mission, they should move on (Mt 10:14). He was looking for receptive hearts, not a sales campaign – terms of reference we can and must learn from today.

He outlined their logistics as minimal, their expectations as high, but the responsibility for all results was His (Mt 10:20). If they were not received as befits His representatives, He promised judgement upon the hearers' heads. The whole process was between God and the hearers, not the disciples and the hearers. This included reward as well as punishment.

When they returned rejoicing after a successful campaign, not only in preaching but in spiritual power, Jesus knew that the Kingdom was in formal operation because He had successfully delegated the authority given to Him. *The train of delegated authority is the proof of rule.*

This whole lesson of us taking on His mantle under delegation is summed up by His: 'Take My yoke upon you and learn from Me, for I am gentle and lowly in heart, and you will find rest for your souls. For My yoke is easy and My burden is light' (Mt 11:29–30). For if we shift the responsibility onto His shoulders for the success of our efforts to proclaim the

Kingdom, then we can relax in our own capabilities. That is now His problem; ours is to hear and obey.

The Ideas Battleground

First clashes: Obedience vs tradition (Mt 12:1–50/ Lk 6:1–11)

> At that time Jesus went through the grainfields on the Sabbath. And His disciples were hungry, and began to pluck heads of grain and to eat. And when the Pharisees saw it, they said to Him, 'Look, Your disciples are doing what is not lawful to do on the Sabbath.' But He said to them, 'Have you not read what David did when he was hungry, he and those who were with him: how he entered the house of God and ate the showbread which was not lawful for him to eat, nor for those who were with him, but only for the priests? Or have you not read in the law that on the Sabbath the priests in the temple profane the Sabbath, and are blameless? . . . But if you had known what this means, 'I desire mercy and not sacrifice,' you would not have condemned the guilt-less. For the Son of Man is Lord even of the Sabbath. (Mt 12:1–8)

First of all Jesus points out to the scribes the contradictions in their law (Mt 12:3–5), and that compassion overrules in the service of the Lord as evidenced by their own scriptures, unless they miss it in their haste to condemn the innocent.

> And they asked Him, saying, 'Is it lawful to heal on the Sabbath?' – that they might accuse Him. Then He said to them, 'What man is there among you who has one sheep, and if it falls into a pit on the Sabbath, will not lay hold of it and lift it out? Of how much more value then is a man than a sheep? Therefore it is

lawful to do good on the Sabbath.' Then He said to the man, 'Stretch out your hand!' And he stretched it out, and it was restored as whole as the other. (Mt 12:10–13)

Secondly, by repeating the exercise of healing a crippled man on the Sabbath to see if they had learned anything, He saw that they had not, and their hardness drove Him to anger (Mk 3:5). He caught them in their own trap (a favourite device of Jesus) by comparing the value of a man and a sheep; that is, if it is legal to help a sheep then how much more is it legal to help a man! They were again equating doing good with working on a Sabbath, whereas the Lord desires us always to do good and to show compassion.

It can be hard when we go against others' expectations, as the disciples were to learn later (Acts 5:29). But we have to learn how to obey Christ rather than tradition or usual practice.

Character training: experience of obedience (Mt 13:1–14:36)

And the disciples came and said to Him, 'Why do You speak to them in parables?' He answered and said to them, 'Because it has been given to you to know the mysteries of the kingdom of heaven, but to them it has not been given.' (Mt 13:10–11)

Jesus talked to the people in parables. Those who wanted to know more – that is, the meaning of the data presented to them – pressed into Him to find out what He was revealing (Mt 13:10). *If God has not placed that cry in our heart to know more, then no amount of selling will change a straight-forward 'believer' into a disciple-learner of Christ Jesus.* Disciples are undoubtedly called by God (Mt 20:16), but here we see that the process seems to be self-selection; truly His ways are past finding out!

Another point of interest is that Jesus tells us that we are in a special time, for many holy men have sought the key that has now been given to us by His appearing upon the earth (Mt 13:17).

He then launches into perhaps the most famous of all His parables, that of the sower (Mt 13:18). This has long been used to persuade the 'lost' to come into the family of Christ. It is also primary teaching for all of us who seek to follow Him into kingdom ways. The first thing we learn is that progress with Jesus is optional; we can opt out if we want to and He checks us out every so often by presenting us with hurdles to jump, just to make sure we are in the programme! He continually gives us choices to take the kingdom way, and if we do so, we commit ourselves deeper and deeper all the time to the way.

Jesus is warning us that that path is increasingly demanding and we all have to move up a stage constantly in our following of Him. It never stops – there is no plateau experience of complete and unassailable holiness or obedience. We can be encouraged that in this great journey we have embarked upon, no one is especially qualified and we all have the same difficulty of dealing with ourselves and grappling with this new reality He has led us into.

We must 'have root in ourselves', by which Jesus means that the word of obedience to Him must have some experience of trust to latch on to, and this experience we will have come across in dealing with the six Beatitudes, or motives and attitudes, that are our interface with the world around us. The word of obedience to the Kingdom of God is an opportunity to explore His authority in newer and newer ways. For example, do we ever want to walk on water in our circumstances? Then this is the way! The areas in which He demonstrates this word are usually those areas over which we have some influence but not control; that is, at work, play, social interaction, social influence, home, charity, politics and church life.

He generally asks us to step out into a risk area that we have not really got the background for and which requires a significant input from Him. Should we succeed in obeying Him and seeing the Kingdom at work on our behalf, we will have established the ground for future faith-risk areas; that is, once we have secured a new trust in the Lord's capacity to control the situation in which we find ourselves and His care for us, he goes on to stretch us again. And so on, until we are confident to follow Him wherever He leads us. This is the growth of 'having root in ourselves'.

The greatest competition we find other than our own internal opposition (of our own motives and attitudes) is the deceitfulness of riches and the cares of this world. Money is not the answer to our problems, much as we may have thought it to be, especially as the world crowds in and targets our soft spots of ego, status, achievement, self-actualisation, sex, survival, ambition and so on. We have a straight choice at these times: will we rise to the challenge of His word to us or not? Gideon had that challenge, and so did Elijah, Paul, Peter, Apollos, Ananias (Paul's prophet) and Mark. They all had their moments of truth when they could have jumped one way or another.

Jesus was shortly to provide a practical demonstration in the development of a faith relationship with God in the Canaanite woman in Sidon, when she had to grapple with and overcome her humiliation if she wanted her daughter to be healed (Mt 15:22).

Would the cares of this world choke the word or not? Sometimes it did, according to Paul speaking of Demas (2 Tim 4:10) or Ananias and Sapphira (Acts 5:5).

Once we have made our choice to follow, even reluctantly like Peter (Jn 6:68), God promises us He will take care of the consequences (Mt 6:25–34).

Jesus goes on to express the rule by God in different ways, primarily I think because it is so 'other', and it takes some getting used to without our usual pigeon-hole categories to help us to adjust to the new.

First, He demonstrates His power by feeding the five thousand men with five loaves and two fishes. Then He walks on water to demonstrate that 'even the winds and the sea obey Him' (Mt 14:25; 8:27).

These were by any standards remarkable miracles which we couldn't duplicate today even with our extraordinary technology. However, I have experienced something similar. Once, when we were completely without money, half a loaf of bread and a tin of salmon lasted our family of five a complete weekend. We just kept carving . . . and eating!

As Jesus demonstrated that the physical laws were subject to Him at His command, it was the first step to opening up the expectations of the disciples that the Kingdom of heaven really had come to the earth, and not just with a good leader – this Man was something very special indeed. Remarkably, He delegated this authority to Peter, who also walked on the water for a short time. Delegation is the hallmark of authority, of a continuous chain of power from the very Highest through the Godhead to men, demonstrating that the Kingdom really has come to earth. But Jesus was working up to this understanding gradually so as not to blow their fuses (Jn 16:12).

Second clash – with the Pharisees: Unity of the brotherhood (Mt 15:1)

> Then the scribes and Pharisees who were from Jerusalem came to Jesus, saying, 'Why do your disciples transgress the tradition of the elders? For they do not wash their hands when they eat bread.' He answered and said to them, 'Why do you also transgress the commandment of God because of your tradition? . . . you say, "Whoever says to his father or mother, 'Whatever profit you might have received from me is a gift to God' – then he need not honour his father or mother." Thus you have made the commandment of God of no effect by your tradition. Hypocrites!' (Mt 15: 1–3, 5–7)

Jesus continues to demonstrate His authority by moving on from the physical laws to confront the Pharisees and scribes over religious laws. These intellectuals prided themselves on tying down everyone in the minutiae of law, so it was essential for Jesus to demonstrate His Christness, His kingship, by defeating them at their own game. They were more interested in exercising and preserving their power than in truth and the purposes of God (Mt 15:6).

The Pharisees and scribes thought they had caught Jesus in an elementary issue, that of hand-washing and transgressing the traditions of the elders. Instead they exposed themselves to the Master's mastery of the law when He pointed out *their* gross failings in the area of obeying the commandments of God!

In an aside to the disciples, Jesus explained the basis of His attack: they had wrongly equated the 'defiling' of unclean hands with sin. It was not sin, and He went on to explain that sin came from the heart not from the stomach.

We too have to develop discernment in our own Christian cultures so that we can readily accept those of another who do not conform to our traditions but who *do* obey God; thus we can enlarge a loving brotherhood under Christ. This is not kindergarten teaching, we can all be offended so easily and unnecessarily, but we must take it to heart if we are not to be found fighting our brethren instead of the enemy of our souls.

My wife dragged me off under protest one time to hear a famous Christian teacher, Dr Jay Adams (author of *Competent to Counsel*). Dr Adams was not charismatic, as I then defined it, so he couldn't possibly have anything to teach me, or so I thought! Isn't that arrogant? I found that this great man of God had the wisdom of ages to impart, and over the course of the week I lost my blinkers and grew to love him, a giant in the hall of the greats.

Jesus then takes occasion to teach about the progressive growth of faith and how it can leap boundaries. The Canaanite woman (Mt 15:22) breaks into his rest period shouting, and He takes no notice (apparently). He can no longer avoid her when she throws herself at His feet and implores Him to deliver her daughter. Her faith is building in stages all the time. In fact you can trace the parable of the sower in her actions. He then takes her a stage further by saying she doesn't qualify, but she gets around that and keeps coming! He finally congratulates her on her faith, which has just demonstrated and educated the onlooking disciples how to develop strength and trust in believing God.

The physical rest was necessary because His next mission was to heal all those who came to Him, to whom He demonstrated the effortless power of God over all personal ills. It was such a consummate, experiential demonstration that they had no room for doubt.

Jesus was teaching and doing, the method still seen in training circles today as the best training method there is. He explained the theory, broke new ground, prompted questions and provided complete rationale in the disciples' own terms. Very rarely did He fail to explain when things went over their head. We can learn so much from Him in the growing areas, not fearing that the genuine enquirer and questioner will ever exhaust God's patience, grace or storehouse.

Third clash – with the Pharisees and Sadducees: Setting the agenda (Mt 19:1–9)

> The Pharisees also came to Him, testing Him, and saying to Him, 'Is it lawful for a man to divorce his wife for just any reason?' And He answered and said to them, '. . . So then, they are no longer two but one flesh.' . . . They said to Him, 'Why then did Moses command to give a certificate of divorce and to put her away?' He said to them, 'Moses, because of the hardness of your hearts, permitted you to divorce your wives, but from the beginning it was not so. And I say to you, whoever divorces his wife, except for sexual immorality, and marries another commits adultery.' (Mt 19:3–4, 6–9)

The third clash with the Pharisees came when together with the Sadducees they approached Jesus with a prepared agenda to trap Him into siding with one group or the other in the then current Hillel/Shammai divorce debate. This was instead of the off-the-cuff reactions they had offered previously– the pressure was increasing.

Jesus turned their phraseology and their request on its head, and He did not react to their agenda, but set His own (Mt 19:8). This is a huge lesson for us in how to respond to a challenge. In order to do so, we do not have to use our opponents' language or their debating parameters. Rather we should learn from the Master and drag our opponents onto our ground to flounder and founder. Not only did He reply directly to both the original question and the secondary (trap) question; He continued to put content into His reply by making behavioural demands of them. Their inclination was then not to take the argument further because it might drag them deeper into trouble with Him!

It also teaches us to make sure that all teaching we receive into ourselves is from God and not serving a human agenda (Mt 15:6). I remember seeing a major Christian magazine defending its stance on homophobia. Why did they not see that by even using the newly fashioned word 'homophobia', they had been pushed off their own territory so that all their subsequent arguments sounded weak and pathetic?

Further character training: Rewards for service (Mt 19:10–21:22)

> The disciples said to Him, 'If such is the case of the man with his wife, it is better not to marry.' But He said to them, '. . . and there are eunuchs who have made themselves eunuchs for the kingdom of heaven's sake.' (Mt 19:10–12)

Jesus was a supreme trainer because he mixed theory with practical demonstration; that is, explanations of the underlying dynamics of human behaviour with how to get a handle on understanding the kingdom rule. For example, He used the rebuff and defeat of the Pharisees to explain to His disciples that the condition of a man was such that the calling upon his life was affected by the depth of his desire for marriage, and as such it was different for everyone. He explained that our entering the sphere of His rule was so different that we might as well accept that we know very little in advance about it; we have so much to unlearn and relearn, we really have to go back to school like a child.

When the rich young ruler made his approach to Jesus he was very hungry for reality and truth because he had gone beyond the usual religious satisfactions of the day. But he was pushed further than he was prepared to go when Jesus answered him directly face to face, by presenting the drastic change that would be required if the young man was to progress further. He then consoled His disciples, some undoubtedly middle class, with the assurance that it really was possible for God to replace anything we lose in this world in yielding to His demands of service. Indeed, His rewards are fair and merciful, as He explains in the parable of the vineyard labourers.

Rewards are still on their mind as the mother of James and John asks Jesus for preferment for her sons. Jesus is restrained and does not object at all to this desire for advancement. Indeed He invites them to commit further by drinking the cup that would be offered them. They agree with alacrity to this – an agreement which James was called upon to honour as an early Christian martyr (Acts 12:2).

He wrapped up the disciples' indignation with a further lesson, an apparent paradox that those who have ambitions in the Kingdom have first to learn to serve. He never seemed to waste a moment, further demonstrated with the healing of the two blind men calling out to Him as they were travelling to Jerusalem. But He did not berate or nag or belittle His disciples, rather seeking continually ways to increase their faith.

Faith and holiness

Constant preaching about holiness (or the lack of it) can induce a kind of paralysis in the church, leading to a lack of conversions, a lack of purpose, a lack of life in the Christian community. Do we never consider that Peter had to struggle against his racism well into his post-Pentecost ministry; that Paul suffered from covetousness like all Pharisees, or that John and James were sneakily ambitious? Think for a moment about the tax collector and the Pharisee at worship (Lk 18:9). This was a heart-cry from Christ for reality between God and man.

There is after all overwhelming provision for the consequences of sin, but there is no provision for not crying to God and not contending for the faith. Christ made this quite clear in the parable of the talents, and a further reaction of the Godhead is seen in Psalm 78 when He castigates Ephraim for turning back in the day of battle, 'even though armed'.

Let's face it, our faith is just not strong enough to cope with the demands God makes of us. We are therefore obliged to abandon ourselves to God so that He might make up the shortfall. In this increased intimacy, we learn in our desperation that we need Him more than we ever imagined, and our hearts become pure because of our love relationship with Him. The more we are exposed in the battles of the Kingdom and the more we are fearful of the wind and the storms, the more we are obliged to depend upon Him; we can get holy and repentant pretty quickly when pushed by circumstances, which is of course the very essence of our faith, not the other way round.

Fourth clash – with Pharisees and chief priests: Going on the attack (Mt 21:1–22:15)

There now follows a significant change in strategy by Christ as He takes the fight to the chief priests themselves with three major provocations:

1. His triumphant march into Jerusalem, a scriptural fulfilment.
2. His clearing of the Temple of the merchants, which also fulfilled Scripture.
3. The children crying out their praise to 'the Son of David', also a scriptural fulfilment.

This is a very important principle of progression to understand. First, God provokes a rethink in those of us who are called to the Kingdom of Christ with confirming demonstrations of power. Then we respond to the criticisms of outsiders, confounding their criticisms by overturning their nostrums (Lk 21:15). Then when all is ready we attack the presuppositions of those who rule our nation with a radical agenda of values, provoking either their compliance or their repression, although either way the values go into the soil of our nation to flower sooner or later in the battle for the minds of the people.

> And seeing a fig tree by the road, He came to it and found nothing on it but leaves, said to it, 'Let no fruit grow on you ever again.' Immediately the fig tree withered away. And when the disciples saw it, they marveled, saying, 'How did the fig tree wither away so soon?' So Jesus answered and said to them, 'Assuredly I say to you, if you have faith and do not doubt, you will not only do what was

done to the fig tree, but also if you say to this mountain, "Be removed and be cast into the sea," it will be done. And whatever things you ask in prayer, believing, you will receive.' (Mt 21:19–22)

All this time Jesus was caring for the minds of His disciples, to keep their new worldview fresh and radical. The teaching of the fig tree and the moving of mountains was to keep them on board at a critical and worrying time for them, for unlike us they had not seen the end of the book yet!

The next day He clashed again with the chief priests and elders over the nature of His authority:

Now when He came into the temple, the chief priests and the elders of the people confronted Him as He was teaching, and said, 'By what authority are You doing these things? And who gave you this authority?' But Jesus answered and said to them, 'I also will ask you one thing, which if you tell Me, I likewise will tell you by what authority I do these things: The baptism of John – where was it from? From heaven or from men?' And they reasoned among themselves, saying, 'If we say, "From heaven," He will say to us, "Why then did you not believe him?" But if we say, "From men," we fear the multitude, for all count John as a prophet.' So they answered Jesus and said, 'We do not know.' And He said to them, 'Neither will I tell you by what authority I do these things.' (Mt 21:23–27)

Of course they had not given this authority so it was essential that they check Him out, as we say nowadays 'to see where He was coming from'. But, as usual, they got more than they expected. Jesus caught them in a scandal, that of their non-recognition of John the Baptist, who had shown all the characteristics of a prophet, the first for centuries, and the memory of whom was very precious in the sight of the common people.

And we too should learn from this, that the exercise of temporal power inevitably requires hard decisions to be made between expediency and principle. Without God, expediency usually wins, but yields unwholesome and hypocritical fruit. There is usually plenty of material in these areas which we can use if we wise up to how Christ won these exchanges with His opponents.

We must be as wise as serpents but as harmless as doves. In other words, this kind of material should be used in the direct defeat of a spurious argument which has been couched in moral indignation; it is a warning to our opposition that we have done our homework and we can be dangerous if illegal arguments are used against our mission.

Christ goes on to underline the lesson about authority with His story of the two brothers who had different reactions to the will of their father. One was clearly condemned and one was clearly exonerated, each of their fates being decided by their actions. Christ even drags out the fact that the elders of the people had not even repented of their attitude to John after his death when he presented no threat! He did not let them off one iota of their guilt.

Christ then challenges them again with two parables in which He unmistakably makes His claims for the condemnation of the chief priests and the Pharisees, who are powerless to act against Him because of the favourable opinion of the people. He is challenging them to come out and fight in the open before the people who are assembling for the Feast of the Passover. Seeing their impotence, He proceeds to up the stakes by telling yet another parable against them about who would be welcome in the Kingdom of heaven and who would not; He leaves them in no doubt as to which constituency is which.

The lesson: Engulf or don't start it!

The Christian stance has all too often been to respond on their opponents' territory in the areas of their choosing. It is a long time since Christian thought dominated our nation's agenda with timing and contemporary wisdom, as Christ is doing in this passage. His opponents are not only losing the war but they are being routed, for Christ piles argument and accusation upon the same so that they do not know which way to turn to get out of the fire. *This teaches us never to enter this kind of fight until the Holy Spirit has given us more than enough ammunition to engulf our opponents.* The power of our attack, however, is underlined by the winsomeness of the love of Christ in us that shows mercy even in determination.

When God gives us the ascendancy we must press forward to win the argument because in so doing the onlooking people (who are watching very closely indeed) can have the freedom to make their choices between the forces on display. If we falter, then we let the argument go by default and the watchers can be lost – in fact, wilfully lost. However, we must not forget our commission also includes how to win; that is, with the compassion, love and poverty of spirit that marks out a servant of the King.

The response of the Pharisees was to call a counsel of war between the chief protagonists; the Pharisees, Herodians, chief priests and Sadducees. Their thought was that between them they surely ought to be able to trap Him. So they sallied forth to tackle Christ one by one.

Provocative argument is OK, but we must expect retaliation. Our storehouse must be full of good material, gathered under the guidance of the Holy Spirit, who will give us what to say at the crucial time (Lk 21:15).

Fifth clash – with Pharisees and Herodians

> And [the Pharisees] sent to Him their disciples with the Herodians, saying, 'Teacher, we know that You are true, and teach the way of God in truth; nor do you care about anyone, for You do not regard the person of men. Tell us, therefore, what do You think? Is it lawful to pay taxes to Caesar, or not?' But Jesus perceived their wickedness, and said, 'Why do you test Me, you hypocrites? Show Me the tax money.' So they brought Him a denarius. And He said to them, 'Whose image and inscription is this?' They said to Him, 'Caesar's.' And He said to them, 'Render, therefore, to Caesar the things that are Caesar's, and to God the things that are God's.' When they had heard these words, they marveled, and left Him and went their way. (Mt 16:16–22)

The famous clash of 'rendering unto Caesar' is much admired by all who read it and frequently misapplied. But there is inherent in the riposte a marvellous description of how the Kingdom of God works in tandem with the state. Each citizen must decide which authority he obeys depending upon the issues involved, as the apostles were later to demonstrate in front of the Sanhedrin (Acts 5:29). God puts authorities in place (Rom 13:1) and expects us to obey them with the proviso that if we are unable to, we must be ready to take our medicine. This is anathema in our western age of rights. However, injustice that is endured by suffering saints focuses outsiders' attention upon issues of principle. Brian Souter, when defending the principle of protecting schoolchildren from homosexual propaganda, was threatened by the London mayor-elect with the withdrawal of his Stagecoach franchise from the London area. He did not back down, even when his vehicles were attacked and damaged in London under the inactive eyes of the authorities.

Although this is a subject deserving separate and careful attention, let it suffice to say that our role vis-à-vis the state is as an influence; to guide rather than to rule. We are a nation of priests, not kings (1 Pet 2:5–9). This is a marvellous guide to our actions and statements, particularly if we are in any form of governmental power. President George W. Bush had a complete oppositional stance against abortion, but he pledged during 2001 to uphold the law that currently supported abortion as an officer of the law and not use his station to unlawfully implement his belief. His role as president is part of his nation's institutions and he has correctly understood the difference between his private conviction and his public duty. He is like the rich man that Jesus said (Mt 19:23–24) would find great difficulty entering the Kingdom, the rule, of God; however, 'with God all things are possible' (Mt 19:26).

Sixth clash – with Sadducees (Mt 22:23–33)

It was then the turn of the Sadducees. Their great idea was a convoluted story of a woman who had seven husbands. Jesus despatched that one with a simple use of the present tense in His explanation and a clear interpretation of Scripture: '. . . spoken to you by God, saying, "I am the God of Abraham . . ." God is not the God of the dead, but of the living.' God describes Himself as the present-tense God of the living not the dead. It is so simple, so clear, so obvious.

There is so much content in Jesus' answers that the questions seem almost irrelevant beside the value-added content of His replies. His opponents found themselves drowning in a sea of answers, not knowing which way to turn, and we too must immerse ourselves in the subjects of our calling, going as it were beyond the required mile so that we not only give value for money but threaten those who are looking for single, Greek-type responses which they can then debate.

A similar approach was taken by Paul in the Areopagus (Acts 17:22–32) when he too gave his inquisitors more than they could handle, necessitating their withdrawal from the contest to reconsider their position.

There is usually an opening in our opponents' arguments to point out the truth. After all, we have access to *the* truth, and they can only hazard a guess, a guess moreover that has self-interest as its base. It will inevitably be flawed, and the Spirit will lead us into identifying and destroying this man-made wisdom from within itself if we ask Him to lead us.

Seventh clash – with the Pharisees (Mt 22:34–46)

> But when the Pharisees heard that He had silenced the Sadducees, they gathered together. Then one of them, a lawyer, asked Him a question, testing Him, and saying, 'Teacher, which is the great commandment in the law?' (Mt 22:34–36)

Now it was the turn of the big boys again, the Pharisees, who had chosen a legal expert to present their case. He asked an unanswerable question on the relative values of the Commandments, but Christ gave them a lesson in logic by picking out the two upon which all the others depend. Taking advantage of the opportunity of the Pharisees gathering together to see their man overwhelm the upstart, Jesus quickly turned the trap to His advantage by setting them an unanswerable question:

> Jesus asked them, saying, 'What do you think about the Christ? Whose Son is He?' They said to Him, 'The Son of David.' Then

He said to them, 'How then does David in the Spirit call Him
"Lord," saying, "The Lord said to my Lord . . ."? If David then
calls Him "Lord," how is He his Son?' And no one was able to
answer Him a word . . . (Mt 22:41–46)

The Pharisees, gathering to see the fun, were put on their
mettle when Jesus asked them His question, a scriptural
dilemma about the identity of the Son of God. They did not
know the answer of course – an inevitable outcome outside of
the revelation of Jesus as the Christ (Mt 22:46).

His position was so well thought out, He knew what they
knew and He had developed their thought pattern to an
extreme that would trap them. So likewise we must master the
portion of our calling allocated to us by God so that we can
move lightly and effectively as the Spirit leads us in the dance
of a master swordsman.

Seeing His foes vanquished, Christ turned to a public attack
upon the scribes and Pharisees. He began with a withering
analysis of how the scribes and Pharisees fulfilled their roles.

Facing Conflict

Matthew 23:1–39

Then Jesus spoke to the multitudes and to His disciples, saying:
'The scribes and the Pharisees sit in Moses' seat. Therefore whatever they tell you to observe, that observe and do, but do not do
according to their works; for they say, and do not do.'

It is clear that Jesus had set His face towards the cross (Mt
23:39; 26:2), as His fresh provocations were designed to

reveal the self-serving hypocrisy of the spiritual leaders of Israel, which would in turn provoke the heaviest penalty. In other words, He had been given a strategy by His Father (Mt 26:39, 56). This should also be our priority when engaging in warfare, whether small local skirmishes or major national high-profile warfare. We must know the underlying strategic plans of the Father and our place in them, for without this we are beating the air (1 Cor 9:26); indeed we may get seriously hurt (Acts 19:16), and our mission may be compromised.

Before the attack, Jesus addresses His followers, guiding them with essential attitude training. Without the right attitude, our opponents can catch us in anger, self-service, ignorance, hypocrisy, ego or the love of status. He gives a very handy behavioural check-and-balance device: 'But he who is greatest among you shall be your servant' (Mt 23:11). This sets us in the right posture for attack.

Christ's target was the Pharisees and the scribes, who administered and legislated the spiritual life of the nation. His epithet for them was 'hypocrite'; that is, play-actor. Their religion was make-believe, a stage play into which they co-opted all the people as bit-players and cast themselves in the title roles.

Seeking the rule of God, both in the nation and personally, is the urge in all who aspire to follow the God of Israel. But the Pharisees' behaviour and rules declared their games, while at the same time preventing others from seeking reality and truth in God. Christ denounced them with specific charges and evidence, the succinct language carefully chosen. He charged them with lies, murder and cheating, and making a mockery of the holy burden that had been offered to them.

But notice that this is not a mud-slinging exercise by Christ. Rather it is an attack with a fullness of content. We too must do our homework and make sure that not only do our cases hold water, but they also demolish the man-made customs, practices and laws that our opponents cling to as external proofs of their position.

Prophecy: Its role and place at times of conflict (Mt 24–25)

The disciples came to Him privately, saying, 'Tell us, when will these things be? And what will be the sign of Your coming, and of the end of the age?' (Mt 24:3)

There comes a time when God reveals prophecy to us, especially when issues of a national nature are involved. He does not leave us comfortless at these times, and the prophecy goes on to strengthen our sinews at the time of testing, reassuring us that God is with us, even though the circumstances look grim. The prophecy can of course warn of specific things (Acts 11:28), but often it comes in code that we can see work out as the time (Mt 24:15) comes upon us. This is not arbitrary awkwardness on God's part; it is just that we 'cannot bear them now' (Jn 16:12), or that we will not be able to make sense of them from our present viewpoint. It does, however, behove us to write the prophecies down and, like Mary, to keep them in our heart, so that we are ready for shifts in our landscape and not shocked into helplessness like the apostles after the crucifixion of Jesus Christ. 'He said to His disciples, "You know that after two days is the Passover, and the Son of Man will be delivered up to be crucified"' (Mt 26:1–2). It is interesting to note that Jesus warned the disciples about His imminent crucifixion before the chief priests and elders had actually met to plan it. We must bear in mind at all times that when we are on the Lord's business it is His business, we are His servants, emissaries, and He has all things in His hand, including the heart condition of our enemies and all circumstances.

I was in Hadera, Israel, in the office of a general manager, trying to secure an exclusive supply of material for my business when the telephone rang with a major complaint from a very angry London client of mine, who had traced me all the way to Israel! Boy was he mad, and I was thinking, 'Of all the things to happen to a salesman at such a critical meeting!' However, the Lord gave me the ability to settle the complaint promptly and satisfactorily on the telephone as I sat in the Israeli manager's office. The manager gave me the contract without further discussion because he had seen me in action. I could not have planned a better demonstration, but at the time I nearly panicked. I had forgotten that 'all things work together for good to those who love God, to those who are called according to His purpose' (Rom 8:28). But when we engage with the enemies of the gospel we must be sure we *are* 'called according to His purpose'. If we are not, our presentation will depend solely upon our personal skills, which do not have the comprehensive follow-up of the Holy Spirit.

In Matthew 26:7, Jesus breaks the expectations of His disciples, as usual, by accepting the offering of the woman's anointing with expensive perfume; He does not conform to expectations of outward piety – that is, by selling the perfume and giving to the poor – but to His Father's provision for His hour of trial. It is essential we understand the point or we will be derailed at critical moments. We must be sure of our calling, our mission and our ground. We answer to the King when we are on His business, not to expectations, and this alone can provoke the apparently tolerant to reveal their true heart. You may note, for example, that it was this action that finally triggered Judas Iscariot to betray Jesus.

I was somewhat humbled and embarrassed when someone with an international ministry for whom I was organising a conference managed to offend most of the people she came into contact with. I had to face the fact that bull in a china shop or not, this lady was sent by God, was on His business and we were not to touch her in any way at all. Hands off the prophet! This can be very difficult for us, but God uses it to reveal to us our heart and help us make our resolution for Him or otherwise. It helps to have a (rueful) sense of humour and, make no mistake about it, the truth will come out, sometimes even from the rooftops, as it did with Judas.

The prices that are paid

The whole Gethsemane experience (vv. 36–46) is a trying one when we undergo it, especially when we just do not see the logic or the sense of what is going on. But sometimes there are bigger issues than we could possibly see or understand; it is essential we play our part to the best of our ability and courage, albeit blindly sometimes, and that we trust in God. He will reveal all we need to know and understand in due time.

The great evangelist Hudson Taylor apparently saw little reward for his sacrificial efforts in China. However, when his tired body was finally lowered into the soil a great explosion of conversions to Christ took place which even withstood the ravages of the red Cultural Revolution. Even Wilberforce did not live to see his abolition of slavery bill become law, but the ramifications of his work reverberate today 200 years later. The important thing is that we find the role God has prepared for us (Eph 2:10) and that we play our part to the limits of our ability and conviction.

Spiritual struggle is exhausting, as the disciples demonstrated by sleeping on watch. Just bear in mind that if you are so engaged on God's business, the internal and external struggle has every mental facility of our brain working overtime and it is exhausting; do not be surprised at this often overlooked cost of serving the King.

The physical assault upon Jesus and the disciples (vv. 47–56) and Jesus' admonition to put away the sword of defence is a practical demonstration of the famous Ephesians 6 scripture: 'For we do not wrestle against flesh and blood, but against principalities, against powers, against the rulers of the darkness of this age . . .' (v. 12). The real battle was to come in the arguments and refutations between the Christ and His accusers. Our conflict likewise is in the ideas battleground and seldom in the physical. We must learn how to fight these battles and realise that behind the flesh and blood representatives lie the real or unidentified organisations that spawn them. These entities are only overcome in the battle of ideas.

Sometimes the ideas are so powerful that they turn one world force against another. Such was the case in 2001 when Kansas Christians turned the free thinkers against the determinist Darwinists so that Christian ideas of the creation could now be taught alongside Darwinist theory in Kansas schools, overturning the court decision of the famous Tennessee 'Monkey Trial' of 1927.

Although the forces are spiritual, the troops are flesh and it can be difficult for us to see that our dispute with flesh is to be directed at the spiritual wickedness in the heavenly places behind them. So it is not much good spearing individual representatives, except on the points of our ideas.

Grand confrontations such as Jesus faced may come to some of us selected and trained by God. However, it is much more usual that we face smaller scale trials, and we must be ready and listening for the preparations of the Holy Spirit on a daily basis. We must carefully note that our ideas of 'justice' have nothing to do with these tests. God may have arranged them so that others may see the contest and how we stand in the evil unjust hour. Our demeanour, especially when unjustly accused, is as important as our verbal combat, for it reveals the clarity and integrity of our heart and the One by whom we have been called. Peter and John later faced this kind of test when their accusers marvelled and observed their confidence, and had nothing to say (Acts 4:13).

Books have been written about the illegality of Christ's trial from start to finish, especially when He was found guilty on a charge that had not actually been brought. Suffice it to say we may expect nothing less. There was an article in the London *Times* (27 December 2001) accusing Christianity of being complicit in the death and destruction of the twentieth century, when in fact the twentieth century was the atheist century of all centuries, with such as Lenin, Stalin, Hitler, Pol Pot and Mao Zedong in charge of the destruction of countless millions of lives. The big lie is as difficult to break down as an accumulation of small lies.

How do we respond? As the Scripture demonstrates for us. Jesus Christ, Paul, Peter and Stephen were all called upon to defend the faith (Acts 22:1–21; 3:12–26; 7:1–53) in a most public manner and we can learn from them how to do it.

Some of the wisdom is to refer to a common heritage and then make a divergence with the course the hearers have taken, pointing them to the truth, managing as we do so never ever to compromise the sovereignty of God over all.

Jesus quoted Psalm 110:1 in His response to the high priest (Mt 26:64) who represented the people of Israel; appropriate evidence for His audience. Paul quoted the Greeks' own poets (Acts 17:28) to engage them with his message – again an appropriate use of material. Likewise we must ensure that we are equipped to engage with material familiar to our audience and use it fearlessly in the defence of the gospel.

Winning the actual contest is not always God's intention. For example, Jesus was the sacrificial Lamb that was to take away the sin of the world and He proceeded to do so by accepting the death verdict of the Sanhedrin. Jesus held true to His purpose before Pilate when He had the opportunity to make fools of the chief priests and get His sentence thrown out. We must do likewise by holding to that commission that God hands us and never letting go, as for example Paul was able to do as he testified to Timothy (2 Tim 4:6–8). It is our commission and ours alone to deliver to Him on that day.

We disciples are latter-day actors in the momentous event. The watchers are being worked upon by the Holy Spirit as they take their stand in the valley of decision. We owe it to our fathers in the faith to do it properly even in the face of persecution, injustice, politics, fashionable thought or overwhelming odds. Once we engage in this battle we must endeavour never to turn back like Demas (2 Tim 4:10) or 'put Him to an open shame' (Heb 6:6) by falling away, because by doing so we betray the offer of hope God is making to the watchers.

But we need leaders who, like Paul and Wilberforce, are able and willing to lead us in this enterprise of bringing revival to our nation.

Apostle: Man for the Hour!

'He is a chosen vessel of Mine to bear My name before Gentiles, kings, and the children of Israel.' (Acts 9:15)

'I think myself happy, King Agrippa, because today I shall answer for myself before you.' (Acts 26:2)

The cry for revival

All of the Christian movements in this nation during the twentieth century – the Pentecostal, the charismatic, the Restoration and the national revival – all had the expectancy of an imminent national outpouring of the Spirit when thousands of people would be swept up into a glorious national revival and the churches would be swelling to bursting point with new converts. I have been expectant of imminent revival for nearly forty years, but have yet to see it in our nation.

However, in 1996 I was privileged to accompany an internationally known English preacher as his prayer partner to the Lithuanian national Charismatic Conference after that country had been freed from Soviet Communism. I saw there for the first time the outpouring of the Holy Spirit, with 'chains falling off' and 'prisoners walking free' – in this case from the decades of tyrannical Communism. I was deeply shaken by the experience, and the memory still brings me to tears. I know first hand, therefore, that revival is a very real and dynamic experience, and the cries and yearnings of our congregations for thirty or more years have a basis in reality.

But my friend the English preacher later confessed to his own congregation that he did not know why the revival had not happened here in England. This was despite the very best heart-searching, prayer, cries, fastings, repenting, campaigns and programmes, with foreign speakers trying to duplicate their own national revival successes here in the UK. As observers, we found this increasingly dispiriting and bewildering, and our hearts' cry became, 'Where *is* God in our nation?'

Apostolic leadership comes first

A man went out to fish for his hungry family. The lake was frozen over. He cast his line again and again but caught nothing because the ice was too thick and his hook couldn't penetrate the surface. He fished all day until he was exhausted. He looked up to the heavens and said out loud, 'There must be another way, for there are plenty of fish in these waters.'

Just then, a man happened by who was a carpenter and with him he had a big wooden carpenter's mallet. He saw the man's plight and, getting out the mallet, he struck the ice several times with great force. The ice couldn't resist the attack and yielded a big hole. The man cast his line again, but this time into the hole and deep down into the water, and before very long the weight of his catch was almost too heavy to carry. He even had enough for his hungry neighbours. He told his wife the story and she said, 'Common sense. Why didn't you think of that before?' 'Because I am not a carpenter, and I don't have a carpenter's mallet,' was her husband's reply.

Preaching evangelism ahead of the apostolic conflict is like fishing on top of the ice. We need *the* Carpenter's mallet to break through to the waters where the fish are. Who or what is the carpenter's mallet that can break through for the evangelist and the local church that does the work of the evangelist? Why, the apostle called and anointed like Paul (Acts 9:15) to stand before kings and the debaters of this age, of course! He is the mallet that breaks through the ice of contemporary culture to reach the hearts of men and women and place them squarely in the valley of decision.

A different kind of apostolic leader: Standing before kings

We recall that Paul, as the apostle of Christ, contended with religious leaders of both the Jewish and the Christian congregations, with national parliaments, with the Sanhedrin, with mobs intent on his blood, with individuals intent on discrediting him and with city fathers. And also that he did so at great cost and risk (2 Cor 11:23–28), possibly a prerequisite for this kind of leader (Acts 9:15).

Paul contended using ideas of the Godhead and the Kingdom of Jesus Christ, insisting that all things were created by Him, for Him and through Him (Col 1:16; Acts 17:23). The ideas were expressed differently for Colosse than for the Areopagus, for the Sanhedrin than for the tetrarchs of Israel, because he connected with people where they were, without any kind of presuppositions. He struggled and often won the contests against the best of his day, as King Agrippa attests in Acts 26:32, for example: 'This man might have been set free if he had not appealed to Caesar.'

And in the wake of the battles, God honoured the struggle by allowing either the proclamation of the gospel or the growth of the church; this is always the case. Even lost struggles rarely failed to bear fruit as truly the darkness could not put out His light, as Gamaliel testifies in Acts 5:38–39, or the Philippian jailer at his conversion (Acts 16:30).

It is clear from the record of Paul's great work in the book of Acts, and from his own writings, that there are several roles of the apostle. First, there is the one who builds or sets up churches, setting elders in place and having concern for them (Titus 1:5). Then there is the one who interprets Scripture for the contemporary day (2 Tim 2:15). And then there is the apostle, called and trained and anointed from birth to stand before kings (Acts 9:15).

The first two we are fairly familiar with in contemporary experience. The charismatic renewal has revealed many of the first kind of apostle and we honour them as they act within their calling. We think of those in the second category such as C.S. Lewis, Francis Schaeffer, Martyn Lloyd-Jones and possibly Derek Prince. But the third?

John Wesley, two weeks before his death, advised Lord Wilberforce that in his (Wilberforce's) desire to end slavery he was engaged upon a holy enterprise, and so confirmed the calling to end the iniquitous slave trade in bodies in the British Empire that burned within Wilberforce. Wilberforce was trained, called and was obedient, and God gave him the power of Revelation 2:27 to carry out the task He had set him. The power even rolled on after the noble lord's death, ending in the total abolition of slavery in the British Empire in the 1830s and thence throughout the Christian nations in the world. What an anointing!

Who have we had in our nation who has been anointed by God to stand before the rulers and kings of our land at high personal risk to reputation and career, disputing with the philosophers of this age so as to release a few of the multitude who are listening to the debate? I can think of the late Mary Whitehouse, and the recent Brian Souter/ Cardinal Winning combination, and the late Baroness Young (who successfully led the Clause 28 retention debate in the House of Lords, defeating the government three times).

Angela Mason, the CE of Stonewall, the powerful and effective homosexual lobbying organisation, said in an *Observer* article that the only opposition her organisation was worried about was from Christian groups. She perceives something about us, even if we do not!

God has historically sent the men and women to 'stand before kings' and disciple the nation when His body starts to cry to Him for deliverance. This was as true for the enslaved Israelites in Egypt as it was for the pre-Pentecostal intercessors in Azusa Street, the Orkneys and Sunderland. And so this cry for the Kingdom of Christ Jesus to disciple our nation once again must be articulated long and loud by the praying church, even though the full effect of the prayer cannot be discerned and understood.

This kind of fervent prayer of the righteous achieves two things: it prepares us for change and challenge, and it releases God to extend His rod of ruling to a ready people. It would be disastrous if He extended His kingdom power to a church that was unready and undisciplined. We must all be ready to back these new leaders and movements with resources, networking, research, materials, publicity, assistants, encouragement and protection (from friends and foes) in establishing the infrastructure that such modern Wilberforces need.

Conclusion

From the house of our personal life we have constructed with Jesus Christ we are able to come together as Jesus constructs *His* house in order to fight the good fight in the areas for which He has planned, prepared and commissioned us, His body. Therefore let us follow the apostolic leaders He sets among us to enjoin battle in the most fulfilling, exciting, unpredictable, worthwhile and rewarding life that it is possible to live together with the brothers and sisters God has given us.

To sum up the preparations for revival of the church in which Jesus Christ our Lord leads us, let us remember to:

- contend only in the areas He designates;
- contend only when He confirms we are ready;
- contend only according to the rules;
- do our homework;
- respond only to the Holy Spirit's prompting;
- follow the apostles whom Jesus appoints.

May the Lord be with you and with your spirit. Amen.

Part 3: National Revival

We are in a very strong strategic position to serve our nation in providing choices for righteousness and opening the doors of opportunity for all who would be saved:

- We are already in place in the media, medical profession, education, parliament, business and commerce, the factories and dealer desks, married and unmarried, young and old, privileged and poor.
- We are in the religious culture of Christianity, which effortlessly crosses race boundaries, social boundaries, language boundaries, educational boundaries and national boundaries.
- We are placed in every social station in life there is.
- Our reputation for goodness in all the charity fields gives us a credibility that cannot be bought. Roy Hattersley, a convinced propagandist for atheism, wrote following the Hurrican Catrina disaster: 'The Salvation Army has been given a special status as provider in chief of American disaster relief. But its work is being augmented by all sorts of other groups. Almost all of them religious in character. Notable by their absence are teams from rationalist societies, free thinkers clubs and atheists' associations' (*Guardian*, 12 September 2005).

So what is holding us back?

In Part 3 we will be looking at how the church can make itself ready under the Holy Spirit's guidance to deal with major issues such as the social dominance of secular humanism and the place of our Hebraic roots in our affections, and to train for conflict on the national stage. Then and only then may we dare venture to contend for the faith in the national arena of ideas, philosophies, pressure and interest groups. Part 3 also shows us how He can give us the forums we need to get our national message across, and how He can enable us to overwhelm the practitioners of the philosophies which run our country.

When we are ready, the Lord is able to give us all the responsibility we can handle for the discipling of the nation.

CHAPTER FOUR

CONTENDING FOR THE FAITH

> And Jesus came and spoke to them, saying, 'All authority has been given to Me in heaven and on earth. Go therefore and make disciples of all the nations, baptizing them in the name of the Father and of the Son and of the Holy Spirit, teaching them to observe all things that I have commanded you; and I am with you always, even to the end of the age.' (Mt 28:18–20)

When we look at the word 'nations' more closely we see that it has two elements:

- *people*, i.e. persons, tribe, ethnic group, population, stock, football fan clubs;
- *realm*, i.e. community, republic, country, monarchy, dominion, kingdom.

In other words, the word 'nation' contains two thoughts: one of people and one of institutions that govern. When we look at the church's current activities, we see that it tends to concentrate upon one aspect only, that of discipling numbers of individual people. Discipling the realm or rule of the nation today by guiding the way it should go, influencing its passage and its government of the people is largely ignored (with some honourable exceptions) as impossible or 'not our business'. Discipling the nation is *not* the same as so-called reconstructionism or dominion theology for, as we warned in the early pages of this book, we who are serving the Lord as priests in His Kingdom will rarely end up ruling anything!

English history is full of examples of the church discipling the nation without actually displacing the ruler of the day. For example, the bishops who brokered the Magna Carta, or the Christian influence that led to the abolition of slavery in 1807 and 1833, or the modifying, in the 1830s, 40s and 70s, of the working conditions in factories and mines for children and women, or the 95 per cent coverage of the country by 1900 of free primary school education, or the new factory working practices introduced by the Quakers such as Edward Cadbury, or the aiding of the administration of care for the paupers, or even the emergence of leading Trade Union figures from a Christian background such as Joseph Arch (a Methodist lay preacher).

Contending for the faith in the past

During the later 1990s God gave me the desire and the opportunity to research the impact of Christianity upon the social, economic and political life of our nation from the beginning of the eighteenth century onwards. I became aware that the body of Christ had similar problems then of lethargy, ignorance, Mammon and the simple process of survival which presented the same overwhelming resistance to revival as it does to us today. The church then, however, seemed to be more aware of the precedents set by their own fathers in the faith, and set to work, from a very low level, in the early eighteenth century to work for the best part of two centuries for the betterment of their nation in justice, working conditions and education. They managed to bring about mind-blowing social changes that affected the nation at every level of industry, politics, education and society, and of course the filling of churches!

In the British Industrial Revolution, there was a colossal social change from a rural society to an urban one, and the social safeguards of the yeoman rural scene ceased to operate in a very short space of time. Industrialists were brutal in their exploitation of these people who came to live and work in squalid and dangerous conditions. At the same time, that is from the early eighteenth century to the mid-nineteenth, the church grew in influence through the work of such groups as the Christian Movement for the Promulgation of Christian Manners, followed by the great evangelistic campaigns of Whitworth and the Wesleys. Seeing the distress of the common people and the disregard that the new industrialists had for them, the Christian church started to work on the conscience of the nation to develop the novel concept of a 'duty of care'. Thus gradually throughout the nineteenth century, employers were obliged to introduce humane working conditions, and the authorities more hygienic town environments. This was accomplished under great opposition and much protest, but the victory of a Christian idea, 'duty of care', propounded at some considerable risk by Christians, enabled the Lord to triumph over self-interest and greed, over expediency and philosophy, by destroying the wisdom of the wise (1 Cor 1:19) from within the system.

It is interesting to note that this powerful expression of discipling the nation (Mt 28:19) was accomplished by probably not much more than 20 per cent of believing Christians at the height of the Victorian reforming period. The Lord appeared to use a three-pronged approach, with the working class being addressed by the new cell-group Methodists, the commercial class by the Quakers and the ruling classes by the Anglicans. Each class was addressed in its own terms.

Christian contention for the faith over the 200 years from the early eighteenth century was by the principle of salt and light influence, which moderated the iniquitous tendency of the powerful, who had been recently liberated by the secular philosophy of utilitarianism to dehumanise and use people like workshop expendables. Sure it took 200 years, but it worked well and thoroughly. Contrast that to the present times when there is no co-ordinated moderating force capable of contending with the philosophies of global, unelected and unaccountable Mammon of global capitalism, of centralised continent-wide government, of the fashionable faiths of new age, humanism and liberalism. Only Christ the King is capable of dealing with them, for only He is powerful enough to confound their wisdom and bring their schemes to nought.

Is this all just cant or biblical hyperbole? The nation's upheavals in the Industrial Revolution, when hundreds of years of developed societal fabric was brutally torn asunder by unscrupulous, greedy men of power, required an equally powerful opposition to confront them. This long-term challenge from the body, not acting on its own behalf but for others, meant the wholesale discipling or teaching of the nation (Mt 28:18–19) in order to reclaim justice and mercy and the rule of law for all. The need was quite clear to these men and women of faith, who would most certainly not have regarded their national mission as cant and posturing.

The effectiveness of this campaign may be seen in stark contrast to the lack of cross-church support our modern campaigners such as Lord Alton (abortion), Mary Whitehouse (depiction of violence in the media), Gillick (teenage morality) and Souter (homosexuality in schools) have had in their attempts to teach the nation some balance in moral issues. These discipling campaigns must take place across the nation and be conducted by all of us in whatever circumstances we find ourselves. Others today include the Romance Academy (combating teen sex outside of marriage), CAP UK (debt counselling) and the City Link movement (effective prayer and social action to reduce crime).

All battles for the course and conduct of a nation are fought in the minds of the people, illustrated by scriptural examples like Elijah before the people at Mount Carmel and the young David before the armies of the Philistines. Or contemporaneously, over 30 per cent of registered adult voters in the 2000 Scottish referendum carried out by Christians voted against the reintroduction of homosexual propaganda in primary and secondary schools. To put this showing in perspective, if this had been a parliamentary election, this would have been enough to give a majority in the Scottish Parliament! The people had been watching the struggle between the Christian lobby and the government and took an overwhelming decision to back the Christian position.

Paul warns against the wiles of the world in Romans 12:1–2; 'I beseech you therefore, brethren, by the mercies of God . . . do not be conformed to this world, but be transformed by the renewing of your mind, that you may prove what is that good and acceptable and perfect will of God.'

Contending for the faith, therefore, is no less than the Great Commission (Mt 28:18–20) 'to disciple the nation'. It is clear that not only are radically different strategies needed from and powered by our interventionist God, but also the ordinary people of Christ's church had to have a new understanding of contending for the faith. The seven spirits in Isaiah 11 (of the

Lord, of wisdom, of understanding, of counsel, of might, of knowledge, of the fear of the Lord) are needed to lift us out of the mindsets we are all in, evangelised as we are by the subtle, patient and ruthless enemy of secular humanism.

How then do we, the body of Christ, set about placing ourselves under the Holy Spirit's guidance for a common move to bring the nation once again under the divine influence, protection and blessing of Christ? First of all we learn what this discipling means. Second, we train to contend for the faith at the level where we find ourselves through our personal calling. Third, we follow the appropriate leadership that the Holy Spirit has put in place for us.

If we set about this holy task, the people of our nation may hear the distinctive Christian voice of guidance giving them real choices about life and society at the national, local and personal level, and may be given a fair chance of making informed decisions.

Contending for the faith in the present

A Christian-discipled nation comprises three types of individual: those who are righteous, those who are unrighteous and those who are amoral. We in the church are fairly familiar with the first two because our nation has been discipled for over 1,800 years by Judeo-Christianity and has an understanding of right and wrong and the concept of law. But there is a generation growing among us that does not have this background of 'law', so it finds the concept of repentance completely alien.

This amoral secular pagan generation requires something different again from the earlier straightforward approach of 'repent from your sin' because in order to preach the gospel of good news of repentance towards faith and the revelation of the

Kingdom of God, those of an amoral secular society first need to understand the bad news; that is, there are immutable laws given by an eternal Lawgiver which all have wantonly broken. Those are two very big steps for an unbelieving pagan to make, for the very basis of the proposition is outside their experience.

Pagans must then acknowledge this Lawgiver, the King Christ Jesus, before it is even possible for them to receive the opportunity offered by the Saviour and His saving grace. This is not a simple message because our nation is captured by the philosophy of liberal ideas based upon freedom without accountability which has been consistently developing since the publication of Darwin's *Origin of Species* and the writings of Nietzsche and Rousseau.

Thus, if we are ever to release the captives we have to first break down these imprisoning ideas, just like David against Goliath or Elijah against the prophets of Baal. Furthermore, if the 'ideas battle' is public the people may watch the process and have the opportunity to make up their own minds in their personal valley of decision.

Paul demonstrated this at Mars Hill (Acts 17:22) by first establishing the authoritative lordship of our God in the people's own terms of philosophy and poetry and then going on to describe the opportunity that God offers through Jesus. This is how 'captivity is taken captive' and the captives are set free, so should we wish to have Paul's impact upon our amoral secular nation then we have to follow his lead and example. Nothing else will do.

The fruits of clashes with the world systems in Scripture

As the church moves out of its protective enclaves into the causal areas of society's failure, there will inevitably be clashes with those who resist Christian ideas. However, according to our own national history and the clear examples in Scripture, this can fall out to the furtherance of the proclamation of the Kingdom of Christ Jesus, as long as we know how to conduct ourselves (Is 6:8). The table below shows some of the many examples in the book of Acts.

Some examples of confrontation and kingdom growth in the book of Acts

	Acts	Brief Description
Clash	4:1–3	They seized Peter and John, and put them in jail
Growth	4:4	But many who heard believed, and grew to about 5,000
Proclaim	4:8–17	Stone builders rejected has become the capstone
Clash	4:24–31	Why do the nations rage?
Proclaim	4:33	With great power the apostles continued to testify
Clash	5:26–28	The captain went, brought the apostles, filled Jerusalem
Proclaim	5:29–32	God exalted Him to His own right hand
Growth	6:1	Those days when the number of disciples was increasing
Growth	6:7	Word of God spread, numbers increased, priests obedient
Clash	8:1–3	A great persecution arose against the church
Proclaim	8:4–25	Preached the word wherever they went
Growth	8:14	Samaria had accepted the word of God
Clash	9:23	The Jews conspired to kill him
Growth	9:31	The church grew in numbers
Growth	11:21	A great number of people believed
Proclaim	13:16–43	Men of Israel and you Gentiles who worship God
Clash	13:45	Jews, filled with jealousy, abused them
Growth	13:48	When the Gentiles saw this they believed

Discipling the Nation

The discipling process

In the closing years of the eighteenth century Christians saw two major social factors of change. First, the Industrial Revolution that had started in a big way in the middle of the eighteenth century was changing the population from two-thirds rural based to two-thirds industrial town or city based. Second, the common land which was the freeman's source of survival was being systematically fenced off (2 million hectares up to 1845) by the new rich landowners, financed by the growing power of commercial banks such as Barings. These freemen either had to starve (as some did) or move into the new industrial towns.

What were the effects of the change? Once the yeoman lost his independence and his status he effectively became the property of the industrial factory owners. There was no duty of care by employers (it hadn't been necessary hitherto), and whole families, including children and pregnant women, were all drafted into factories and mines for the creation of the Victorian industrial model of national wealth.

What was the reaction of the church? Both high and low worked to establish what became known as 'duty of care' by an employer towards his employees. Over the years of the nineteenth century, the Christians forced the pace and through sheer tenacity and force of argument obliged the nation to implement humane hours and conditions of work in factories and mines. This was all the more remarkable as there was no precept for this anywhere in the world. Thus the Christians were working at the frontier of a new social, economic and even legal system.

By the end of the century, 95 per cent of the nation would be receiving primary education, and those like the Cadbury family, Fry, Clarke, Rowntree, Shaftsbury, Wilberforce even Joseph Arch had changed the face of the nation at a frontier time in its history. Or, as Matthew 29:19 would have it, they discipled the nation.

The two areas of opportunity

So how should the church be exposed to the world systems of men in this current era? By the scriptural examples of challenging the status quo of the world in its value systems and also its institutions, which (in the Western world at least) are beginning to seriously fail. The resulting clashes will fall out to the benefit of the government of God, as was the case for Moses clashing with Pharaoh; Nehemiah clashing with Artaxerxes; Daniel with Darius; Joseph with Potiphar; even Jonah and the nation of Nineveh.

The clashing of the two kingdoms of light and darkness always results in either proclamation of the Kingdom of God (see Darius's national proclamation of Daniel: in chapters 26–27, Paul's in Acts 24 and 26, or Stephen's in Acts 7) or the increase of the people of God. Either way, the gospel of King Jesus Christ is preached. The New Testament is full of examples, especially Acts (see the table at the end of the section on 'Contending for the faith' for more detail).

It's in the mind: Influence vs power

Christ outlines His strategy for His rule in the Gospels, that is by salt and light (Mt 5:13–16), which seems lightweight until you recognise that the devil has copied this divine technique throughout the ages, and the great or notorious politician Machiavelli (whose ways are copied today by management gurus) ruled by just that manner – that is, by influence over his prince. So influence is not a pie in the sky idea for Sunday school, but a potent weapon which the church has neglected in our nation for a century or more.

Nothing has changed from Psalm 2 then: Jesus Christ still wants to reign over His inheritance through the salt and light of His body, the church. His gospel is therefore one which seeks to teach that the Kingdom is near, among us (Mt 10:7). So how is the salt and light of influence exercised? Through great numbers of people being saved? Through big churches? Through Christian prime ministers? Not really, although this might help under certain circumstances. The battle of ideas is won on the public stage in the minds of the people.

Influencing the popular mood, therefore, and winning the battle for the minds of people is the weapon that the church must master. Influence, as a method of ruling a nation – that is, being salt and light and a city set on a hill (Mt 5:13–16) – avoids the triumphalist and reconstructionist positions, and is a practical demonstration of the rule of the King Jesus Christ in a nation by way of the apostolic church (Eph 3:10, 21).

Influencing rulers is very potent, as can be seen by examples in the Bible (Mt 21:46; Acts 4:21; 5:26), and it is not necessary for a Christian to be prime minister and flood the chambers of parliament with believers in order to vote through legislation to disciple or influence the national and local course of the nation. Penetrating the world systems or rule has been amply demonstrated as highly possible and effective by such Christian pioneers as the Englishmen Wilberforce, Shaftesbury, Barnardo, Arch and Temple.

The church, local and national, therefore, has to move into its heritage of discipling the ruling of the nation by first repenting of its neglect of this duty, and then by finding the expert men of faith in its ranks, new kinds of leaders, who can help them frame their resistance to the propaganda war of ideas in all national forums, and organise their response to the failure of the institutions. These are the new Pauline apostles, called as he was to 'bear My name before Gentiles, kings, and the children of Israel' (Acts 9:15).

'King of kings' is a political statement

Bob Mumford commented that in seeking to understand the meaning of the term 'Kingdom of God', he had collected over thirty-seven definitions by various great saints, and after some twelve years of searching myself for the meaning of this central proclamation of Christ I now understand a little of the difficulty of the problem of definition.

I note also the times even Jesus Christ seems to search for a way to convey the truth. For example, He says twice in Luke 13: 'To what shall I liken the kingdom of God?' But He also warns about giving up the search to understand in Matthew 13:19: 'When anyone hears the word of the kingdom, and does not understand it, then the wicked one comes and snatches away what was sown in his heart.'

However, we do know that 'kingdom' means the zone of rulership, and that is what Jesus Christ says He is seeking in the Lord's Prayer (Mt 6:9), and in the famous 'seek first the kingdom of God' scripture of Matthew 6:33. This idea of God ruling on the earth is seen much earlier, in Psalm 2, which encapsulates the claims of God over His creation: 'The LORD has said to Me, ". . . Ask of Me, and I will give You the nations for Your inheritance"' (vv. 7–8). The New Testament confirms the development of that offer in: 'All authority has been given to Me in heaven and on earth. Go therefore and make disciples of all the nations' (Mt 28:18–19) and in the commission in Revelation 2:26–27: 'And he who overcomes and keeps My works until the end, to him I will give power over the nations . . . as I also have received from My Father . . .', which richly echoes Psalm 149, where it talks about the honour of all the saints being to bind the kings and nobles of the nations and execute upon them the written judgement.

So the Lord Jesus Christ is King over the nations, indeed over all things in the heavens and the earth (Eph 1:20–22), and He intends to rule through His body the church until such time as He appears and every knee shall bow and every tongue confess that He is Lord (Phil 2:10).

But this 'ruling' by the church is not the reconstructionist's vision of direct power upon the earth – the English have already tried that with Cromwell and failed – but rather through the indirect power of influence. Influence gives guidance by providing true options about which people may make informed choices and be responsible for the progress or otherwise of their society.

Some of the perceptual problems we ourselves face

This idea of 'contending for the faith' may not be what we were expecting, of course, when we first considered national revival, but that was true of the holiness movement praying for the second blessing when speaking in tongues unexpectedly came instead! Or of Jesus the son of a carpenter coming when the nation was expecting a king, and so on.

I asked a leader of the Pentecostal movement in the 1970s what he thought of the charismatic movement in the church of England. 'If it is from God,' he said, 'they will come and join us.' But of course it was and they didn't. And now this same Anglican movement has promoted the Alpha course, one of the most compelling and influential Christian discipling movements since Wesley.

Christ warned us of this in the Gospels when He described the way the Kingdom comes unexpectedly and without traditional form, using the picture of new wine and old wineskins. The implication of His warning is that there is no room for us to incorporate the Kingdom into *our* church structures, but rather it is the other way around, whereby Christ is willing to incorporate us into *His* Kingdom. For at the end of the day, the Kingdom *is* Christ by definition, and the church will not pidgeon-hole Him, incorporate Him, organise Him or tame Him. He is the Christ, the King, and it is He who holds *us* in the palm of His hand. It really will explode old wineskins of church cultural practice asunder if we try to adapt and tolerate instead of embrace and change, so it is essential for our role as good servants of the King not to split and schism but to move together like the Israelites in the desert, willing to move and to change the moment His cloud is seen to shake and move (Num 9:17).

The people in the valley of decision need to see the presentation of ideas clearly to make a choice between the two kingdoms of Jesus Christ and our enemy. This principle is clearly seen in Scripture of the watching, cowed Israelite army under Saul turned into a rampaging tiger of a military force by the triumph of the single idea of being the army of the living God (1 Sam 17:26, 45). And the watching Israelite people at Mount Carmel seeing the contest of wills between the

triumphant Elijah and the priests of Baal, and again the transformation of the cowed nation into a triumphant army after
Gideon's demoralising of the Midianites, or in the New
Testament with Peter in the temple courts propounding the
prophet Joel's prophecy. And in contemporary times, 1.2
million out of 4 million Scots voted for the Christian notion
to retain the ban on the promotion of homosexuality in
primary schools. In all these cases, the people watched the
contest of ideas in the valley of decision and voted, but they
needed the opportunity! This is 'contending for the faith' and
is the duty of every church generation.

Securing the forum to speak

I asked the principal at a theological seminary why his skilful
apologetics were restricted to a Christian audience and not
proclaimed (as it were) from the rooftops of our nation. He
replied that there was no opportunity allowed in the national
media or national forum to which he and his seminary had
access. I grieved over this admission of our lost heritage and
role to address our own nation until the Lord opened my eyes
to the simple fact that a forum is opened to those who are seen
to be experts on issues of a critical nature. So when I saw this
very same principal being interviewed on TV news over the
scandal of a homosexual being selected as a bishop, I understood then that the Lord has given us in His timing the very
issue which will not go away in the long term and will guarantee the church a forum that will dominate our thinking and
our presence in the nation. That issue is Israel and I have
described at more length in the following section how this will
attract and keep national media attention on us. Within this
opportunity is the parallel opportunity to disciple the nation

not only about Israel but about the paths of righteousness discussed above.

How is discipling the nation done?

We dropped the ball somewhere after the voyage of the Beagle and the publication of *Origin of Species* (1859) by failing to get the strategy from God our King to counter this pernicious determinist philosophy and retreating instead into our religious ghetto, rarely to venture out. Even our charity functions were taken from us with the introduction of the welfare state, itself a Christian phrase and concept taken from Archbishop Temple's 1942 pamphlet *The State and the Individual*. But it need not have been so, and it need not be so now either.

Our fathers in the faith did not rest but insisted on discipling the nation by winning the contest of ideas (the salt and light principle), an interesting example of which has occurred in the USA regarding the teaching of creationism in schools. The education authorities in Tennessee lost the famous 'Monkey Trial' of 1927 when they were arguing to retain the ascendancy of the Bible creation story, but seventy years later the Kansas Christians won the return match and they, together with a few other states, now teach creationism alongside the theory of evolution in their schools. How? They set the determinists (Darwinists) against the free-willers (humanists), using the same biblical strategy where God divides the enemy against themselves (Acts 23:7–9; 2 Chron 20:22). This is an example of destroying the wisdom of the wise (1 Cor 1:16), which we have examined in more depth in Chapter 2. We could have won the same Darwinian battle following 1859 in this country had we only resorted to God for the strategy, like David (2 Sam 5:23) and the modern Kansas creationists, instead of being forced onto our back foot and a whole-scale intellectual retreat and defeat ever since.

As it is, Lady Young demonstrated that battles of ideas could still be won in 2000, even in our national parliament, by three times defeating the government's bill that encouraged the promotion of homosexuality in our schools. Even with the odds heavily weighted against her campaign, this apostolic act succeeded because she was God's anointed, empowered representative in this particular debate in this particular forum.

God has definitely promised us (1 Cor 1:19) that He will defeat the debaters of this age through us and the reason He allows generational challenges is so that each generation of Christians can exercise their arm for war (2 Cor 10:5), and each generation of non-believers may see the battle and have a fair chance of proclaiming, 'Now we believe, not because of what you said, for we ourselves have heard Him and we know that this is indeed the Christ, the Saviour of the world' (Jn 4:41–42), and, 'As for me and my house, we will follow the Lord.'

But there are debates which are going largely unanswered in our nation, the high ground of which liberal thought is garnering to itself. We will miss the contention if we do not realise that our nation's fate is hanging in the balance and it might be generations before we have another opportunity to influence its passage. Already our long, rich history has been largely robbed of its Christian-Judeo laws because they have been dismantled by a self-serving, short-sighted, merciless new middle class wanting freedom without boundaries.

Christ said, 'I will build My church' (Mt 16:18) and Scripture exhorts us to 'contend earnestly for the faith' (Jude 3). Perhaps we have got these two the wrong way around. Do we say in effect, 'Jesus, leave the church building to us and *You* go out there into the world and contend for the faith'? If this is so, we have forgotten our eighteen hundred years of national history and been deceived into allowing the enemy to have a free run in the nation with no real opposition. We are living in a unique moment, but it is possible that we could miss our cue.

The moment we engage under the leadership of men or women who are anointed by God expressly for the purpose of leading the nation by contending for the faith (Acts 9:15) we can expect Christ the King to move on our behalf and give us the victory we have chorused about for decades; that is, the victory of souls who are won in the valley of decision as the two kingdoms clash. The first three chapters of 1 Corinthians are dedicated to explaining how Christ guarantees victory over the wisdom of the wise from within their argument! Jesus did it all the time, of course. For as He is the truth, all opposition to Him must have internal contradictions within it by definition, so all we have to do is find them and exploit them. What are we waiting for? It is all there for the taking, just like Canaan was before the army of the Israelites.

Absenting ourselves from the conflict

When we retreated after our defeat by the Darwinians to nitpick over interesting details of scriptural interpretation, or to build the Lord's church for Him, or to engage in spiritual non-involvement in our nation, we lost the battle for the souls of the watching generations. And for that, judgement will most certainly start with us, the house of God.

Jesus the Christ wants His inheritance back, and He will get it with us in this generation, or without us in another. Judging by scriptural precedents (Acts 7:34), He brings extreme pressure to bear upon His people, who then cry out in anguish over many years until the cry reaches fever pitch, and then He hears from heaven and heals our land. Does it have to be that way? Do we now face a Kadesh-Barnea choice of judgement (Num 13:30)? Already prophetic Christian writers such as Dr Christopher Hill, David Pawson and Dr Clifford Hill are warning of judgement coming upon us.

It is almost unbelievable how long He has restrained His hand in mercy on our nation. One might think He has restrained it because of the integrity of the centuries of our forebears who honoured Him, but it is really difficult to think of a contemporary reason. Maybe it is because He still respects the Coronation Covenant oath 'to promulgate the Protestant faith of Jesus Christ', taken by our nation's Sovereign in 1952, never revoked; and which she confirmed in her November 2005 speech.

Whatever the reason, there are signs of a window of opportunity to contend for the faith and enable the multitudes of our nation to once again make clear choices in the valley of decision. The signs are there in the newspapers, the TV discussion programmes, the parliamentary votes, the scientific *faux pas*, of the Lord getting behind His servants in power just as He promised us in Revelation 2:27. City Link reports falls in crime rates in the areas where they have organised systematic cross-denomination prayer campaigns.

As we have seen, our best opportunity to seize the media limelight is to take up the issue of supporting Israel, but of course we must first settle the issues that Israel raises within our own ranks and we have addressed this as our first priority in the following section, as this is the gateway in God's timing that will enable us to fulfil our calling in this generation.

The church must quickly repent of blindness, self-interest and fear, and then seek Him to reveal the real issues which are visited upon us at this time. We must take confidence that He has prepared the apostles and anointed them to stand before the rulers of our nation and its institutions and rebuke them like David (1 Sam 17:26) for opposing the army of the living God, and that His people will be willing in the day of His power to take up the walk of the cross and find the works that have been prepared for each of them.

References

Christian Institute website <www.christian.org.uk>
Evangelical Alliance website <www.eauk.org>
Transform UK website <www.transform-uk.org>
The Institute for the Study of Islam and Christianity website <www.isic-centre.org>

The Issue of Israel, Michael's People

The status of the Jews as a nation before God has become clouded in Christian thinking, largely due to the popularisation of replacement theology, a radical view of God's people first propounded in the second century by Justin Martyr and the first five Principals of the Alexandrian Seminary (Pantaenus, Clement, Origen, Pamphilus and Eusebius the friend of the Emperor Constantine). This Greek seminary invented the idea of merging Greek philosophy with Christianity by using Greek philosophy's allegorical method of interpretation, particularly of the Bible, leading to the teaching that the church was the 'New Israel' of God which replaced literal Israel and the Jewish people in God's plan of redemption. Origen interpreted literally the Scriptures that spoke of curses on the Jews, but allegorised those that spoke of blessings for the Jews so that all blessings henceforth were considered to be for the church only!

This is reflected in our modern replacement theology, which posits that the Christian church has replaced the Jews as the 'New Israel' in all of God's covenantal promises, fully superseding the nation God had previously called His own. It claims that only the New Covenant remains active, with the first covenants made by God (primarily with Abraham, Moses and David) now invalid or void. Now, under this rewrite of biblical history, all references of blessings or promises to Israel in the Old (and most controversially the New) Testament are to be considered allegorical or symbolic. A full exposition of this history is contained in Dr Richard Booker's excellent *No Longer Strangers* (Sounds of the Trumpet, 2002).

Of course this made the hitherto very *Jewish* Christianity more acceptable to the Greek-thinking world, as did Constantine's appropriation of the pagan festivals of Ishtar (Easter) and Mithras (25 December) for Rome's pagans. This would never have survived as a philosophy in the first 135 years of Christianity because of the preponderance of Jewish believers, but after the second Jewish revolt of AD 132–135 these Jewish believers died out and the *de facto* governance of doctrine passed to the Gentile Christian church. The de-Judification march continued with the change of the Jewish Sabbath of Saturday to the 'new' Sabbath of Sunday and statements by the new theologians of how anti-Christ the Jews and all aspects of the faith that had Jewish connotations were.

In sum, belief in the Jewish Messiah Jesus passed from an internal Jewish sect called 'The Way', which included external

Gentile believers, to a fully Gentile, separated movement adopting the name of 'Christianity' given it in Antioch. And this has largely remained the case ever since, with the exceptions of the Puritan movement and the evangelical Zionist movement, which both pleaded a special case for the Jews in the purposes of God.

While a moment's reflection reveals that the 'replacement' view flies in the face of what we know of our unchanging, faithful and covenant-keeping God, the result of the unthinking acceptance of replacement theology has led to horrific consequences throughout the last 2,000 years. Jews have been mercilessly persecuted by Christians for centuries, with triumphant pogroms and expulsions from one country after another (including Britain in 1290) rendering them a people in permanent exile and vulnerable to the worst human war crimes in history by such as Stalin and Hitler (the latter of which quoted the writings of Martin Luther in justification for persecution of the Jews, although this was undoubtedly to cover the true philosophical base of his creed derived from Nietzsche's 'Superman' and the determinist writings following Darwin *et al.*).

But while the consequences for the Jews of our Christian forefathers' beliefs and actions may leave us appalled and even repentant, it is also important to realise that the relentless hacking away at the Jewish olive tree spoken of in Romans 11 also has enormous implications for the Christian church, the 'grafted in' olive branch (Rom 11:17). After all, it is our own roots that we are cutting away. Thus the stupidities and consequences of some of the heresies of replacement theology are as follows:

First, if we claim to replace the Jews rather than join from them, we deny our inheritance, our line, our heritage, indeed our very *identity* as Christians. For, as Jesus reminds us, 'salvation is of the Jews' (Jn 4:22). We are partakers of the natural olive tree (the remnant of believing Israel) and are planted in among them, not in place of them (Rom 11:17) . If we claim to replace the Jews we become like a brother who denies his Father's firstborn, His first love, thus rending the family in two. *The consequences of this denial* are twofold:

1. We have an identity crisis. If we ignore our spiritual heritage, our family, then how can we claim consistency, or even a consistent God, in the face of conflicting and proselytising philosophies? How do we engage with secular humanism, the modern incarnation of the spirit of Greece (addressed earlier in this book in the section on spiritual warfare)? How do we expect blessing from our Father when we damn our brother?

2. Islam is able to build upon this self-inflicted separation of Christianity from its Jewish roots and claim a replacement theology of its own; that is, that Islam now replaces Christianity, and owes nothing to the Hebrew Scriptures and covenants. Islam is then free to divorce the Jews and Israel from any legitimacy, making them appropriate targets for destruction. (Of course Islam also divorces Jesus Christ from His Jewish heritage, promises and status as King of the Jews and Messiah by a convoluted interpretation of His virgin birth, claiming Jesus Christ as an Islamic prophet rather than as the Son of God and Saviour of the world.) *Once the slippery slope of replacement theology is contemplated, it then becomes hard to refute that Christians have only the logical step of submission to Islam to avoid the wrath of Allah and Islamists.*

Second, competing worldviews (especially humanism) can see, even if we cannot, the potency of the Judeo/Christian common heritage joining forces, and so seek to separate them. Consider, for example, in an attempt to isolate Israel, how America's pro-Israel Christian president is vociferously blamed around the world for the current Middle East crisis and, in consequence, the Christian world as well. Humanists paint a picture of recent history that is desperately one-sided against the Jews and the nation-state of Israel, and the Gentile church often does nothing in response.

The consequence of this is that the Christian church is provoked into having either to dare to defend the Jews or to join the noisy throng condemning them, often on false and malicious information. Sadly we so often falter, take the easy path and side with the dominating liberal humanistic view and condemn Israel, our own family, isolating Jews and driving a wedge between them and us.

Third, we deny having a viewpoint that is rooted in God's covenants with the Jews; that is, one that is biblically historical. We should take our example from Paul, who in his address to the Areopagus, took his authority to proclaim his message from the historicity of the Israel story when he appealed to his Gentile hearers and to us to repent and to acknowledge Jesus (Acts 17:17–31). Or from the lips of Jesus Himself, who confessed His title of King of the Jews to Pilate (Mt 27:11).

The consequence of this is that the Christian church has no historical or rational basis for a defence of its beliefs, and can only suffer and submit to the forces of this world instead of being enabled to contend vigorously for the faith.

Fourth, we no longer seek to help these, the least of Christ's brethren.

The consequence of this is that we are condemned by Jesus Himself, who could not be clearer on this point (Mt 25:30–46). Other scriptures, such as Joel 3:1–2 and Deuteronomy 30:5–7, confirm this warning of God's judgement in prospect for us, the Gentile church, if we fail to seek to help the Jews.

Fifth, we cut ourselves off from the 'root and fatness of the olive tree' (Rom 11:17–18) and the support that naturally brings.

The consequence of this: How many churches do we see springing up and flourishing richly for a short while before sinking into lassitude and even despair as members sneak off to find another centre that offers a 'new thing'? Even traditional churches are not immune – witness the church buildings that are sold for redevelopment, perhaps as meeting centres for other faiths. They were not connected to the root and support of the olive tree, Israel, and they withered and died. However, if we seek to help Israel, God will help us as the Scripture promises (Gen 12:1–3).

Sixth, we ignore a potentially massive strategic spiritual warfare weapon in our struggle against the spiritual forces of secular humanism and Islam in the form of help from Michael the prince of Israel (Dan 10:21).

The consequence of this is that we are left weakened against a formidable enemy, secular humanism, which during the last 200 years has run roughshod over the church in Western Europe, pulverising our structure, heritage, cultures, laws and history and which now also cleverly suborns Islam to join its attack upon Christianity. I have addressed this issue at greater length in the section on spiritual warfare.

However, we can learn from Scripture how to understand this difficult issue, since hostility to the Jews is not only a *post*-apostolic problem, for the apostle Paul clearly warns the Gentiles in Romans 8–11 that God has not cast away His people, as they still have the covenants and the promises that God, by His very nature, cannot abandon.

Modern scholars have also revisited anti-scriptural Christian prejudice and arrogance towards the Jews in such books as Ronald Diprose's *Israel and the Church* and Sarah Teplinsky's *Why Care about Israel?* and the aforementioned *No Longer Strangers* by Dr Richard Booker. Derek Prince, in his book *Prophetic Destinies*, lists seventy-nine Old Testament prophecies regarding Israel, and forty-six regarding promises about the land of Israel. Indeed Dr Prince emphasises three oaths God gives to His people which are also accompanied by covenants. These two things simply cannot be broken without changing the very nature of God. Consider for a moment the concept that God could ever break a covenant; that He could ever be unfaithful to a promise (Heb 6:17). Those who press the case for replacement theology are saying exactly that.

However, there is an alternative that our faithful God has planned for us, and which I believe will bring the Christian church much fulfilment and our place in His Kingdom, but it requires a radical rethink of who we *think* we are, and God's purpose for the church.

Jew and Gentile joined together

The roots of the nation of Israel's relationship with God (Rom 11:16–18) are the covenants He made with the Jewish patriarchs and prophets. We Gentiles have access to the rich grace of those covenants (Gal 3:20) through the last covenant promised through Jeremiah to 'the house of Israel and . . . the house of Judah' (Jer 31:31), which we celebrate as the New

Covenant (Heb 9:15). In this covenant Jesus 'is the Mediator of the new covenant, by means of death' (Heb 9:15) and so it is the one we ourselves depend upon to be saved.

Thus we Gentile Christian 'branches' draw from the covenantal roots by our engrafting into Israel, the historical entity. This relationship links Jew and Christian inextricably as we partake of the richness of their root, their covenant with God, our New Covenant. It is worth noting that the Greek word used here for partaking (Rom 11:17) is *sunkoinonos*, which is to do with companionship and co-partnership together. The Scripture warns us that the root supports us (Rom 11:18) as it does the natural branches (the Jews, who are the elect of God). As Jamieson comments regarding this passage, 'From Israel hath come all that thou art and hast in the family of God; for "salvation is of the Jews"' (Jn 4:22). We are wild branches that are grafted in among them – not instead of them – and if we boast against them God may not spare us, as He did not spare some natural branches that were broken off (Rom 11:17).

So it can be seen that if a wedge can be inserted between the roots of God's Israel and the branches of His Gentile church, either by secular politics or by Islam's version of replacement theology or by our own, then the church ceases to partake of the 'root and fatness of the olive tree' (Rom 11:17). The roots are then unable to support the church, leaving both the church and Israel to be picked off by their enemies more easily. I believe that this lies at the very heart of one of the prime causes of the weakness and ineffectiveness of the Christian church in the West today. I think it worth noting that *where the church is flourishing in the world today, there is no history of Jewish persecution*, whether it be in South America, China or the American Mid West. Where the church has been in decline or decay, there is usually a long history of persecution – for example, in Europe, Russia and the Middle East. Of course we must be clear that we are not discussing the effectiveness or otherwise of a few anointed men and women of God, or our personal salvation, but rather the corporate Christian church as a unit, a family, a bride, an army.

We can thus begin to see that if, as a corporate church, we succumb to the propaganda of Israel's enemies we are spiritually chopping at our own roots, and thus will become an irrelevance both to the purposes of the kings and rulers of the nations, and even, as Scripture and history demonstrate, to God. On the other hand, if the Gentile church were to see its survival and prosperity and expansion in a vigorous support of Israel, it would draw deeply from the richness God would then provide and become once again the major force that the Roman, Ottoman and British empires had to come to terms with.

As usual, of course, this attitude can lead to extremes such as the so-called 'Dual Covenant' movement, which denies that Jews need to come to Jesus in order to access this New Covenant and be born again of incorruptible seed, justified by means of Jesus' sacrifice on the cross and become sons of God through the resurrection of Jesus from the dead with access to the Kingdom here and now (Jn 3:5). There is no dual access to the promises of the New Covenant, otherwise as the Scripture says (Heb 8:7) there would have been no need for one in the first place! Apart from church politics, there is genuine confusion over the status of Jews and their 'old' covenants, particularly since the Jews do not have temple sacrifices for sin. The major point to grasp is that there is a significant difference between the state of being justified by faith (open to the Hebrews, famously Abraham) and that of being regenerated or born again, which includes justification, and which is only through Jesus Christ.

Clarifying the status of the Jew – regenerated or justified?

Luke 7:28 says: 'There is not a greater prophet than John the Baptist; but he who is least in the kingdom of God is greater than he.' This scripture is fascinating, and to many Christians confusing. How can there be two classes of believer? But Jesus is contrasting the state of regeneration (us) with the state of justification only (John the Baptist), as he deliberately separates the status of those justified by faith through the old covenants and those justified by faith by the New Covenant.

The New Covenant – regenerated children of the Kingdom

This New Covenant status is one we are most familiar with but is worth clarifying in order to contrast the status of the Jews before God. The child of the kingdom is not only justified, he is also regenerated with the nature of Christ, sanctified and justified by the blood of Christ, and crucially now has free entry into the holiest place, following his Saviour Jesus, who has provided the sacrifice once and for all. This extraordinary status is accorded to all, both Jew and Gentile, who are regenerated according to Romans 4:24–5:2 and are 'a new creation' in Christ Jesus; 'old things have passed away; behold, all things have become new' (2 Cor 5:17).

The old covenants – the justified Jew

However, it must be noted that Jesus does not say that Jews of the old covenants such as John the Baptist do not have access to Him. Indeed, the two persons identified as Moses and Elijah on the Mount of Transfiguration are of course Hebrews who have been justified by faith through the old covenants. Paul discusses this kind of justification at some length (Rom 4:1–13), with particular reference to Abraham. The apostle James confirms this status (Jas 2:23), as does Jesus Himself, who also extends it to Abraham's descendants Isaac and Jacob, who sit down with Him in the Kingdom of heaven (Lk 11:8). David himself talks as if from experience when he says, 'Blessed are those whose lawless deeds are forgiven, and whose sins are covered; blessed is the man to whom the Lord shall not impute sin' (Rom 4:7–8).

The clearest demonstration of justification for the Jew who does not believe in Jesus but applies by faith through the covenants of the patriarchs is from the mouth of Jesus in Luke 18:9–14. Here He describes the humble and contrite tax collector who depends upon God justifying him going down to his house justified rather than the seemingly upright Pharisee who is depending upon his own efforts. This condition is emphasised in Psalm 51:16–17: 'For You do not desire sacrifice, or else I would give it; You do not delight in burnt offering. The sacrifices of God are a broken spirit, a broken and a contrite heart – these, O God, You will not despise.' Similar scriptures are found in Isaiah 66:2; Psalm 34:18 and Isaiah 57:15. Clearly then the Jew who does not believe in Jesus but who is calling upon the name of the Lord (Joel 2:32) can in humility, brokenness and contrition for his sins still be justified before God by faith because of the covenants God has made with Israel. However, his place in the Kingdom is one that is located in eternity (Lk 11:8) whereas the regenerated man has access to the Kingdom of God here and now through Jesus. Clearly such a Jew who is unregenerated needs to be evangelised (Rom 10:14–15), following in the steps of the apostle Peter (Gal 2:8), so that he might enter that state in the here and now. *It is a serious mistake to try and equate New Covenant regeneration with Old Covenantal justification, as we have seen above.*

The common criticism of the Jew's status by the contemporary Gentile church is that he cannot be justified because the Jews no longer have a temple or temple sacrifices for sin. This is anticipated in Scripture and answered by God to the prophet Habakkuk, who raised the same issue of Jews going into the dispersion without a temple and without sacrifices: 'Behold the proud, his soul is not upright in him; but the just shall live by his faith' (Hab 2:4). The Lord confirms in this passage that the Jews in exile may still be justified by their faith even though they have no access to either temple or sacrifices, so the criticism is unfounded and even mischievous with regard to present-day Jews who still do not have a temple for sin-sacrifices.

Finally, it is also errant to say that the time of the Jews is past; that they have been bypassed. It is wise to remember that the justified Jew is one of the 'elect' or 'remnant' of God who are Jews He picks for Himself to maintain a witness within the nation (Rom 11:28–29). But does this mean that being a descendant of Abraham, a Jew is automatically justified? By no means, otherwise Jacob and Esau would have been equal in the eyes of God!

The unjustified Jew

Romans 9:31–32 says: 'Israel, pursuing the law of righteousness, has not attained to the law of righteousness. Why?

Because they did not seek it by faith, but as it were, by the works of the law. For they stumbled at that stumbling stone.' Justification, in order to be effective, must be imputed and imparted by God, as only His righteousness is adequate to avoid deserved judgement. Establishing our own righteousness apart from faith is the major stumbling block at which we can all fall if we are not careful, particularly the Jews by their blindness in thinking they can attain the righteousness of God by any effort of their own, or by their lineage from Abraham. For if indeed it is possible to establish sufficient righteousness by your own efforts then you are equal with God, which is heresy under New and Old Covenants. It is the wise man who recognises his inadequacy in this area and appeals to God early, whether Jew or Gentile!

Identities: A summary

If we are able to understand the several categories of people referred to by Paul and others in his teaching concerning the relationship between the Jews and Gentiles found in his letter to the Romans chapters 9–11, we may better understand the issues involved for us today. So who then are the Jews, the elect, the remnant and the Gentiles? Who is justified before God and who is not? Let us identify the status of seven sets of individuals before God:

1. The Jew who does not believe in Jesus but who depends in faith upon God to justify him through God's covenants with Israel

As we have seen, this Jew is part of the elected 'remnant' that God always reserves for Himself through any persecution of the nation of Israel. These are described by Paul as follows:

'Concerning the gospel they are enemies for your sake, but concerning the election they are beloved for the sake of the fathers. For the gifts and the calling of God are irrevocable' (Rom 11:28–29). This individual is unregenerated and does not enjoy the full and present provision of the New Covenant (Jer 31:31) promised to the house of Israel and the house of Judah but is nevertheless an heir by faith of the provisions that Paul describes in Romans 9:4–5. Jesus poignantly describes this character in the parable of the publican and the Pharisee (Lk 18:9–14), when He describes the abandon of the sinning tax collector throwing himself upon the mercy of God. Paul also refers to David's description of the blessed state of this kind of man to whom God ascribes righteousness apart from works (Rom 4:6). This Jew is availing himself of the patriarchal covenants which have never been revoked and the Lord's promise to the prophet Habakkuk, echoing Abraham's own justification (Gen 15:6): 'Behold the proud, his soul is not upright in him; but the just shall live by his faith' (Hab 2:4). This promise of being justified by faith still exists, but the full and present provisions of the New Covenant are denied him unless he is born again of incorruptible seed through the atonement of Jesus on the cross after hearing the gospel preached (Rom 10:13–15).

It is this Israel that the body of Christ as a whole must seek to support and serve, even if they regard us as enemies (Rom 11:28), so that the church may benefit from the richness of Israel's roots, and jointly participate in the heralding of the end-time purposes of Christ (Rom 11:12, 25).

2. The Jew who believes in Jesus

Known nowadays as 'Messianic Jews', these are Jews who enjoy the full provision of the New Covenant. They are complete Jews in every sense; they are regenerated and already live in the Kingdom of Christ, and with them the middle wall of partition with the Gentiles is broken down. This Jew may now enter the holiest place by the new and living way (Heb 10:19–20) instead of the high priest. This high place of justification is an extraordinary provision and must be brought to mind when contrasting the justification of the believing Jew in Jesus with the unbelieving Jew. He has no dependence upon any aspect of temple service that involves justification for his sins/sinful nature, for these are already met by Jesus' sacrifice.

Messianic Jews may consider themselves to be a bridge between the Gentiles in Christ and the commonwealth of Israel, but they will be regarded as enemies by Israel, just as the Gentiles in Christ are (Rom 11:28). There is no bridge or 'halo effect' until the fullness of the Gentiles has come in (Rom 11:25). However, Messianic Jews are a vivid demonstration of the grace of God in Christ that Jews of the elect may see for themselves and can understand (Rom 10:14).

3. The Jew who does not believe in Jesus and depends upon his 'works of the law' to justify him

This individual is in unbelief and is 'broken off' from the olive tree (Rom 11:20). However, if he does not continue in unbelief, God is able to graft him into the natural olive tree again (Rom 11:23) and this condition Paul describes as 'life from the dead' (Rom 11:15). Paul also makes the interesting comment in Romans 11:12 that their contribution will be 'riches for the Gentiles'. This clearly has implications for the church too wide-reaching to discuss here.

4. The Jew who trusts solely in his Abrahamic ancestry

This person is 'not all Israel who are of Israel' (Rom 9:6–8) because physical ancestry alone is not the qualifier. Paul explains, 'The children of the flesh, these are not the children of God' (Rom 9:8).

5. The Gentile who believes in Jesus according to Romans 4:24–5:2

This Gentile is the Christian, born again of incorruptible seed, who now has access to the New Covenant by the provision of Christ, and can enter the holiest place by the new and living way provided by Jesus the sacrifice (Eph 2:17). He is now described as one of 'My people', 'Beloved of God', 'sons of God' (Hos 2:23; Rom 9:25) as now he is in a new state: 'But now in Christ Jesus you who once were far off have been brought near by the blood of Christ' (Eph: 2:12). However, although this man is going to heaven, Jesus warns him that being born again is but a start on the road to life; it is not an end (Mt 7:21–26). He amplifies this warning elsewhere (Jn 3:3–8) that the new birth is but a preliminary requirement to seeing and entering the Kingdom of God. So the new birth is not a Christian club we join but rather an obligation for service.

6. The Gentile who does not believe in Jesus

This Gentile has no access to the covenants made with the patriarchs and is described in Ephesians 2:12 as being 'without Christ, being aliens from the commonwealth of Israel and strangers from the covenants of promise, having no hope and without God in the world'.

However, should God choose to confront him with His claims of righteousness and an offer of salvation in Jesus, this man will have an opportunity to access the life-saving New Covenant promised in Jeremiah and confirmed in the resurrection of Christ to the right hand of God (Rom 4:24–5:2).

7. The Gentile who thinks he is a Christian but is not

No doubt there are unregenerate members of the Gentile church who are not members of the living body but who are there for cultural or social reasons alone. Jesus condemns them with those dread words 'I never knew you' (Mt 7:23). Jesus explains that even if this man has done miracles in His name, if He does not know him, he is doomed (Mt 7:21–23). It is our duty to make quite clear the call of Christ for 'all men everywhere to repent' (Acts 17:30–31) to our generation so that they have a fair opportunity to make the right decision.

Is the church already under judgement?

The answer to this question depends upon whether one believes that Christianity is a private, personal religion or whether it is a calling to proclaim the government of Christ Jesus on earth.

If it is a private religion then to avoid the judgement of God we should seek greater personal holiness in order to be increasingly like Him. It can be convincingly argued that the evangelical church has concentrated its preaching in this way (together with evangelism) for forty years. I believe this exclusive concentration upon personal holiness – especially by personal effort – has emasculated the church and distracted its members.

If, on the other hand, Christianity is not a private religion but the carrying out of a commission from God to proclaim His Kingdom and disciple the nation (Mt 28:19), then clearly judgement will depend upon the measure of our obedience to

Him, rather than our ability to try to be like Him, which is a quality He imparts rather than one we secure for ourselves. The Lord approved the severest rebuke that was meted out to the unprofitable servant (Lk 19:20–27) who neglected the task allotted to him and adopted a passive attitude to his duty of minding his master's interests. Likewise, if our commission from God is to proclaim the government or Kingdom of Christ in our present time upon the earth, then we can anticipate the same scrutiny and the same rebuke if we too are neglectful of our duty in our own generation.

Elsewhere in this book we describe how the proclamation and influence of the government of Christ in our nation's history has guided the nation in the ways of righteousness and how its neglect has led to the capture and control of the church by the secular world. If we are to assess ourselves objectively, then we must look at whether we have been a profitable or an unprofitable servant, since we delude ourselves if we believe there is a semi-detached third option such as 'keeping ourselves to ourselves'. That prevailing condition of the church, which is perhaps our cultural Achilles' heel, is being disturbed by the goads of God (Acts 9:5) as secular humanism increases the pressure upon us by its co-opting of Islam in its cause. Of course they may only do what God permits! God has used the Chaldeans before to judge and chastise His people (Hab 1:6) and it looks as though He is using them again (together with the humanists) as millions of global Muslims leave their homes and come to this nation with their alien culture and their mission of Ummah (see page 246).

It is time we woke up to our destiny and privilege in being called at such a time as this, for if we are not under judgement then we are most certainly under challenge!

A frank appraisal

We see a patient spiritual enemy in the form of humanism's political correctness not only evangelising the media, politics, education, science and medicine in the ways described in this book, but also encroaching upon the territory of the church, both in its public influence and its private administration. Cleverly, this enemy of the cross suborns Islam to inhibit the church's expression of the faith by pretending to protect it (that is, Islam) from offence. For example, the secular world is seeking to bind the church into secular employment law, into limiting what might be proclaimed in the name of Christ, even banning public signs of Christianity such as Bibles in hospitals, hot cross buns, crosses in graveyards, Christmas decorations, all in the name of 'non-offence'. These are but the first signs of the hatred of Christianity which secular humanism is stirring up.

Combating this tidal wave is not to be undertaken without adequate planning, preparation and resources, both at the corporate and the personal level. We do not have the natural centre-stage opportunities any more that once enabled us to more easily influence the nation, so our contention for the faith has to take different strategies to make the most of the attention we can attract.

I believe two priorities face us. The first one, which we have detailed elsewhere in this book, is we must arm ourselves with maturity and the knowledge of our faith and also of those faiths with which we are in conflict. The second priority is to start seeking to support Israel. Supporting Israel will thrust the church into the public arena like no other issue, for not only will we be obeying God in drawing upon the richness of the roots of our own faith, we will also be empowered to contend for the faith in our ancient role to proclaim Christ's claims of righteousness upon the nation.

Starting on the road to support Israel

I believe that we face a simple, four-fold plan to changing our corporate direction from being a burden to and persecutor of Israel, God's elect, to being a blessing, which is:

1. seeking Scripture to properly understand how we are linked with the Jews;
2. repentance for our attitude to them in the past;
3. changing attitude from persecution and indifference to love and support;
4. proactive support.

Seeking Scripture

One way and another the Scriptures, particularly Romans 9–11, give an extremely plain and heavy warning to us to treat the Jews with respect, with brotherhood and friendship, not only for their sake but for our own. Scripture also warns us both in the Old Testament (Gen 12:1–3; Joel 3:1–2) and the New (Mt 25:40, 45) that poor treatment of the Jews will result in judgement and punishment. So for our own sakes and self-interest, both now and in eternity, we must try to turn around and do our utmost to befriend the Jewish people in the way Jesus describes at some length in Matthew 25:29–46. It is my personal horror that the Judge might consider the messianic scripture in Zechariah 12:9–14 to apply to the Gentile church as well – that is, that we will look upon Israel whom we Gentiles have pierced through over many bloody centuries – and that Jesus included us when He said,

'And the King will answer and say to them, "Assuredly, I say to you inasmuch as you did it to one of the least of these My brethren, you did it to Me"' (Mt 25:40). May God have mercy on us!

Repentance

And should we not repent of our ways towards the Jews, we will get trouble from the instruments of God's judgement, such as the political and media world of secular humanism and the Islamic movement (Is 60:12; Rom 11:21–22). Mind you, it might be difficult for our repentance to be believed by the Jews, for apart from nearly 2,000 years of Christian persecution of the Jews, we have to take note of the scripture which advises that the 'sons of the election' are the 'enemies of the gospel for our sake', although 'they are beloved for the sake of the fathers. For the gifts and the calling of God are irrevocable' (Rom 11:28–29). Unsurprisingly the Jews are suspicious of Christian motives and we are unlikely to get much thanks as we try to make up for our centuries of persecution and neglect.

Changing our attitude towards the Jews and our worldview towards Israel

The other, obvious, difficulty is that our own attitude varies from support of the Jews through the sidelining of replacement theology to outright persecution and obstruction of God's people such as Martin Luther's raging 'We must drive them out like wild dogs' (*The Jews and their Lies*, 1543), the giving away of their land by Winston churchill in defiance of the Mandate provision, the barring of Jews fleeing Hitler from landing in the Promised Land, the betrayal of the Jews by the British who refused to resupply arms to Israel while they were being attacked not once but twice, and the latest phenomenon of church networks linking in a united stand against the Jews. This latter disgrace is evidenced by the World Council of Churches' anti-Israel one-sided stance in reporting its 'violation of human rights', the national Council of churches of Christ (USA) condemning Israel and the churches for Middle East Peace seeking to promote the Palestinian cause. (All quoted in detail in Sandra Teplinsky's book *Why Care about Israel?*). The Anglican church also has withdrawn investment from Israel.

Proactive support

However, movements such as the Love Never Fails coalition of committed Christian pro-Israel groups and the Joseph Storehouse are growing in our nation and it would be a good first step if we made a stand with them. It is a start that British Christians have already declared a confession of our sins against the Jewish people in the public demonstration in Westminster Hall on 1 November 1999, the anniversary of Edward I's expulsion of Jews from England. This was followed by the handing to the deputy lieutenant of Greater London, a Jew, of the Solemn Declaration of our part in the persecution of the Jews, which sought God's forgiveness for ourselves and His blessing upon His covenant people, after which the church bells of London rang out. The Vatican, too, has offered repentance for the Catholic Church's sins against the Jews.

This is strong, remarkable leadership and is of the type we must all strive to follow and contribute to in the contending for our faith in this nation. We must acknowledge our roots and be faithful to the Scriptures, refraining from closing our eyes and hearts against God's clear warnings to us. We have everything to win and nothing to lose, except our chains of secular humanism.

The Issue of the Prince of Persia

The 1982 Declaration by the Islamic Foundation (Leicester) stated in *The Islamic Conquest of Britain* (20 December 2002):

> The Islamic Movement is an organised struggle to change the existing society into an Islamic society based on the Qur'an and the Sunna and to make Islam, which is a code for entire life, supreme and dominant, especially in the socio-political spheres.

How is it possible for this alien culture to make such a statement in the land that has benefited from a Judeo-Christian political, legal and cultural framework for over 1,800 years and which now revels in the luxury of postmodern behavioural licence?

Well, things they are a-changin' and this Islamic ambition is neither laughable nor improbable. The 2001 national UK census revealed that about 73 per cent of the nation registered themselves as Christian, which is about 43 million, with about 1.2 million Muslims, about half a million Jews and the same number of Hindus. However, according to a British government delegation to Cairo in 2002, the Muslim figure had then risen to about 3 million, and according to Migration Watch the annual immigration of legal and illegal immigrants, mostly Islamic, is about 180,000, which suggests a projected Islamic population of about 6 million by 2013.

The ISIC Report of January 2005, 'Islam in Britain', details the broad penetration into all levels of British politics, law and society media and education, and in particular:

- Charles Clarke (Secretary of State for Education) launched The Muslim Council of Great Britain (MCB) project in October 2004 called 'Books for Schools', which aims to place a large Islamic resource pack in every school in Britain.
- The government and the Bank of England have accepted sharia-compliant financial products in Britain and have even changed the law on stamp duty to accommodate it.
- The MCB has identified twenty-three marginal Westminster constituencies where Muslims could precipitate a change of seat, and the Muslim Public Affairs Committee stated on its website that MPAC made history in the UK as the first ever parliamentary candidate was defeated by a Muslim bloc vote in the Brent East by-election of September 2003.

Islamic tactics

Islamic policy operates strategically and tactically in their three stages of national Mission. Their first step is to move into specific areas in the nation, for example London, Birmingham and North West England, and then unite locally in order to form a bloc population. Then secondly they seek to present a striking public presence by establishing a mosque and then working towards building a new mosque as large as possible. They also establish such things as local recognition of Islamic festivals and Islamic dress. Then they demand recognition by local government bodies and begin to input their voice in order to influence the law, the customs and even the language of the host culture. For example, Muslim police officers are now permitted to wear sharia-compliant headdress as part of the uniform in the UK. Also, when visiting a senior member of a mosque, some senior non-Muslim police officers will change out of uniform and into a sharia-compliant form of dress. The third stage is to establish the ascendancy and political sovereignty of Islam. If this claim is then put forward clearly and convincingly 'then the Muslim would proceed to involve the necessary powers to invoke it' (Zakaria Bashier, 'A model for Islamization', *The Muslim*, August/November 1977).

This is, to coin a modern phrase, a 'grooming' of the unsuspecting by the ill-intentioned. It happens step by step until we wake up in an Islamic-dominated society like the proverbial slowly boiled frog that was initially too comfortable but suddenly too incapacitated to move or protest.

Why are we so vulnerable?

What has been the vulnerability in our nation that has made it possible for such advances by Islam? First, we have dismantled our spiritual defences in the name of postmodern tolerance and comfort-zone maintenance and second we face a very determined and long-term plan to subdue the Christian world under submission to Allah, the Islamic god, bringing into this fold all other pagans that rebel against him. In tracking this analysis we have first to retrace Christianity's steps in this nation.

The Venerable Bede in his eighth-century *History of the English Church and its People*, records that the British king Lucius wrote to the continental church in AD 156 for a representative to come to England to help him and his kingdom convert to Christianity. His request was granted and the conversion process commenced the same year. England has been Christian (to varying degrees of piety) ever since – that is, for over eighteen hundred years. Thus the English culture of race, language, literature, law, tribe, history, custom and societal rules has been impacted through and through by its Christian roots, which have anchored the identity of the English. Despite the busyness of the liberals over the last century and a half, that Englishness remains a potent, latent force, even if it has few or no champion advocates. However, that very fact contributes no doubt to the conclusions of observers such as Jeremy Paxman in his *The English* (Penguin, 1999), who writes, 'Being English used to be so easy . . . but now the English seem to have entered a collective crisis of identity.' The definition of Englishness proves to be extremely elusive in our multicultural amorphous society which eschews political and religious history, preferring instead the belief of myths that owe more to political speech writers than the sacrifices of our forebears.

Tony Blankley (editorial editor of *The Washington Times*) writes in his *The West's Last Chance* (Regnery, 2005), '. . . if current unthinking tolerance of the intolerant continues, if current thinking in Europe doesn't change, Western values and lifestyles will be supplanted in Europe by the values of radical Islam.' How could this be possible in England after these 1,800 Christian years?

When the church began its ridiculous retreat following early modernism and determinism in the late nineteenth century, it left the cultural middle ground to anyone who had a contrary agenda, and the English identity was then put at risk. The first belief system to fill the vacuum was socialism, followed by its offspring the freedom-loving sixties generation with its symbol of freedom, the birth control pill. Next came the so-called 'baby-boomers' whose creed was 'You can have it all', whose family policy was abortion on demand, and whose view of history was rewritten by the Marxist and socialist academics. Now we have 'Generation X', so-called because it is a generation that has lost its heritage, its culture and its identity, and possesses only a creed of fashion in all things, including beliefs. The parents of Generation X took their eyes off the parenting ball as they divorced and aborted on demand, worked for ever higher mortgages, and watched their equity disappear in crashed endowment policies and decimated investments in ISAS, TESSAS, PEPS and managed funds.

So when the liberals and socialists began to demolish the Christian heritage in earnest in the 1960s and later, they were actually finishing off the English identity. They have done such a good job that when mass immigration of other religious cultures started there was no real argument raised against the imposition of a so-called 'multi-faith' and 'multicultural' society because any real counter would have to be based upon a clear sense of national identity. And as the English sense of identity is inextricably bound up with Christianity, no secularist worth his salt could bring himself to defend it, and so the cause was lost by default. The church of course was at the forefront of dumbness and culpability, as it was when Darwin's theories were first gladly seized upon by secular academics.

Clearly this contemporary open society is now very vulnerable to any strong political or religious creed that can present itself as a defender of the present comforts and even offer a strong ethical promise to develop the current position even further. Into this vacuum has stepped the new culture and community of Islam, gladly accepting the tacit offer to take over the cultural high ground of England. Islam picks up the benefits of centuries of soul-searching Dissenters, Anglicans and Catholics who sacrificed all for their children's future. It also enjoys the international encouragement of the EU, which is positive in its promotion of Islam and Islamic interests because this enhances its standing in the oil-rich Islamic nations and its anti-USA ambitions.

Islam finds itself virtually unchallenged as it presents its alternative society to a nation which assumes its core British values of current freedoms and privileges would only be enhanced rather than exchanged as it picks and chooses elements of this alien culture. But the real danger of Islam to our nation is not the bombs, distressing though these are; it is the neo-colonialism that it reaches for. Having this exotic guest in its midst is rather exciting and fashionable, so the nation is urged by apologists in government and media to forget the bombs and the strife emanating from Islamic societies everywhere (even our own), and believe that the major postmodern tenets of tolerance and non-offence cannot be wrong. In fact the bombers are only enacting the third stage of Islamisation ahead of their companions, the 'Moderates', who are still in the second stage. The bombers only succeed in driving us into the arms of the Moderates, whose Islamisation aims are identical.

What is primarily not perceived, however, is that this is the role any society must play that falls into *dhimmitude*[1]; that is, a subservience to Islam. Democracy has no place in *dhimmitude*, and neither does criticism, reformation, protest or change – Islam is more than a little different from Christianity then!

---

1 *Dhimmi*: Arabic word for meaning subservience to Islamic power.

And so now there is another god in our midst in England: the Arab Allah and his prophet Mohammed, the god of Ibrahim and Ishmael, not the God of Abraham, Isaac and Jacob whom Christians and Jews worship. Islam can clearly be seen as the latest spiritual descendant of the 'prince of the kingdom of Persia' (Dan 10:13) and it is quite clear that Islamic leadership and inspiration today comes from the Islamic revolution in Iran, Persia of old. This prince has sought to destroy Israel since the days of Haman (Esther 3:6) and Daniel, and has waged war on Christianity since Islam's inception in the seventh century. It is ideologically, socially and governmentally opposed to Christ as the Son of God, to Judaism and to the societies that have prospered historically by following their frameworks.

Islam, now the second largest religion in the UK, originated in the early seventh century AD by means of a series of dreams of Mohammed, an Arab trader in what is now Saudi Arabia. The major religious faith at that time in Asia Minor and Europe as far as England was Christianity in its various forms.

It is perhaps noteworthy that the Koran originated with one man as the source, whereas the Bible has about forty-one authors, each writing over a period of some 1,450 years with remarkable consistency. The Bible requires that something be established by two or three witnesses; for example, a 'witness' had to be found to replace Judas Iscariot: 'of these men who have accompanied us . . . beginning from the baptism of John to that day when He was taken up from us, one of these must become a witness with us of His resurrection' (Acts 1:21–22).

Moreover Moses wrote the Penteteuch in about 1445 BC from which Islam gets its own story: there are no equivalent contemporary Muslim writings. Thus in criticising the biblical writings which name Israel as God's own people with oaths by God, Islam criticises its own history.

Mohammed had two major dreams: one in Medina and one in Mecca. When his contemporaries did not accept his peaceful dream, his second dream, a military one, energised the formation of an army that marched upon Mecca and conquered it. Flushed with success and forced conversions, his imperial ambitions beckoned and his generals marched into Christian Syria and Palestine to take them by force. They continued westward along the North African coast to Portugal and Spain, and to Poitiers in France, and they were only stopped in their central European invasions at Vienna. We will never know how close we came then to losing Europe and Britain to Islam. In fact 'there was nothing to stop them sailing up the Thames', as the historian Gibbons remarked. He was perhaps a little hasty in judgement, however, as his own university, Oxford, will soon sport 'a prayer hall with traditional dome and minaret tower' at its new Centre for Islamic Studies.

Nothing has really changed in Islamic ambitions over the centuries, and it is generally agreed that Islam has never had what might be called a 'Reformation', so it is still mired in the mores of the seventh century. Amir Taheri, an Iranian commentator, writing under the byeline 'And this is why they did it', a lead article in *The Times* the day after the 7 July 2005 bombing atrocity in London, explains:

> But sorry old chaps, you are dealing with an enemy that does not want anything specific, and cannot be talked back into reason through anger management or round table discussions. Or rather this enemy does want something specific: to take full control of your lives, dictate every single move you make around the clock and, if you dare resist, he will feel it his divine duty to kill you.

Islam has always been, therefore, a warlike religion which will not tolerate dissent, criticism or competition. In fact *Operation World* (2001 edition) reports that there are forty-two Muslim nations in the world with significant restrictions on Christian belief (the Islamic practice of *dhimmitude*). It estimates Islamic adherence in the world at 21 per cent of the world population, growing by conversion and reproduction, whereas Christianity is currently about 32 per cent of the world population, growing mainly by conversion. Christianity generally grows by conversion alone because, as the Pentecostal pioneer David du Plessis pointed out, 'God has no grandsons'.

Kalim Siddiqui, in *The Muslim Manifesto* (The Muslim Institute, London, 1992), warns us:

> Of all the major religions of the world, Islam is the most politicized. At its inception Islam created a political platform from which Muslims were to launch themselves on a global role as founders of great states, empires and a world civilisation and culture. Political and cultural subservience goes against their grain.

And:

> Despite being a minority, Muslims here can define and pursue goals compatible with the goals of the global Ummah, the world community of Muslims of which they are an integral part.

Of course 'subservience' and 'minority' translate to the Islam mind as *dhimmitude* (that is, 'second-class citizen'), as Islam was conceived as being the pervading power and does not feel itself properly constituted if it is obliged to accept a minority role; hence its drive to become the majority culture either by numbers or by influence. And gradually they are succeeding in our nation as the secular liberals concede ground under the multicultural, pluralism agenda which was originally cast to displace Christianity in the nation's affections. Liberals will of course live to rue the day when they replace the benevolence of Christianity for the implacability of Islam, but then the field may have been won by this foreign prince of Persia who will toss aside the PC protests of liberals as so much confetti. A modern example of the Islamisation of a country by using its culture against it is Pakistan, which now has the Christian population under subjection as *dhimmi* to sharia law.

How do we counter the march of Islam in our nation? Well, we will not counter anything until we understand how the Kingdom of God is manifested through Jesus Christ. Until that point it is as though we are grappling with an octopus in the dark. The Kingdom of Christ has all the answers, first in the discipling of the individual, then of the church and then of the nation. Nothing changes from the principle Jesus first taught in Matthew 28:19: 'Go therefore and make disciples of the nations . . . teaching them to observe all the things I have commanded you.'

Once we have come into obedience to the King, then the King brings all other things into obedience (Rom 1:5; 2 Cor 10:6). Far-fetched? Not really, because all major battles are in the mind, inspire the imagination and commit the life. When Jesus commands us in this way, all things are possible. But we must first learn how to follow Him in the walk of faith, understanding Him and His mission and following in His power.

Happily, that 73 per cent profession of Christian adherence reported in the 2001 UK census is still there, a legacy of a Christian national identity lying dormant, buried under layers of ludicrous philosophical, socialist and liberal solutions to the problems of life and community now being exposed for the self-serving hypocrisy that they are. And it is to that 73 per cent that we must direct our efforts under the guidance of the Holy Spirit to win the battle of ideas, whether or not they take final steps to follow Christ. Are twenty-first-century Christians up to the same challenge that has faced their fathers in the faith for two millennia?

We have seen elsewhere in this book how we can embrace the spiritual, moral and political imperative of joining with Israel if we are to vigorously counter the claims that this fearsome and powerful prince of Persia is making upon our society aided and abetted by his secularist apologists. However, we must recognise that should we review and even repent of our hostile attitudes towards the Jews and Israel, we will attract virulent propaganda, making immediate enemies in the liberal metropolitan elites, the academic elites, the political elites and of course from the Islamic culture itself, which cannot abide competition.

For Islam's advance is spiritual, not secular, and can only be countered by spiritual means (2 Cor 10:3–6; Eph 6:12), in spite of the obviously physical manifestation of bombings made in the name of *jihad*. We must see the realities of the world and counter the enemies of Christ where it is most effective, where our spiritual weapons are most use and where our contending for the faith can yield real results in the minds of the people of our nation in the valley of decision.

When we consider that the princes of Greece and Persia are working side-by-side to defeat God's people and enslave the nations (Ps 2:1–6), then we understand why we must resist pro-Islamic legislation flowing from our lawmakers, and the framing of public opinion in the image of Islam (Mt 5:11–12). For example, the Religious Hatred Bill and the sharia-compliant local legislation, as well as the petty general political correctness agenda that bans hot cross buns and public signs of Christianity, must be opposed whenever we can oppose them.

But we cannot stand up for our beliefs if they have not been tested in the furnace of experience, for we will fold at the first fiery trial. The discipling outlined in this book is designed to mature the believer and the church as fast as possible; the steps to follow to disciple the nation will open before us as the Holy Spirit leads us. Remember, the church of Christ looks like an army terrible with banners, and both secularists and other religions view its awakening with fear. When we align ourselves with Israel we will present a truly awesome spiritual terror that will be like that visited upon the land of Canaan before the advance of the Israelites (Josh 2:11), and as then also now God promises to bless us if we bless Israel; indeed, 'who can be against us?' Discipled believers have everything to win and nothing to lose in this struggle for the minds of our people.

Addressing the Issue of the Prince of Greece

Introduction

In the 1940s and 50s the American philosopher Leo Strauss predicted that the then current promotion of a no-holds-barred era of personal freedom would usher in a time of a nation that would became ungovernable. Much of what he said came to pass in the 1970s with the widespread riots in the US in the name of freedom. His prescription for government was that they should draw the nation together by pointing out external threats, even if they had to be exaggerated or invented. US governments bought into this solution, hence the rise of the domino theory of the spread of communism, the connection between widely different insurgent groups throughout the world, the 'evil empire' (of the USSR), and the apparent current cataclysmic threat of world terrorism.

The UK reacted in a milder way with its Toxteth and Brixton riots, but nevertheless the political philosophy lingers on, such that it is commonly held that our nation in the early twenty-first century can only be politically 'managed' rather than led. The development of social freedom in this nation has been promoted by white middle-class liberals in the fond belief that a so-called multicultural, multi-faith society would necessitate the destruction of our Christian heritage and identity and release them into an unparalleled freedom of action and thought without the censure that would surely be theirs were the Christian church alive and active.

Censure? Without the Christian prophetic reins, this nation has no defence against the strongest elements in its midst because it soon descends into a slavery to Mammon, whereby everything has a price, and price rather than righteousness becomes the measure of all things. The most vulnerable of course are the poor, the victims of the law of the jungle, who are vulnerable economically, societally and morally. The church has always fought for the poor because it is the right thing to do: the rich look after themselves. The poor of course include more than the financially dependent; it also means the old, those without a social support mechanism, the pregnant, the uneducated, all those without a voice either within themselves or speaking for them.

In worshipping Mammon, our society is given over to a standardising of ourselves. We become 'consumers', mono-culturised so that we can be the better controlled in matters of law, finance, consumerism, societal structures and morality, owing our sense of identity to the state alone. Popular culture has already reflected this trend in films such as *Logan's Run* and books such as *Brave New World*, and its elements spring from Rousseau's vision of the state as family. As the respected political commentator Andrew Rawnsley observes, '[government ministers] . . . are pouring out legislation to monitor and regulate the lives of law-abiding citizens' (*Observer*, 30 April 2006).

The destruction of 1,800 years of Christian national culture had to be done because it was the only way to uproot this powerful stable English culture, which had bred the provision of safe dissent. The main weapon used against Christian principles, paradoxically, has been Christian guilt in the face of arguments that quote fairness and equality as undeserved legacies of a colonial past instead of the fruit of following a Christian faith at great cost to many individuals. With no Christian defence, there is *no* defence, and our political and industrial leaders can do what they desire to enhance their control, reward, pleasure and status.

The true paradox of the day is that we are controlled in our day-to-day lives by the ideal of freedom, or rather the *idea* of freedom, which is the new religion, whereas Christianity is freedom within form, a commitment to limits, which enables the growth of communal trust and security in safety. Christianity includes in its package the idea of dissent, that most slippery of social concepts to legislate for, because it is after all a contradiction to allow for dissent within a form of authority. Freedom without Christianity's safety factors is like planting tropical plants outside in the cold, snow and storms instead of within the safety of the greenhouse.

Consumerism is apparent freedom leading to anarchy, to which the state of course must move in to try to moderate and control. The liberals have thus made a rod for their own back because without the provision of dissent against current fashionable correctness, they must be conformed to what has grown under their sun. It is becoming common already for magazines and newspapers to complain, albeit discreetly, about the introduction of foreign cultures into our society without a murmur of protest being allowed; for example: 'Multicultural liberals especially are reluctant to criticise Islam because they view it as an ally in their campaign to revolutionise Western culture' (The *Mail* leader, 1 August 2004).

And this could well lead to the development of authoritarian, centralised national governance, with more interference in personal lives and freedoms, and more restrictive laws and institutions. As Andrew Rawnsley writes, '[This New Labour government] . . . is mad for writing new laws, but bad at ensuring that laws that exist are effectively applied' (*Observer*, 30 April 2006). Consequently, there will be less opportunity to appeal, for the determinist form of government cannot tolerate dissent, as it exists for itself and is not interested in right dealing for its own sake. I well remember the TV news showing the face of our prime minister, white with rage, as he addressed the so-called 'petrol rebellion' of 2000 in a Downing Street statement.

There are many issues of pressing societal significance today, and there are admirable organisations in the UK today such as the Lawyers' Christian Fellowship, the Christian Institute and the CARE organisation which research and organise a heavyweight Christian response in depth at both local and parliamentary levels.

We shall now look at some of the more pressing issues which the church must move into and dominate.

Overcoming fashionable philosophies

Overview

A society's philosophical infrastructure is the means by which the whole may continue to function whether or not some of its constituents are aware of the facility being accorded.

The philosophical infrastructure of a society is always helped by its source of influence being outside the reach of the society's capacity to change it. Thus a Christian society might reasonably be expected to last a very long time, but a communist one, which has its gods within its control, may be expected not to last much longer than a man's lifetime, as we saw in the twentieth century. Even the great empire of Rome began its downward descent when the emperor required his subjects to worship him as a god co-equal or superior to all other gods. Gods that are replaceable tend to lose credence and thus the fundamental structure that holds that particular society together begins to unravel, particularly if vested interests see a (temporary) advantage in hastening its decline.

The philosophical infrastructure of English society has been established as Christian over centuries since it first came to these shores in AD 156. Alfred the Great in the tenth century, a devout Christian, was trying to arrange universal education as well as the rule of common law to which all were subject, from the least to the greatest. He started a process which went on for centuries, carrying with it even the invader Norman ruling classes.

The bond of common values that was the social philosophical infrastructure then and for the 1,000 years since has been Christian. Reference used to be continually made to the Christian precedent, hence the upheaval in the Middle Ages when Scripture was gradually infiltrated by practice, the 'authority of the church' and Greek philosophy, stealing away from society one of its precious balancing weights, that of the rule of Scripture in practice.

When Martin Luther rediscovered the biblical truth of justification by faith in Christ, the Bible was 'placed in the centre of the church congregations of Europe and the altar screen removed'. This was a statement of the principle that the Scripture had total precedence over all the rules and detractions man could devise. In England this began to bring about King Alfred's dream that all men would be equally subject to the rule of law, an incredible feat of social engineering.

But today, liberal thinkers and commentators do away with the Christian philosophical infrastructure in a bid to exercise petty fashionable freedoms. This has already happened in most areas of social institution or practice, but now the unwritten social cohesion of society is being attacked.

'It's not fair' and 'My rights . . .' are very common sentiments heard today because we have an instinctive feel for justice brought about by the rule of common law. It is in our bones and our speech patterns because for centuries we have been deeply discipled by Christian morals. We as a people have in the past tended not to rebel but to rely upon the checks and balances of English justice and fair play under the watchful eye of the prophetic church. This is not a common value in the world; it is a rare value and one of which we, and especially the liberals, are unaware.

The liberals forget that the nation's social infrastructure supports them – they do not support the infrastructure. The infrastructure is a bargain of power between the various competing interests in society. It takes decades, if not centuries, to come to a common balance between interests. In fact conflict does not ever cease but rather diminishes in intensity.

However, should someone wake up to the fact that in the absence of an outright war between competing interests they might wage a private campaign to further their cause, they endanger the checks and balances that have been painfully established at much cost. They think that the infrastructure will continue for ever and their liberty can be guaranteed by simple inertia. However, once the ogre of social competition is awakened, the other forces, until now in equilibrium, come out to play, for their interests are now being disregarded.

There is rarely a simple gain and always a loss to equal or surpass the gain. If the disturbance goes on long enough the local disturbance becomes national as the waves disturb established social bargains. The resultant upheaval can change the society beyond all recognition.

There is no going back to a previous period perceived as better balanced. Rather the whole of the balancing bargain has to be fought out again over the same number of generations that brought about the new changes.

The core of the infrastructure is the common belief of the people in the established checks and balances they have been party to over hundreds of years. This is the solidity of the body of the society and when this unravels we are back at a place of the rule of the strongest interest, the rule of the jungle, just like the Roman predecessor. This is an entirely predictable result of replacing the ministry of the influential prophetic church with desperate determinist hedonism.

The danger signs for our current age may be seen in the completely unpredictable petrol rebellion of September 2000, the marches of the Countryside Alliance and the Paedophile Protestors, the votes against the Clause 28 abolition and against the lowering of the legal age of sodomy to sixteen. These national protests are an entirely predictable result of replacing the prophetic influence of the church with a deterministic 'fittest survival' philosophy of community response. 'Going to the barricades' has been a typical French response since the 1790s, precisely because there is no other way the popular sentiment may be heard by the government other than through the apostolic church, and in following the French into their secular solutions of government we too will have to develop a mindset of minor rebellions in order to halt unpopular or grossly unfair measures.

The peace of a balanced bargain within a society is society's greatest achievement, but without the Christian prophetic warriors who fought to put it in place, it will be lost by the ignorant bowing to the unscrupulous. And that is what is happening, for little if anything has been achieved by the national protests listed above.

So where did we miss it?

The trite answer is that we, the church at large, did not recognise the 'time of our visitation' starting from the closing decades of the nineteenth century when scientific discoveries and hypotheses began to overtake commonly accepted axioms and scriptural truths. Before that, Christ's church, His body, provided the apostolic guiding reins for the governing and operation of our society, achieving great societal change for the particular benefit of the inarticulate and the powerless. This apostolic movement worked with considerable success against deeply entrenched interests for the abolition of slavery, for the care of working women, for free universal education, for humane conditions in factories, for chimney boys, for the ending of press gangs, for decent housing environments, and so on. The reforming movements started in the early eighteenth century in the wake of the epidemic of addiction to the new Dutch aromatic gin which had gripped the poor and was well on its way to killing them off in London. The average lifespan for a man in London at this time was about forty to forty-five. It was a social (and economic) disaster for the capital city which was rising to the heights of becoming the leading trading centre of Europe.

But towards the end of the nineteenth century, the church seemed to lose its way, facing new philosophies promoting the 'freedom' of the individual, the rebellion against authority and, most particularly, lifting ideas from Nietzsche and Darwin which promoted the concept of the fittest and strongest dominating the rest as a right. It was a recipe for anarchy, and indeed revolution spread through Europe as similar ideas became dominant.

Although there was plenty of discontent in England, it did not have sufficient immediate momentum for a revolution. Nevertheless the long-term effect upon the institutions of state and the cultural norms of its citizens has been profound. These new philosophies have gradually corroded the established raft of social deals that had been continually modified over centuries, and the practice of gradual modification has been hi-jacked by pressure groups that have seen a sectional inter-est in sudden and immediate change.

A clear example of hijacking would perhaps be the promo-tion of completely immoral behaviour in our daily TV soap operas, where anger and fractured relationships are considered the norm, educating viewers in new paths of relationship dynamics. This is not in the interest of some societal higher goal, but in the interest of better viewing figures and profit. This care-lessness and greed contributes to a gradual change in societal

interaction towards increased lawlessness, high teenage preg-
nancy and disease and the various so-called 'rages' – road-rage,
queue-rage and trolley-rage – where there are real victims.

The main benefit of determinism and monoculture to a
controlling entity is that individuals are reduced to the status
of commodities to be 'managed' and marketed to. Indeed even
politics is being seen as managing the nation rather than
leading it. Thus, to facilitate this, Mammon is interested in
promoting any overarching culture or cultural philosophy
that helps to destroy individual identity. As identity comes
from external references to self, the significance of external
reference points must be reduced or eliminated. This is prin-
cipally done by the various postmodernist philosophies of
individual freedom, or rather the freedom to do your own
thing, and the key to this must be the destruction of any influence which binds people together in a framework of law, such
as Christianity. The result of these philosophies of so-called
'freedom' is the sense of personal rights without responsibilities, a sense of grievance, a sense of not getting what is due to
us, clearly spelled out in adverts such as L'Oreal's 'Because I'm
worth it . . .'. Of course, establishing 'rights' is essential if the
Christian counter-culture is not contending on our behalf.

It is clear from Jesus' statement that we worship either God
or Mammon, and Revelation 17 and 18 confirm that the ultimate conflict will be between Christ and Mammon. So far, in
the Western democracies, Christian morality has moderated
the excesses of the frightening power of Mammon. But
Mammon seeks as always to throw off those restraints and co-
opts rulers, multinational industries and other global agencies
to do just that (see Psalm 2:1–2).

The EU Constitution, for example, will divorce the English
voter from its own legislating body (which will become the EU

Commission) for the first time since 1833, and England will be broken down into nine (EU) regions for the first time since King Alfred. The EU intends to become a massive power engine with a new legal identity of its own in the economic warfare of the future.

The church must recognise its apostolic stance within the English nation and resist the *arché* that would reduce the national identity to a brand name like a can of beans. Only the Christian church is able to make this move by way of its arguments, its history and its standing as the body of Christ in the nation.

And so the contention of the faith against the anti-God philosophies of postmodernism is a very real struggle for the soul of the nation which is up for sale. Whatever the political future for our nation, if its character is overwhelmingly and overtly Christian then the political destiny will determine itself, for anti-Christ-like bureaucracy cannot abide the stand for righteousness (the EU Constitution, for example, specifically exempts its officers and departments from any legal liability whatsoever, whether or not their actions have been illegal), and will either reform or spit the offending Christian culture out. One way or another, England in or out of the EU will work Christ's work – without forming a political party of its own.

But the church must win the identity arguments and the nation must revive its undercurrent of Christian identity (73 per cent in the last national census) to bring this about.

Science in the grip of Mammon

Overview

The scientific industry, for that is now what it is, is linked umbilically to multinational companies, particularly the pharmaceuticals, who look to it to contribute huge profits and who inject funds into scientific companies, universities and laboratories to secure that end. This has become the only way a scientist may now reach the dizzy heights of fame and fortune and firmly secure his future.

Once when I was interviewing a scientist in a Birmingham university laboratory, he offered to design for the mill which supplied my paper a designer bug that would dispose safely of the waste produced by the mill. It was a simple *quid pro quo* and this was an eye-opener to me of the way the system works. Gone are the days of some higher, more noble goal of increasing knowledge and good works for all men; of men such as Alexander Fleming who, having discovered the miracle drug penicillin, gave it to the nation. Millions of dollars were made from the discovery of course, but not by him!

Issues of so-called 'ethics' are manipulated without scruple to blind the unwary; and the unwary includes most of us. We rarely examine the difference between the terms 'ethical' and 'moral'. An ethical code for a drug company, for example, may be decided upon in its AGM by bureaucrats and accountants to suit its convenience and its shareholders. A moral code, however, has connotations of conscience in doing the right thing and in the West, of course, it is a shadow of Christianity.

The real issues raised by scientific 'research' can hide fundamental interference in the stuff of life, whether of food, genetics or cloning. When a politician or scientist uses the term 'principle' or 'ethics', we must immediately look for the vested interest; for example, will this lead to promotion, to a TV sound bite or to further consultancy work? This is not cynicism on our part, it is acquainting ourselves with the world's ways by taking appropriate mental precautions.

So when it comes to scientists, their worldview has changed from the search for pure knowledge to the search for profitable knowledge, but ours regarding them, generally, has not changed. We must now learn to sift their 'advances' and proclamations of a rosy future. Scientific advance nowadays is measured not by altruism but by the number of papers published, by the sponsorship of the laboratory, by a scientist's paid lecture value and by the rewards scientists may command in salary, status and consultancy.

The idea of a noble research scientist striving away in the back room with no reward save the knowledge that he is 'doing good' has gone for ever, if it ever existed. But we still have our respect for his integrity and lack of self-interest, and this blinds us to the fact that the scientific community will use our ignorance and silence for their own ends for rewards and money. So when a scientist is caught up in issues that concern our everyday life, we should first look for the real arguments, which usually centre around money, and secondly for the spurious arguments which seek to use an 'ethical' argument for concealment in much the same way as Adam used his fig-leaf apron.

Typical recent issues have been GM food, reproductive medicine, genetics, spare part surgery and farming methods. When we hear the proclaiming of a 'scientific breakthrough' with expected social rewards, let us draw back and consider the ethical justifications against the size and value of the likely commercial market. We particularly need to examine the so-called ethical considerations in the light of basic Christian principles. In other words, do the 'ethics' hold morally good water? What are the moral alternatives? Is this procedure an unnecessary foray into needless experimentation with only short-term consideration of the possible downsides for the generations that follow?

A specific area of science that is constantly in the news is of course the biological sciences, primarily because of the break-throughs in mapping the human genome, but also because it is now possible to concoct specific characteristics of living things by changing the genetic makeup of the organism. Thus by mixing fish genes with strawberries, it is possible to grow strawberries under cold conditions. One of the main problems of this enforced 'species jump' is of course that the normal inter-species safeguards put there by God cease to be effective, so it is possible to also import antipathetic elements such as disease to the new organism for which it has no natural defence.

Professor Postai, for example, found that his laboratory rats developed cancers when fed with GM potatoes. He was unwise enough, in a laboratory funded by a GM company, to publish his results, whereupon he was promptly suspended, then his research results were 'lost', as was his job and reputation. No wonder God repeats some ten times in Genesis that species are to 'reproduce after their own kind'. Was that a warning for latter-day scientific wannabees?

You can see that not only does the average Christian need to keep abreast of general scientific progress, we also need our own precious scientists who can argue the kingdom of God corner with power and effect. These will be the apostles in their area, speaking to the 'kings' of their profession, be they institutional heads, government officers, industrial barons or media bosses. So, although there are many issues in the scientific world to be addressed, it is this specific one which we will be examining closer – that which I call the 'modern Eden catastrophe'.

The modern Eden catastrophe: The original temptation – again!

We are reminded that behind the Eden tragedy there was Satan in the form of a serpent, using clever arguments of perception to persuade Eve of the desirability of long life, power and independence, or what we call these days 'enhancing her quality of life'. The same Satan is behind the modern Eden catastrophe in the form of Mammon promising very great rewards of wealth, fame and power to research scientists. However, the apple *they* have to eat is the scientific possibility of enhancing our quality of life, with the promise of healing, improved performance and extended lifespan; in other words, to find the wisdom to break through the age-old barrier that God set over the tree of life and the tree of knowledge in the first Garden. Perhaps one can perceive a parallel with their modern equivalent of the tree of knowledge of good and evil (DNA string) and the tree of life (the genome) and see that nothing has changed since Adam's decision to experiment in like manner.

The scientists' new foray into Eden majors on two main themes – cloning and genetic engineering – most of their reasons for which are hidden in crocodile tears about suffering humanity, but in reality promise the researcher fame, wealth and power.

Cloning, the major miracle from this latter-day Eden, holds forth the promise of replacement spare parts for worn-out, diseased or damaged bodies. These are to be grown in human or hybrid human-animal form, harvested like corn and transplanted into the patient. Sounds marvellous until you realise that the clone has to be murdered in order to harvest the 'spare part', making a commodity out of the bodies of persons. We already carry this out, of course, in the despicable trade of body parts purchased from starving Third-Worlders. Nevertheless any trade in bodies is evil Mammon in its anti-person form, as the slave-trade reformers convinced their contemporaries.

The act of creating a new species (the so-called 'second creation' or eighth-day creation) suddenly introduces a significant new creature to our delicately poised ecostructure with absolutely no understanding of how it might upset that balance. This whole area subverts God's original command to 'Reproduce after your own kind', repeated ten times in Genesis 1. The nightmare scenario of the movie *Alien IV* does not seem so far-fetched in its body form.

Aligned but separate to this is the uneasy fact that some percentage of mitochondrial DNA from the host animal (pig, mouse, rat, etc.) will pass into the cloned part and will be passed on in the germ line into the human generations that follow, with unknown consequences. For example, the propensity for or vulnerability to a species-jumping viral disease is completely unknown.

Genetic engineering is experimenting with the very stuff of life itself. For example, the DeCode Genetics Company has claimed it has isolated the gene that creates a protein in the body that confers old age on individuals, earning it the sobriquet of the 'Methuselah gene'. DCG now holds out the prospect that one day it will be able to create drugs that will extend human life (other diseases and ill-health permitting) to those who can afford the treatment (*Observer*, 3 February 2002).

A legitimate area of genetic research, however, is adult stem cell research, an exciting and worthwhile enterprise producing tangible results of regrown tissue, muscle, nerve cells and so on ('The ultimate stem cell discovered', *New Scientist*, 23 January 2002), sneered at by most of the scientific community because it does nothing to unlock the very stuff of life, unlike embryonic stem cells, which they would much prefer to experiment with. This obscuring of moral alternatives by scientists is perverse and contradicts their own *raison d'être* for the experiments in the first place; that is, the promise of hope for the afflicted and in support of which, without mercy, they even wheel on the sick to speak for them. It does, however, reveal their real motives, which is to have little or no obstruction in their pursuit of the keys to life, and to have the most open opportunity for their personal enrichment and fame. James Watson, Nobel laureate, for example, has said, 'If we can make better human beings by knowing how to add genes, why shouldn't we?' This is not so far removed from Hitler's Dr Mengeles and his eugenic experiments looking for the 'superman' of the fascist ideal.

The arguments used against cloning and immoral genetic engineering are highly technical but entirely effective and sound in seeking to reinforce the contention that it is bad science chasing mega money.

First, the interdependence of the human species and the natural world can be upset if we introduce a new species, or if we alter a species or its immediate environment, or indeed if we wipe out a species. For example, our experience with feeding cows with cows (possibly including human remains) led to the species jump of CJD from cows to humans; the introduction of foreign species (such as the grey squirrel in England, the lamprey eel in Canada, the starling in America) to a local environment can lead to the gradual elimination of the home species. The US federal government estimates that the annual economic costs of invasive species in America are over $100 billion (US OTA 1993). In the year 1999–2000 some 400 Indian farmers committed suicide because the GM corn seed they had been persuaded to buy was non-reproductive and they went bankrupt; the Indian scientist speaker at the 2000 Reith lectures begged the Western commercial world to stay out of the Third World's delicate agricultural economies: an impossible dream, for Mammon knows no mercy.

Second, the cross-species adaptation by genetic means of plants (fish genes in strawberries and tomatoes, for example), or of human spare parts grown in animal/hybrid carriers, is being carried out with unpredictable consequences in generations to come. The mistakes cannot be recalled or eliminated, for once the germ line has been changed, it stays changed, unless the 'mistakes' are sterilised or killed. Is there provision or even laws available to clear up such a mess? Of course not.

Third, the promise of 'designer babies' (where babies may be programmed by introducing genes that enhance their lives physically or mentally) presupposes that each birth will be perfect and will have no unwelcome germ line side effects. The downside of this of course is the wastage in human babies of the 'mistakes' and deformed embryos that are produced, and even the tragedy of birthed children if 'mistakes' arise some time after birth. Of course if the practice ever proves practicable for a chosen (rich) few, there is also the nightmare scenario of a superior sub-species elite brand of humanity completely distorting the cohesion of our society.

Taking these three together, we have no idea how this might upset our delicate ecosystem which has developed over a considerable period of time if one accepts the Genesis carefully arranged sequences, or in Darwinian terms squeezing a few million years of evolution into a decade. Either way it is a recipe for disaster, for which the authors will not be held culpable nor will they pay. Rather society at large will have to clear up the mess of scientists playing with the construction set of life. Ordinary men and women will pay by having their various life-hopes cruelly raised and dashed, and of course the luckless creatures being experimented upon, grown, birthed and killed will pay the ultimate price, all in the name of scientific prestige, money and power.

Thus we have a legacy of at least three laws from the first Eden catastrophe that we are in danger of flouting. These are:

1. 'Reproduce after your own kind.'
2. 'Don't try to remake My laws.'
3. 'Don't try to live for ever.'

And it is these three laws we violate when we enter into God's creation territory, for it is these three that He abrogates to Himself, even when He first released us to rule the earth under His delegated authority.

The first law is repeated ten times in Genesis and is a fairly clear instruction not to mix our basic parts with those of animals and also defines the limits of sexuality by the injunction, 'Male and female He created them'; that is, there are no middle genders at all. As the marriage relationship mirrors Christ and His bride, any distortion is a rejection of Christ and His end-time scenario of the marriage of the Lamb.

The second law instructs us to work within His laws in genetic engineering so that we should not try to construct different building blocks of life that may lead us anywhere but the nirvana the biotech industry might claim. Murdering foetuses is just one of the nightmare scenarios that are presented to us as humane, efficient and beneficial to our lifestyle comfort.

Similarly, of the third law, when we try to change the tree of life to make man after our own image by biological enhancement, we are actually seeking to change the stereotype and do away with the Genesis pattern of 'So God created man in His own image; in the image of God He created him' (Gen 1:27) and 'Before I formed you in the womb I knew you' (Jer 1:5). We swap the God of the Bible for Professor Watson and his colleagues. An edifying prospect?

To summarise, if we try to take to ourselves a role that God has reserved for Himself, such as lawgiver or creator, we follow that kind of progress which Lucifer attempted when his ambition was to become like the Most High (Is 14), and Adam, which prompted the divine comment, 'Behold, the man has become like one of Us' (Gen 3:22).

We are on dangerous ground and we invite His wrath upon our heads if we proceed without care and consideration of His proper part in all this. The prophetic church in particular will be guilty if it fails to take effective action after seeking the kingdom lead of Jesus Christ.

The liberal agenda and the homosexual lobby

One of the recent main issues before the church has been the reach of the homosexual lobby to control the secular liberal agenda. The homosexual lobbies have used the trick of equating homosexuality with feminism and race – the other two great social issues of the day – and has taken advantage of their genuine grievance and years of painful and dangerous campaigning.

But the feminist and racial reach for equality is not an adult lifestyle choice as is homosexuality, and neither of them seeks to proselytise to their way of life as homosexuals do, especially among the young. Being black or female is not an adult lifestyle choice; it is demonstrably fixed in the original makeup of the person. There is, however, no evidence whatsoever of the determinist gene that would make a homosexual, and indeed many homosexuals would confirm that their sexual choice has been the conscious and deliberate decision of a thinking adult.

The campaign for tolerance of this adult lifestyle choice has already been won. Indeed we have had avowedly homosexual politicians in some of the highest offices in the land, so the campaign has moved on to the schools, because if you control the college, you control the organisation, as Schaeffer would say. If homosexuals can gain control of the agenda of schools, they not only have a recruitment opportunity their predecessors could only have dreamt of, they have the long-term opportunity to control the liberal agenda.

Presently only about 1 per cent or under of the population are practising homosexuals, and only about 0.15 per cent of the nation's households are homosexual, but already their influence by political lobbying and opinion-forming is way above their actual numbers. Already it is almost impossible to refute their arguments on moral grounds; indeed they have seized the moral ground themselves by way of their 'equality' argument. So we have to think differently and ask God which weapons we should employ. Brian Souter used some of the following arguments in his Scottish campaign to prevent the promotion of homosexuality in schools:

1. Homosexuality is an adult lifestyle choice.
2. Protect the young against promotion of an adult lifestyle choice.
3. Parents have rights to safeguard the lifestyle choice of their children.
4. We know same-sex crushes happen to adolescents, but they are a phase. Homosexuals seek to continue that phase and not let the child escape into mature heterosexuality. (I would add to this that same-sex crushes happen for a

very good reason: they are usually set on empathetic role models such as the top sports person, musician or academic. When that age or status is reached, or the social aspiration changes, then the crush drops away, having served its purpose.)

Souter recognised that he best served his purpose by financing Cardinal Winning and by networking among business people providing feedback from the world so that Winning could orientate his approach for the best effect.

Another approach is to realise that homosexuals trespass upon fathers' rights. Fathers do not resist because they have neither arguments nor lobby that can effectively articulate their stance, and so they have been cowed and outgunned by the liberals. The danger to families coming from the homosexual agenda is that it proposes a different alternative to God's family pattern that He has established as the basic building block in a society. And as homosexuals proselytise, they progress from winning tolerance from a generous society to dominance of the agenda of that society.

They also trespass on the Father's territory by declaring an inadequacy in His original creation: 'male and female He created them'. So their real contest is with the rules and parameters of normal human relations that God has laid down for our benefit, and in the end of course they will have to deal with Him in that aspect of their disobedience.

We should note that the Scripture teaches us that homosexuals worship and serve the creature rather than the Creator (Rom 1:25). This would suggest that homosexuality is a belief system, even a kind of religion, and so it would be extremely difficult to extricate someone from its clutches and combat the self-righteousness of its claims. We must, however, attempt to frustrate the homosexual advance upon the liberal agenda, demolish its arguments and confront its *arché*.

It is clear of course that individuals may be caught up in the homosexual movement because of disastrous personal experience and they may have found comfort in the homosexual society, which can be extremely sensitive and caring of personal hurt. It is, however, a wrong way out of unfortunate and perhaps agonising personal circumstances although it may seem right as a possibility. The Scripture warns us against the way that seems right to man, and however the homosexual course may be justified, it is in direct conflict with God's commands, confuses the difficult social problems we have and stores up trouble for the future. It is, however, an extraordinary opportunity for the church to understand first how the postmodern idea of inclusivity and community can work against God's laws, and then to seek God for the power to rescue as many as possible from this lifestyle.

We need God's strategy to see how this radical social agenda may be countered, but already there are some indicators of how this might come about. For example, the internal upheaval of the Anglican Communion has raised the issue of homosexuality from the unmentionable to the unholy, with 'issues of unscriptural practice' being bandied about in the press quite freely – something unheard of in previous years. Another issue is that the recent developments of an awareness of 'too much immigration' have placed the liberal-homosexual axis in a dilemma. To suggest that Islamic immigration should somehow be curbed as the right-wingers suggest is to be accused of the liberal mantra of 'racism'. However, to accede to the Islamic demands for their value system to be validated would mean that homosexuality, for example, would be outlawed. A court case reported nationally in June

2004 stated that a judge had upheld the right of a secular school to maintain its secular character by refusing admission to a pupil who wished to wear religious attire – that is, hijab costume – which created outrage in the Islamic community.

These are classic cases of the agendas of two opposing *archés* being set against each other, and within the limits of loving our fellow man we could seek God as to how this conflict of philosophies, which both vehemently oppose Christianity, might best serve the Kingdom's interests. If we were to seek God for strategic directions so that we succeed in establishing a right framework to oppose the main thrusts of social policy, we could emulate the early nineteenth-century church and not the late nineteenth-century church. The latter failed in the face of determinism, with the inevitable growth of oppressive political creeds and world wars.

Who knows where our slackness in the face of another determinist challenge would lead us during this century?

CHAPTER FIVE

PROPOSITIONS

Implications

The shock of change

Introducing the Kingdom of Christ Jesus to the church brings about fundamental changes to all the issues in church affairs we can see. Therefore our part in it requires a deep commitment to the lordship of Christ Jesus and respect for the leading of the Holy Spirit.

Understandably we try to encompass anything new within the framework of what we know already. But when we cast our mind back to when we were first saved, or when we were introduced to the idea of the baptism in the Holy Spirit, we recall that we were obliged to radically change our set of useful frameworks/metanarratives as we realised that in fact we really knew nothing about this new dimension and had nothing to measure it by. On the contrary, we found that in order to enter, we were obliged to radically rethink our standard position, as Nicodemus discovered

(Jn 3:9–12) when he questioned Jesus about being born again.

Jesus explained the principle of grasping new frameworks when He described the process as putting new wine into new bottles (Mt 9:16–17). This is particularly appropriate when considering the implications of this book, for there are kingdom principles involved here which do not allow us to read the instructions and introduce a new system as though marketing the latest self-help technique. It just does not work like that.

So, how does it work?

The expansion of the Kingdom of Jesus Christ by the work of the Holy Spirit does not take place the same way we would expand a secular empire, business or organisation, as may be seen by comparing the expansion of the first-century church to the expansion of the Roman Empire. The characteristic of the Roman Empire's expansion was to impose by force a systematic infrastructure of roads, language, politics, trade, law and governance on every nation that came under its dominance. The early church, on the other hand, expanded by working with whatever opportunity presented itself under the leadership of the Holy Spirit rather than by planning a structured campaign. The opportunities varied in form as suited the local conditions. For example, we see Paul mixing with women at a market, or addressing the Greek central forum, or attracting the unwelcome attention of the local authorities, who promptly jailed him. Every church 'plant' was different and in fact the only thing they seemed to have in common was the recognition of eldership and the central core of doctrine which Paul was at great pains to explain, publish and follow up by personal visitation if that was within his power.

The common thread of church culture throughout various Middle Eastern nations was likewise liberating (Acts 15: 23–29), with a light burden of common requirements. Even the finances of the early church were conducted in a unique manner, i.e. they 'had all things in common' (Acts 2:44) and Paul collected for the church at Jerusalem (Acts 11:29–30).

The principle of kingdom expansion, therefore, might be summed up as: 'The wind blows where it wishes, and you hear the sound of it, but cannot tell where it comes from or where it goes. So is everyone who is born of the Spirit' (Jn 3:8). This principle of the sovereign action of the Holy Spirit is extremely difficult to learn to live with and I fear it has the downside that many good Christians will not be able to convert from the Roman *system* to the kingdom *way*.

The upside

However, should we be willing to grasp this nettle, we can see that the Holy Spirit way of unpredictability brings with it several kingdom advantages.

First, the Holy Spirit can choose those whom He judges best suited to bring about kingdom change in a particular situation, for as He formulates the job description He is also best suited to choose through whom He may act.

Second, it is difficult for the enemies of the gospel to second-guess the Holy Spirit's leading.

Third, it is a beautiful illustration of the many-sided splendour of the body.

Fourth, each situation is treated individually and not as a common 'one solution fits all'.

Fifth, the unexpectedness of the kingdom way keeps our interest and attention at full throttle (we do not get bored).

Sixth, we are all encouraged to keep close to Him, as He might call upon any one of us to move out in faith at any time.

Seventh, it gives an opportunity for *everyone* in the body to function as the Holy Spirit gives them opportunity, providing of course they are building each other up in love.

The modus operandi

The operation of the Kingdom depends upon the *power* and the *unpredictability* of the Holy Spirit to produce an organic, unique growth of believers whom He is then able to use to impact their particular sphere of influence for the glory of Jesus Christ (Eph 3:9–10).

The sphere of this operation is through the life of the Christian individual, the conduct of the church and the impact of the church at large upon the nation. This is not only a personal challenge to each of us, but it also presents the greatest opportunity the national church has had in 150 years to change our nation by rolling back its culture. Francis Schaeffer refers to this challenge in his *The Church and the West* with a strong longing and yearning, as though he could see this time of our visitation.

The challenge for personal revival

The kingdom challenge opens up all kinds of possibilities and talents within us and opens the way for the Holy Spirit to lead us into a new life. For instance, after my son read the manuscript draft of this book he opened up to the Holy Spirit, who promptly poured new music into his heart from which he cut a worship CD. He then created a website to exchange new kingdom music free of charge with the church at large. He even started a part-time apologetics course at Oxford University while expanding his high-flying City consultant post and leading the local church worship group in which he has sought to develop a corporate leadership sharing model. Jesus empowers us as well as inspires us.

An accountant friend of mine was challenged to develop his (many) good works in the business world and seek to serve Christian business people more effectively. He is now the general secretary of an international Christian business organisation represented in seventy-two countries, bringing his wisdom and expertise to a far larger canvas.

A young mother of five (not all of them her own children) asked what she could do in and for the Kingdom. From the valuable lessons of faith both in her conversion from the Jehovah's Witnesses and her hectic personal life in the midst of a society whose values are diametrically opposed to hers, she is now setting herself to write a book based upon her experiences. She then intends to resume her lecturing career and pass on her experience of faith, hope and love to a floundering generation.

A scientist, retired from her discipline for over fourteen years, was caught in her imagination about the dubious ethics and morality of human genetic manipulation. The Holy Spirit led her to become a world authority on the subject within a year, being asked to write full scientific papers (of the 400 pages kind!) for presentation to the House of Lords' Select Committee and the European Parliament. She has had an immense impact upon the otherwise unstoppable march of Mammon's scientists wishing to experiment with human life for their own purposes, simply because she allowed herself to be pressed by the Holy Spirit to operate far beyond her previous scientific boundaries and experience.

Individuals must discover the purpose God has reserved for them. Everyone is called to work according to the gifts and the measure of faith the Lord has granted them – there are no exceptions. Ephesians 2:10 describes how God has prepared works for all of us to do. Thus if we obey this call of God, out of the shadows will step an army of witnesses to the Kingdom of Christ Jesus, each gifted and experienced and each individually empowered and guided by the Holy Spirit to show the glory of Christ in His diversified body.

The challenge for church revival

The rise of the body to meet the challenge of its many callings means of course that the organisation and leadership must change from the old Roman hierarchical wineskin to a new flexible wineskin. Remember the encouragement of the Jerusalem elders and their forbearance as the phenomenon of the Gentile church exploded in their faces? They only asked for four acts of obedience (abstain from blood, food offered to idols, things strangled and sexual immorality) instead of pressuring them to accept the entire Judeo system! It is that kind of grace the church of Christ needs to employ as it develops and grows into a national force. For should it not do so, not only will the enemies of our faith have a field day with our weakness, but we will look foolish in our own eyes as the sceptics easily upstage Christian amateurs struggling out in an apologetics battlefield they were never trained for and for which they are probably unsuited. The day has gone when trainees or mavericks are the only Christians seen on the open battlefield of ideas attempting to defend the church and the cross.

Styles and operations of leadership must change as well because the unpredictability of the Holy Spirit means He may, and almost certainly will, choose the unlikeliest of candidates in the body to carry out His purposes. Elders must learn to live with that, for releasing the potential within is the precursor to releasing the potential without.

For example, I have seen a church release the Sunday school leader to lead his children to minister in prophecy, healing and words of wisdom to the congregation. I must admit I would not have believed it had I not seen it, especially as an attack of my crippling ankylosing spondylitis was healed in that service (I have not used my walking stick since). Some of the faces of the adults were white with shock as they returned to their seats, with hot words of the Holy Spirit reaching through the children deep into their lives. That kind of release takes the nerve of a strong and secure leadership.

Leaders have to learn to release rather than restrict and control; they must encourage believers to step out of their sinecures and passivity (even at some risk to services and ministries), and help, guide, train and strengthen them as they brave the unknown. When a pastor friend of mine was called to return to the USA from his Sussex church, the over-sight pastor had to call upon the congregation to volunteer exactly how many ministries my friend had released and sup-ported: we counted over thirty-five. It had been joked that it was dangerous to make any suggestions regarding the needs of the unsaved or the church within his hearing because you were in peril of having a new ministry thrust upon you. But it was no free-for-all. On the contrary, the period was marked by strict personal responsibility and this pastor's own deep spirituality, as no one wanted to upset the fun we all had.

This is the true call of leadership as clearly laid out in the Scriptures (Eph 4:12–16). The task of leadership is to prepare us for bigger things, and to help us in this project leaders must always have the bigger canvas of the city and the nation at the back of their minds. Remember Jesus, our model, who seeing the multitude turned His back on them and their needs to take His disciples to a private place to sit down and teach them (Mt 5:1–2). He had in mind at that moment the bigger canvas of multiplying His ministry, whereby He could later release them to go out without Him and minister His healing and deliverance (Mt 10:1–5).

What limitations in our own church or church organisation could be supplied by another group or church near us geographically? Surrendering this kind of isolation will take our leadership pride to the chopping block and deal with it ruthlessly, but joining hearts and lives across the body brings about an interlocking of the body reminiscent of the bones coming together ('with much noise'!) in Ezekiel's prophecy (Ezek 37:7).

For example, a couple in Plymouth, Devon, mortgaged their home, and together with nine Plymouth churches opened up a (much-needed) language learning and culture-guidance centre to serve the 1,000 refugees who flooded into their town under the government's Dispersal Programme in 2001. Against local secular agencies' resistance they have now established their centre as the premier language school in their area and have also set up a similar facility in Bournemouth, in the neighbouring country of Dorset, again with the co-operation of a local church. They are now recognised by the government and attract public funding. Not only is the operation strengthened and more efficient by this inter-church co-operation, but the Scriptures tell us: 'By this all will know that you are My disciples' (Jn 13:35), and this oneness in Christ gives an opportunity for the world to believe that the Son was sent by the Father (Jn 17:21).

And this leads us neatly to the third expression of the Holy Spirit: that of the church at large in the nation.

The challenge for national revival

When the body of Christ seeks to disciple or teach the nation, it must make use and take advantage of all the strengths available – that is, of people, facilities, money, opportunities, access and leadership experience – from whatever branch of the body they may come. If the diversified church acts in this way it looks like an organic whole from the outside, and this gives clear glory to God even before any particular issues are considered (Jn 17:21). Thus the spiritual forces opposing Christ, and the flesh and blood they inform (Eph 2:1–3), are faced, not with a divided and defeated church, but a strong, vigorous and innovative church which has a mind of its own (that is, the mind of Christ) and cannot be as easily manipulated or controlled as it has been for so long.

Leadership will come from unpredictable sources, and pride of tradition – *particularly recent tradition* – has absolutely no place if we wish to avoid obstructing the Holy Spirit in His expression of power. Each challenge will be different and each solution will be different, as King David discovered when fighting the invading Philistines (2 Sam 5:17–25). To his credit, David did not attempt to repeat his first marvellous victorious battle against the invading Philistines, but appealed to God for His strategy for the second conflict, even though the same army, the same terrain, the same logistics were involved. And of course the unpredictable Spirit of God gave David an unpredictable victory.

How many times are we tempted to repeat last year's programme instead of asking our God for the new tactics for the new season? How many exciting moves of God in the church have foundered on the rocks of tradition and ceremony, just because we wanted to take it from here and release ourselves from bondage to God's strategy?

Pride in leadership is often accompanied by arrogance, self-righteousness, envy and jealousy; we really do have to deal with these ridiculous impediments before God deals with them. It is in the jealousy areas that we are severely tested, but if we overcome we will see the power and majesty of God as He manifests Himself through a submissive body.

Another impediment brought about by our spirit of exclusiveness is cold-shouldering the usefulness of inter-church groups such as the EA, FGB, ICCC, CFI, Aglow, Lydia, the Christian Institute, the Zacharias Institute, Prophecy Today and the pressure groups that specialise in particular issues such as genetic exploitation of the unborn. Leaders must see that these groups have been powerfully developed by God; they might be likened to the sinews of Ezekiel's prophecy (Ezek 37:8), pulling the bones together with great force. They are a help, not a distraction, and they are powerful, especially when embraced by the church wholeheartedly and generously. These powerful sinew movements can only be partially effective if they are not allowed to attach to bones; that is, they are not openly acknowledged and supported by the church at large. But should they become a flourishing inter-church phenomenon, the church will not only be enriched and fulfilled, it will begin to function as a national body rather than a road sign for RAC directions.

For example, relatively unknown to the English church is the ICCC's Christian *You Can Start a Business* series being shown on Chinese national TV to well over 40 million viewers; the series is being translated from English into Russian (for the Russian and Ukraine audiences) and twelve other languages, and features testimonies and experience from ICCC Christian business people from all over the world. The Chinese immediately pressed ICCC for the next series! Where in the local church would this kind of expertise and access be available to broadcast kingdom values (albeit without expressly proselytising) across the Communist and ex-Communist world?

Again, Dr Tani Omideyi and the Liverpool Lighthouse project developed their little church in Anfield to meet the need that God had impressed upon them to reach out to the young people threatening older people with violence, house break-ins and the stealing of vehicles. By taking these alien-ated kids into their hearts and homes, the congregation began a turnaround in the kids' lives bringing about behaviour change. The local residents and prominent people changed in attitude from hostile to welcoming as the project got the drug addicts, the homeless, the unemployed and the alcoholics off the streets. The project has now opened an IT training centre, educational programmes for disaffected school-age children, an arts centre, a recycled furniture shop, an employment and skills training centre, a homeless information and advice centre and a drop-in café for the homeless. This church started with no money and yet has refurbished an old cinema as its new operations base at a cost of over £1.7 million.

Another example of impacting the nation is the case of 'God's Estate Agent', as *The Times* byline described Pastor Peter Cunningham of Southport's AOG, church, which in the last five years has set up sixty-eight properties housing 300 homeless people under the Green Pastures Housing Scheme (two-page spread in *The Times*, 8 February 2005). Pastor Pete, as he is known, works closely with the local authorities, who recognise that there would be a hole in the borough council's social welfare policy without Green Pastures! The scheme has now been asked to set up similar ones in Flint, Wigan and Salford.

Another Christian enterprise impacting the community from tiny beginnings is the Genesis Trust in the East Midlands. Starting out with eight people and no money, the Trust now operates from its base in a large converted bus depot: a schools vocational training centre, a dental training school, business incubation units, youth outreach schemes and also a chicken farm to employ out-of-work youths. It is now opening a university-validated academy to train others to manage social change in their community.

When the church finds that it can follow the Holy Spirit as an organic whole in His desire to disciple the nation through the voluntary mutual submission of leaders and church organisations, then the nation can be effectively reached. We will then be able to admit that the ineffective PR campaigns of the past, although well-intentioned, have lacked impact on a nation which needed substantive answers for its lostness.

As we follow the Spirit in this new chapter, burning zeal for our Father's house with goodwill towards all men will replace the defeatist somnolence that we often see today in our Christian groups. Many unsaved may well come to the Lord, but the object of revealing the Kingdom of God in the nation is not only the numbers of converted but glorifying Christ Jesus the King (Eph 3:21), which is seen when righteousness exalts our nation once again.

'The Way Forward' – NOT

This expression, 'The Way Forward', has been the imprimatur of the Labour Party and is the death of any thinking that attempts to understand the ways of the Holy Spirit. The term 'The Way Forward' is taken from the common expression of go-ahead commercial companies of the seventies, later abandoned by them because the world of commerce has too many uncertain and unknown factors to be able to chart ways forward! Political parties and churches unfortunately have not yet spotted that this same condition also applies to them when they view planning and programming for any new project as fundamental. The problem is that rather than being fundamental to *God's* purposes, planning is really only fundamental to *our* sense of security and purpose; this is extremely uncomfortable to face up to.

Thus the question of strategy formulation is a difficult one to address because so much is in the mind and the power of the Holy Spirit; our impatience and irritation must be disciplined and held in check. The planner-minds among us must now face an uncomfortable period, for when the Spirit is given time, space and people through which to move, He does so at His own pace, using who and what He chooses to and He probably will not notify us in advance.

Dear fellow planners, we need to have this printed on our grey matter:

> THE HOLY SPIRIT IS UNPREDICTABLE. THEREFORE IT IS IMPOSSIBLE TO CHART A WAY FORWARD FOR THOSE SEEKING THE KINGDOM OF GOD.

It is simply not possible to plan a blueprint, a pattern, a way forward, sideways or backwards. This is clear from the example of the early years of the church, particularly Paul's wanderings, the travels of the Wesleys or the great Christian outreach of the nineteenth century.

But what we can do is prepare ourselves to grow in intimacy with the Holy Spirit as we build our house, and in the local church as Jesus builds His, so that when He says 'Go!' we immediately seize our opportunity to obey, like a paratrooper when he hears the command 'Jump!'. We must not repeat the error made by the Israelites at Kadesh Barnea when they missed their great opportunity to go on into the Promised Land because of their doubt, fear and disobedience.

However, to go some way to meet the impatient among us, the next section, 'Coursework', gives a suggested outline a typical group might work through in order to begin to understand how the Lord works with us both individually and corporately and what we must do to follow Him.

Additionally, we have present-day examples that we may look to for guidance, such as the church in Korea, which has some of the largest congregations in the world numbering hundreds of thousands. Yoido Full Gospel church's Dr Yonggi Cho confides that he has a deceptively simple 'way forward' for local growth and national influence, which is to *seek the Holy Spirit, hear and obey Him* (Dr Paul Yonggi Cho, *Praying for National Revival*).

So we can set ourselves to *act local* in the development of hope and faith in following how we may build our house, but *think national* by understanding how Christ builds His house, and we can discover how unity for Christ's glory can be sought in our own sphere of influence. Remember Gideon and the choosing of the faithful 300. Those who were ready and looking up and watchful were chosen, while those still with immediate concerns were left until later when the course of the day was already won.

If we can prepare ourselves like this, we make way for the Holy Spirit to take the initiative in publishing the vision of Christ's Kingdom once again in our nation through willing, well-informed Christian believers. If we do, God will build His church in our nation once again.

To summarise

We must:

- prepare ourselves by learning how to build our house and practise meditative listening to God individually and corporately, so that we do not miss the day of our visitation;
- prepare our churches by learning from the Holy Spirit how to release men, women and young people into new and challenging ministries – both inside and outside the local church setting;
- educate ourselves by learning how to challenge the assumptions of the day, looking for God's opportunities in our lives, whether that may be in our personal sphere, the local sphere or the national sphere;
- look to radical sharing of both our personal and our local church time, money, ministries and vision under the inspiration of the Holy Spirit;
- obey the Holy Spirit in seeing how we may best promote the strengths of our local churches in the local or the national scene, and how we may support and encourage the inter-church 'sinew' ministries;

- cry to God for opportunities to be challenged with His priorities, particularly seeking how to show mercy to Israel (Rom 11:18, 32);
- seek the glory of the Lord Jesus Christ with all projects, encounters and sacrifices.

And finally, remember there is no standard pattern that we can construct or discover, but rather we must give the Lord no rest night and day, like the Asuza Street/Sunderland believers seeking the baptism of the Holy Spirit, until the unpredictable power of the Holy Spirit is unleashed in our nation once again.

Having set the scene in thinking about significant change in our own lives and in our group or church in order to play our part in discipling the nation, how may we implement it? The following section, 'Coursework', is designed to get us going, bearing in mind that the Holy Spirit is the course leader and He has probably already taken us through some of the experiences and provoked in us some of the changes that the course describes. So this is meant to be an outline or a suggested roadmap which is flexible enough to allow the Holy Spirit to adapt and develop our lives and calling, bearing in mind the larger canvas God has revealed to us.

Coursework

From manager to leader

In any active response to the serious challenges that this book proposes, leaders will be obliged to move into positive and inspiring leadership from any position that might be described as 'managing' their group, whether that might be a church or an inter-church organisation. These leaders, in taking responsibility for those under their authority, will be obliged to make clear pathways for the others to follow by learning how the dynamic of God's ways is to release rather than control. They do this by searching through the leaves to find fruit (Lk 13:6) and releasing those who are ready, willing and able to take up the calling to which God has appointed them.

In the Kingdom, leaders do *not* send the church members to do their business for them, but rather they set a practical example. Thus by engaging outside of the group's boundaries, they come to be seen by their group as following a kingdom dynamic, and an inspiration to follow.

The leaders must be prepared to find that others of their church may be in advance of them, having been proven by the Holy Spirit in some difficult field such as in business or the NHS or teaching. This must not be seen as a threat to leadership but as a major asset to be utilised; the Holy Spirit's anointing must be seen and recognised by leaders, even to their apparent cost.

The conduct of church services and programmes may change beyond all recognition, but again this is not a threat but a breath of new life: the people will love it and be encouraged in their own budding ministries.

We have noted that leaders are obliged to control and even micro-manage a church group when it is not going anywhere (as people start to squabble about their role, status and exposure), but given a larger canvas such as we are describing, the people want to get into the kingdom action and the infighting falls away. Releasing will come to be seen as the most rewarding part of the leadership experience as leaders see the travail of their soul worked out in people's lives. They move from 'young men' to the father's role (1 Jn 2:12–14).

'Love of the brethren' immediately becomes the imperative

in a kingdom move of God, as only in this environment can the necessary trust develop that enables people to move freely in following the Holy Spirit; it is also the most bracing, fun, exhilarating time.

Leadership reactions

There are only two reactions to the implications that are presented by the Kingdom of God: sterile or hungry. Jesus dealt with the first reaction at some length in Matthew 22:1–14, commenting that 'many are called, but few chosen'. Although refusal to become involved might be our first reaction, it behoves us to consider in this passage the dim view He takes of refusals to serve Him compared to those He calls blessed who 'hunger and thirst for righteousness, for they shall be filled' (Mt 5:6). A sterile reaction in today's terms might be, 'This is too sophisticated, too difficult, makes too many demands on leaders, is too fanatical, too political, too dangerous, too controversial.' Clearly the leader who reacts this way is not ready to take on the pilgrim journey that 'leads to life', but one would hope that he does not delay too long.

The hungry reaction, on the other hand, is that of a seeker who first asks 'How?' rather than objecting with a 'Why?', for he wants to know how to follow the Master in this new way.

Seeker's reaction

The seeker asks themselves, on their own behalf as well as any they are responsible for, 'How do we start, and where do we go from here?' The simple answer is to assess where the seeker is now and then construct a path for them to follow so that they might in time make the way clear for those who come after them. That is the purpose of the following questions.

Where are we now?

To assess where we are we need to ask ourselves:

1. Are we hungry enough, even desperate enough, to hunt out what God has got for us individually and as a group?
2. What risks do we face?
3. What are our strengths and weaknesses as individuals, as leaders and as a group?
4. What opportunities can we see?
5. What areas of the book are we as leaders already familiar with and what areas do we need to revise, research or learn from scratch?
6. Are there areas about which we need to seek help?
7. How soon will we be able to start our own leaders' course, and when would we be able to start the course for our group?

Starting: Overview

We suggest the leaders start their own discussion meetings based upon the book so that they would first study the Beatitudes as outlined in the book and then move on to the chapters dealing with the weapons of our warfare. At a suitable juncture, when they feel comfortable with the material, they can start the first discussions for their group, beginning with the Beatitudes material.

When the leaders master the weapons, they move on to Christ building His house, leading the church into understanding the weapons of our warfare. As the leaders engage in understanding how Christ builds His house, or maybe during that process, they ask the Lord to lead them into the issues in which they should be engaged. These will be both within the church and outside, moving gradually to the outward expression of what is happening in the church.

Course content

The beginning of the course will be fairly structured as the suggested form below. However, as the leadership progress, they will inevitably tailor the course in the light of their experiences and testimonies, and of course to the calling and vision that has been given to their group.

We recommend each leader keeps a personal journal of their journey for review and for passing on their experiences to the larger group who will be following them.

First, we will look at Jesus' teaching of the Beatitudes as outlined in the book.

Second, we will look at the applications as Jesus showed His disciples.

Third, we will try to relate this study to our own experience of the leading of the Holy Spirit in our own life.

Leaders' review

As the leaders and the group as a whole work through the tasks allotted them by the Holy Spirit it is strongly recommended that they hold regular review sessions to assess what the Holy Spirit is saying to the group by way of wisdom and course corrections.

Study outlines

1. Poor in spirit (Mt 5:3):

Discuss the meaning of this expression in the terms of the book.

    a. Explain the parable of the tax collector and the Pharisee (Lk 18:9–14) in terms of being 'poor in spirit'.

    b. Give a personal example which illustrates the principle.

    c. Homework: Prepare for Study 2.

2. Blessed are those who mourn (Mt 5:4)

Discuss the meaning of this expression in the terms of the book.

    a. Read Luke 16:13–15 and explain what there would be to mourn in this encounter if the student were to follow this exhortation of Jesus.

    b. Give a personal example of the lollipop principle.

    c. Homework: Prepare for Study 3.

3. Blessed are the meek (Mt 5:5)

Discuss the meaning of this expression in the terms of the book.

    a. Read Luke 10:30–37 and comment on what ways the Samaritan might be described as 'meek' given Nelson *Dictionary*'s definition.

    b. Give a personal example of the 'meek' principle.

    c. Homework: Prepare for Study 4.

4. Blessed are those who hunger and thirst for righteousness (Mt 5:6)

Discuss the meaning of this expression in the terms of the book.

    a. Read Luke 9:51–56 and explain.

    b. Give a personal example of the 'hunger' principle.

    c. Homework: Prepare for Study 5.

5. *Blessed are the merciful (Mt 5:7)*

Discuss the meaning of this expression in the terms of the book.

    a. Read Luke 11:11–13 and explain.

    b. Give a personal example of the 'merciful' principle.

    c. Homework: Prepare for Study 6.

6. *Blessed are the pure in heart (Mt 5:8)*

Discuss the meaning of this expression in the terms of the book.

    a. Read Luke 18:14 and explain.

    b. Give a personal example of the 'pure in heart' principle.

    c. Homework: Prepare for Study 7.

7. *Blessed are those who are persecuted (Mt 5:10)*

Discuss the meaning of this expression in the terms of the book.

    a. Read Luke 21:12–15 and explain.

    b. Give a personal example of the 'persecuted' principle.

    c. Homework: Prepare for Study 8.

8. *The foundation of understanding His way*

    a. Discuss the function of the motives and attitudes.

    b. Discuss the three overarching principles that help us as we apply the Beatitudes to our lives.

    c. Give a personal example of 'Influence, not power'.

    d. Prepare for Study 9.

9. *The daily tests*

   a. Each member of the group should choose from any of the eleven daily tests the book analyses from Matthew 5:21 to 6:16 to describe how Jesus is disciplining us to examine our reactions and behaviour in the light of Scripture and what we can do about it.

   b. Be personal and apply the test you have chosen to your own life.

   c. Prepare for Study 10.

10. *The modus operandi*

   a. Choose from any of the eight guides in this section, examining what the particular guideline means in daily life.

   b. Give an example from Scripture and an example from personal experience.

   c. Prepare for Study 11.

11. *Review*

   a. Share personal testimony of changed attitudes and behaviour.

   b. Discuss what the course so far would mean to your church or group were they to follow your example in working out these kingdom principles.

   c. Suggest how and when a group or church course can be started.

   d. Prepare for Study 12.

12. *The weapons*

   a. If this material is familiar to the pioneer leaders' group then they can combine the book's chapters as appropriate into single sessions, otherwise each weapon should be dealt with in a separate session. It is essential, however, that these chapters are thoroughly understood by members following in their leaders' footsteps.

13. *Review*

   a. The leaders have now reached the end of their journey into 'The bride prepares', and have now to bring the group for which they are responsible through to an understanding of the 'Weapons of our warfare'.

   b. It is at this stage that the leaders must start seeking the Holy Spirit for the purposes He has in mind for the group as a whole as individuals begin to apply the lessons of building their house.

   c. The individual development that the group as a whole has made may be quite dramatic, with leaders already emerging. An audit of progress is therefore appropriate at this stage to assess the readiness for the outward expression of the callings of God upon the group and also upon individuals.

14. *Development*

   a. Once the leaders understand what they are expected to do in order to follow the Holy Spirit's directions they can begin to obey His instructions and get behind those He has anointed to carry them out.

   b. It will now start becoming apparent which of the lessons of the book in its next section, 'The temple grows', will be needed. It is suggested that the leaders construct their own training course from this point onwards as the challenges present themselves.

Engage!

Why?

The issue of who disciples the nation has to be faced by every-one everywhere in any time; this helps form the identity of the nation and gives identity to its people. I heard some East European migrants in France being interviewed on TV. When asked why they wanted to come to England when they were already in the EU, with all its common provision, their spokesperson replied, 'Well, England is fair and will look after us. As for the French, we don't know what they will decide to do with us.' Regardless of any other issue, can you hear the identity of the English nation coming across in the man's reply? Righteousness exalts a nation and our reputation of an earlier century still hangs over us like a banner. The cultural identity of a nation is variously defined as a combination of several factors, notably blood, belief, religion, family, ances-try, tribe, race, language, history, values and institutions.

Should the church be absent from the fluidity of our chang-ing culture, or should it be in the frontline with divine ideas on the numerous social and institutional factors that will be governing us over the coming century? If we agree that the latter is the case, then we must ask ourselves, 'What is the will of Christ for my generation?' and work with all our strength not to let the current opportunities slip through our fingers.

We can of course choose *not* to fight the fight He has put before us. I suspect that is our first inclination, despite our warlike hymns, our 'Get ready for battle' seminars, our stir-ring pamphlets, our inspiring preaching. Like Gideon at first, we are pretty mouthy until the reality of the conflict strikes us (Judg 6:27).

But if we do not, then who will? Think on this: either we choose to contend for the influence of our faith in the nation, or our grandchildren will have to! The world is already at the doors of the church, with its ban on Christian broadcasting, its threats to ban outside evangelism (Right to Privacy under the Human Rights legislation), its hostility to the Christian position that Jesus Christ is the Way, the Truth and the Life and no one comes to the Father *except* by Him (this 'might' offend other religions in our multicultural society). Do we really want our grandchildren to pick up our burden as well as their own?

God has plans for each generation to contend for the faith for several reasons. First, He trains each generation for war by means of this engagement (1 Cor 1:19); secondly, the contending itself influences the government of the day in its moral framework; and thirdly, the onlooking crowd who willingly place themselves in the valley of decision await the debate in order to make their decision. At the very least we owe them a fair chance of making the right choice. After all, our forefathers made the moves so that we might have the same opportunity.

Where do we start?

Jesus said:

> 'For which of you, intending to build a tower, does not sit down first and count the cost, whether he has enough to *finish* it – lest, after he has laid the foundation, and is not able to *finish*, all who see it begin to mock him, saying, "This man began to build and was not able to *finish*." Or what king, going to make war against another king, does not sit down first and consider whether he is able with ten thousand to meet him who comes against him with twenty thousand?' (Lk 14:28–31)

Make no mistake about it, this is a major enterprise both for individuals and for churches or other Christian groups to attempt; but the issue is, do we want our building to be of God and do we want it to stand against all assault, provide a shelter for those seeking His will and provide a jumping-off point for taking the struggle for our faith to the open forums of the nation? If we do, then clearly the foundations have to be sound, we have to be close to the Holy Spirit and we have to have confidence in the obedience that leads to faith.

First, then, the seeker has to assess where they are now and then construct a path to follow for themselves and those for whom they are responsible.

The suggested path would be that the leader begins the 'We build our house' section of the book, making notes that are appropriate to pass on to the group they are responsible for. It is essential that their experiences are woven into the fabric of the outline, mixing experience with the Scripture so that the latter comes to life for the listeners and interaction can be encouraged and discussed. When the leader has finished the first part of 'We build our house', they should find that they have compiled the first part of the life route map for their followers. They may then progress on to the next section, 'Christ builds His house', while embarking upon the first part with their group. In working through the second part they should be making notes of experience and weaving that into the material and the Scriptures in readiness for sharing up ahead with their group.

The sequence should now be quite well developed so that when the leader has finished the second part and moves on to the third, 'The weapons of our warfare', they should be able to augment the book's material with other reading to give as broad a credence as possible to the attitudes to be taken to the present-day philosophies. By now the group should also be experiencing the working of Jesus' Kingdom in their personal lives, and testimonies should be forthcoming. The wise leader will track these to augment the course that is now taking shape for future use and to base the first 'contending for the faith' projects on this newly developed faith. These are the projects that the Holy Spirit will be introducing locally and even nationally for the group (church or inter-church) to be involved in.

When it comes to seeking Christ for external projects with which the group might be led to engage, it is recommended that the group as a whole meet to seek the Holy Spirit's guidance in prayer, even all-night prayer. It is essential that the group only moves into those areas He has prepared and with those individuals He has called. It is at this point that the leader might find to his alarm that God is calling out others to lead in unexpected areas. This is a cause for rejoicing, not fear, and the leader should take credit that he has been faithful in bringing forth this fruit. It must be said as an encouragement that results in the Kingdom can come very quickly. In fact they will come as soon as the Holy Spirit can entrust the group with them, and the leader must be aware and expectant of this. It can be a hairy ride!

An external project will be presented to the group by the Holy Spirit and will usually be ridiculously ambitious, especially as He will probably choose those we may not consider ready. The group may also find that they are coming into administrative conflict and opposition from local authorities, as we have seen in Chapter 5 ('Implications'), but this is par for the course and the Holy Spirit's guidance must be sought for the best strategy with which to deal with them. Remember Jesus has overcome the world and these obstructions are there to train us for bigger things ahead.

This personal and local experience of the operation of the Kingdom of Christ Jesus will become part of the fabric of our lives. However, the bigger canvas of the nation must always be at the back of our mind. All kingdom projects take their place in impacting the nation, and they have the strategic objective of demonstrating the body to the world of men and women so that they may be presented with objective choices to follow either the course of this world or the cross of the Saviour. We personally may never move outside the local scene, but remember that our part is essential in supporting those who are called to do so. The structure is planned by God so that all support each other in order that a national defence of the gospel can provide a national reference point for the support of those working locally.

What then do we need to do in order to 'finish'? First, we need the will to see that the Kingdom is God's, not ours. Secondly, we need to see that He has already put His generals in place with strategy revealed to them by the Holy Spirit. And third, we must subsume our ambitions under His end-time plans.

The Kingdom is not ours

There is only one body of Christ, one church in our locality, and we must get our act together, not by deciding in committee what denominations we are able to fellowship with and those we cannot, but rather by seeking out those of any stripe who recognise the three criteria listed above, particularly the first: that the Kingdom is Jesus Christ's and His alone.

Listen to Jesus the King again, this time in Revelation: 'What you see, write in a book and send it to the seven churches which are in Asia: to Ephesus, to Smyrna, to Pergamos, to

Thyatira, to Sardis, to Philadelphia, and to Laodicia' (Rev 1:11). And Paul wrote, 'To the church of God which is at Corinth' (1 Cor 1:2) and 'To the church of the Thessalonians' (1 Thess 1:1).

If as a Pentecostal you should find a Catholic who reveres Christ as the present King of kings, you have found unity of the spirit and the Spirit, and if as a sober Anglican you have found the same with a charismatic from a house church who has the same awe of Christ the King, then you are of one spirit and Spirit. Our ideas of unity are not His and we are encouraged to strive to keep that unity in the bond of peace (Eph 4:3), for while it may be straightforward to fellowship with those in the same congregation, it is a lot more difficult to overcome suspicion, fear, jealousy or contempt across the churchy cultural barriers we have all erected.

One Catholic nun taught me, against all my prejudice, to listen to God in a powerful way. Another taught me how to minister to young ministers. I have erected as many barriers as the next man, but I have found that in worshipping Christ Jesus the King, those barriers of colour, creed, culture, background, education even language are *no* barrier, but rather when we find the family of Christ and the Father we have found a wonderful thing, especially when the Holy Spirit goes on to teach us to love one another and demolish those barriers. What treasure of delight! What true friends we make! What an extraordinary creation is the body of Christ!

The Scripture teaches us that we are the body of Christ and members individually (1 Cor 12:1–31). It is not too difficult to recognise the members of the body in our own church, but the real test is whether we can, whether we dare, recognise members of His body across our church cultures. I can testify of precious brothers of different denominations from all over the world whom I have met through ICCC. All are His and I bow before His wonderful creation in different nations and in embarrassed humility at their holiness, power, devotion and intimacy with Him. I have taken myself to task to ask myself, 'How dare I criticise a servant of His?' (Rom 14:4). Believe me, if you have not done so already, it is a traumatic experience to take up your own cross in this manner and begin to strive to keep that unity.

Anointed to stand before kings

Are there Christian men and women who can successfully engage with the debaters of this age? I believe there are, for God reserves for Himself those who have not bent the knee to the Baals of this age. But we have to recognise our need of them and cry to God for the revelation of them, these precious servants He has anointed to 'stand before kings' (Acts 9:15).

The squabbles over the last few years in the international church illustrate for us that we have to be ready to protect these anointed from those of us in the church who violently disagree, as I believe these special servants will be more vulnerable to the church than to the worst the world can throw at them. God has promised to give these servants power to destroy the wisdom of the wise (1 Cor 1:19) as the multitude watch and wait for their revelation. These are emphatically *not* those who belong to a super-spiritual group, but those who have by diligent application sought to follow the Master in His Kingdom.

Of course it may not be fashionable to so engage with the forces of this world, and we may prefer a passive form of Christianity, a costless faith. One international church leader said angrily to me about the 180,000 British babies that are legally aborted every year, 'What do you think *I* can do about it?' There are fifty answers to that question, or maybe none, because if he does not see that even the degree of faith he now possesses rests upon the actions of men and women who have in our past accepted the same challenge in their particular generation, then he is blind, blind, blind. No wonder the Scripture warns that the love of many will grow cold in the last days (Mt 24:12)!

But the apostle anointed to stand before kings (Acts 9:15) in this particular leadership function has in view a great prize, which is nothing less than the inheritance of Christ the King (Ps 2:8). It is a contest that is most definitely not on behalf of themselves, and it is one in which God will follow up by anointing evangelists in their proper role with signs and wonders (Rom 15:18–19) to prove His interest. It is this follow-up role that the evangelists and the pastors will find their most powerful, effective and satisfying purpose, unlike so often in the past when they are struggling out of their depth trying to be all things to all men as though they were apostles, prophets, pastors and teachers all rolled into one.

It is our task to cry, cry and cry again to our God to release His chosen ones to us that we might follow them in the real battle for the minds and hearts of men and women in our nation. We must look for our part, great or small, in setting the frameworks in the spheres of influence that we ourselves have been given (Eph 2:10), understanding the arguments of the day so that once again our nation can offer a lead in righteousness in being discipled by the King. We must not duck this responsibility and leave our nation in a worse state than we found it, smiling weakly to our grandchildren with a limp 'Er, sorry'.

His ways are not our ways

To be ready to follow the Spirit wherever He wishes to go (Jn 3:8) and do whatever He wants us to do, we have first to consider building the tower in our generation (Lk 14:28–31). Second, we must consider the costs of taking ourselves to task in building our house and co-operating in Jesus building His. Third, we have to ask ourselves to strive to keep the unity of the Spirit in the bond of peace as much as it has to do with us.

It may be unusually challenging, but hey! we only have one life and we might as well make it as interesting as possible while it is yet in our power; and maybe we might even go on to hear those golden words, 'Well done, good and faithful servant' (Mt 25:21). I heard a man testify recently that he had been converted to Christ five years previously; that he had been a drinker and a loser until Christ rescued him and gave him a lovely wife and also a vocation to serve the Jews as a principal officer of a British Christian mission to the Jews. He was given a new life when he had had nothing except his gratitude and his willingness to obey Christ in His plans. I would like to be able to say that I too surrender all to Him, for this is the way forward for His body, the church.

CONCLUSION

And so we have laid out for you the issue of the day; that is, there is no revival if we do not contend for the faith.

You will find this walk of faith and the awareness that the practice of it engenders will enrich your everyday life and enrich your Christian experience like nothing else can do, and your thanksgiving to God for being alive at this time will know no bounds.

But this is not for us; it is not even for the multitudes. It is for Him. In seeking to know and understand His rule and desires, we come to know the ache of His heart and to see things in His light and to know Him. To quote Paul: 'Yet indeed I also count all things loss for the excellence of the knowledge of Christ Jesus my Lord, for whom I have suffered the loss of all things, and count them as rubbish, that I may gain Christ and be found in Him . . .' (Phil 3:8).

I beg you: do not be a hearer only, but a doer also. My prayer is that by being a doer of the work set before you, you will be blessed in what you do. And do not tire or turn back once you have started but persevere in the task of knowing Him – whom to know is life – and press toward the goal for the prize of the upward call of God in Christ Jesus.

PROPHECY

We are convinced that the church has been missing something vital by our loss of response to the course the nation has been taking. Our forefathers contended for the faith by stirring the conscience of the nation in their generations to provide justice and mercy in the factories, the mines, for homeless children, for education, for slaves, for the poor and even universal suffrage. The slide seems to have started with the failed response to Darwin.

I asked the Lord why the church did not respond to Darwin as powerfully as Paul did when he slapped down the same philosophy of evolution from the Epicureans.

I believe the Lord replied, *'Paul answered them at their level in that the God of Israel was their Father and they therefore had a duty of response to Him.'*

'But', I said, 'the Darwinians had what they considered evidence and deduction that Paul's argument would not, and did not, satisfy.'

I believe the Lord said to me, *'Do you not suppose there are sufficient hidden evidences in the Scriptures for them as for the*

Epicureans? But no one asked Me. I had no one who felt My pain and who was close enough to Me to hear and respond correctly to this old heresy. This was indeed the day of the Lord when I called but no one was able to answer, and many millions have been lost as a result. The enemies of the earthly body of My Son are now at the gate and will devour that body without thought or mercy, as they think they are the only kings and there is no one to disabuse them.

'*This is the argument which should have been won but was lost, and there have been many others since which have passed by without notice. My church has been preoccupied with its own agenda and did not listen to Mine. Even the current obsession with evangelism is man-based, serves man's objectives and visions, and distracts and deceives My people from the callings I have for each of them.*

'*What does my body know in these days about the operation of My will upon the earth? Is there anyone who can say he has My ear and knows My agenda for this age, even of the last age? The leaders are ignorant of Me, My ways and My voice . . . how can My people possibly be prepared for the assault ahead? Truly "where the carcass is, there the eagles gather", and gather they will, and pick the bones of My body clean. Only bones will remain, and only these bones will rise as an army, a great and terrible army, as through that army I pour out My wrath upon those who have done this thing. They think I am dead? They will find out what "dead" really means; when the anger of the Lord is poured out, there is none to save, none to save.*

'*This process, of continual public defence of My kingdom rule, has been an active part of the function of My people from time immemorial. The process has been lost, and My people will be lost as a result.*

'*Mourn, weep, O earthly Jerusalem, for your army has melted, your walls are down and there is no defence for you. The kings of this world that I have appointed will carry you off to their halls of deceit to play with you, to wile away the years, to stay as children under their instruction and control. You will no longer command the heights of intellectual pursuit, of governmental influence, of social health, of restraint of the mighty and powerful. You have delivered the peoples of the earth into the lap of the evil one, who has had this desire since his fall. There is no comfort for you, only risk as you seek Me, discomfort as you let go of the anaesthetic of this world's playthings and reassurance, and perhaps the knowledge that you are a man, a woman, after My heart. Your satisfactions will no longer be manifest in this world; that opportunity is gone, sold for a bowl of the soup of comfort. Are you really a son of Mine? You will be called upon to prove it like Simon Peter . . . will you fail as your recent fathers in the faith failed? Make up your mind now – not at the point of testing. This is My advice to you.*'

15 January 2000

ACKNOWLEDGEMENTS

The Holy Spirit has led me along an unusual path throughout my life and my gratitude to Him and Jesus my Lord and Saviour knows no bounds. My writing here in this book is as much a record of that journey as it is of a polemic.

I thank two men who have been fathers in the faith to me: the Revd Bob Mumford, who taught me about *archés* and the seven giants of the Beatitudes and much else, and Michael Fenton-Jones, President of ICCC, who inspired me to keep going through some extremely difficult periods.

I owe a huge debt to Oxford's Wycliffe College, where I was privileged to hear Dr Elaine Storkey and Professors McGrath and Lennox, and learn the giving away of one's faith in love by Canon Michael Green.

Inevitably, one realises that one's own family have been so involved in this kind of project that they are almost co-authors. This book would not have been started except for the prompting of my wife June who must have suffered listener fatigue many times.

Lisa, my daughter, joined the project in mind and spirit with exhaustive and faithful research, sharpening and challenging my ideas and presentation, and became a co-writer. Eve-Marie, my other daughter, helped me articulate many of the book's principles so that they were intelligible to the general reader, and Ian and Nicky inspired me with their own working out of these kingdom principles through their lives and through their music, as well as the practical clarification of points I was trying to make.

My thanks to all of you for the adventure of a lifetime.

BIBLIOGRAPHY

Christianity in England, C.A. Alington, Oxford University Press 1942.

A History of the English Church and People, Bede, Penguin edition 1955.

England in the Age of Improvement, Asa Briggs, Folio Society 1999.

Church and State in Modern Britain 1700–1850, Richard Brown, Routledge 1991.

History of England, G.M. Trevelyan, Longman 1947.

A History of the Crusades, Steven Runciman, Folio Society 1994.

A Short History of Nearly Everything, Bill Bryson, Doubleday 2003.

Culture Meltdown, Marcus Honeysett, IVP 2002.

Postmodernism, Kevin O'Donnell, Lion 2003.

Christian Apologetics, Norman Geisler, Baker Book House 1976.

A Short History of the Free Churches, J. Houlder, Dickinson 1899.

Operation World, Patrick Johnstone, Paternoster 2001.

That Hideous Strength, C.S. Lewis, Pan edition 1953.

Mere Christianity, C.S. Lewis, Harper 2002.

Bridge Building, Alistair McGrath, IVP 1992.

Generating Hope, Jimmy Long, Marshall Pickering 1997.

The Difference Between Kingdom and Church, Bob Mumford, Lifechangers.

The Agape Road (video tape series), Bob Mumford, Lifechangers 2002.

Holy Warriors, Frog and Amy Orr-Ewing, Authentic 2002.

The Free Church Tradition, E.A. Payne, SCM 1944.

Pocket Guide to Islam, Patrick Sookhdeo, Christian Focus 2001.

Islam in Conflict, Peter Riddell, IVP 2003.

The God Who is There, Francis Schaeffer, Crossway Books 1982.

Light in the Shadow of Jihad, Ravi Zacharias, Multnomah 2002.

The Challenge of Islam to Christians, David Pawson, Hodder 2003.

Why Care About Israel?, Sarah Teplinsky, Baker Book House 2004.

Prophetic Destinies, Derek Prince, Creation House 1992.

Jerusalem, the Covenant City, Hugh Kitson 2000.

Israel and the Church, Ronald L. Diprose, Authentic Media 2004.

No Longer Strangers, Richard Booker, Sounds of the Trumpet 2002.

Islam in Britain, Institute for the Study of Islam, Isaac 2005.